United States
Department of
Agriculture

Forest Service

Forest
Products
Laboratory

General
Technical
Report
FPL–GTR–150

Directory of Wood-Framed Building Deconstruction and Reused Building Materials Companies, 2005

Abstract

This is a directory of companies involved in wood-framed building deconstruction, dismantling and reused building materials, with an emphasis on those that use, resell, and/or re-manufacture salvaged wood. Companies in this directory range in scope from those that carryout targeted building removals, such as historic barns, strictly for the purpose of harvesting the antique wood in these buildings, to companies that conduct residential and commercial demolition where the primary goal is building removal, and the recovery of materials is conducted opportunistically as a by-product. The bulk of companies listed are those that either salvage or sell building materials. For ease of use, the directory lists companies two ways, alphabetically by state and then alphabetically by company type, and alphabetically by company type and then alphabetically by state.

Keywords: deconstruction, used building materials, lumber, recycling, salvage, building dismantling, building removal, building demolition, architectural salvage

Acknowledgment

Thanks to Vicki Hall, former FPL employee, who helped create the first list of companies from which this directory evolved.

Contents

Originally published July 2004
Revised November 2005

Falk, Robert H.; Guy, G. Bradley. 2005. Directory of wood-framed building deconstruction and reused wood building materials companies, 2005. Gen. Tech. Rep. FPL-GTR-150. Madison, WI: U.S. Department of Agriculture, Forest Service, Forest Products Laboratory. 113 p.

A limited number of free copies of this publication are available to the public from the Forest Products Laboratory, One Gifford Pinchot Drive, Madison, WI 53726–2398. This publication is also available online at www.fpl.fs.fed.us. Laboratory publications are sent to hundreds of libraries in the United States and elsewhere.

The Forest Products Laboratory is maintained in cooperation with the University of Wisconsin.

Preface

About This Directory

This directory was cooperatively developed by the USDA Forest Products Laboratory and the Powell Center for Construction and Environment, University of Florida. Brad Guy, currently Director of Operations, Hamer Center for Community Design Assistance, Pennsylvania State University, was instrumental in creating the database of companies and performing the nationwide telephone survey from which the company contact and general industry information was generated. Information was also provided by the Used Building Materials Association (UBMA).

This is a directory of companies involved in wood-framed building deconstruction and dismantling and reused building materials, with an emphasis on those that use, resell, or remanufacture salvaged wood. The purpose of this directory is to provide a consumer and business resource for locating companies offering a variety of products and services:

- Partial or whole building removals, with a focus on wood materials recovery and reuse

- Brokering, buying, or selling salvaged wood building materials

- Producing, buying, or selling specialized salvaged wood products, such as architectural items or re-milled flooring

- Construction and timber-framing using reclaimed wood in new construction or remodeling

- To a lesser extent, ancillary services such as environmental remediation, recycling, and equipment used in building deconstruction

Companies in this directory range in scope from those that carry out targeted building removals, such as historic barns, strictly for the purpose of harvesting the antique wood in these buildings, to companies that conduct residential and commercial demolition where the primary goal is building removal and the materials are recovered opportunistically as a by-product. The bulk of companies listed are those that either salvage or sell building materials.

To compile this directory, many different sources were utilized. First and foremost, the Internet was extensively searched using several search engines. Lists of contact names were also created from a host of published green building resource guides, the National Wood Recycling directory, lists of organization memberships (such as the Used Building Materials Association), and attendee lists from conferences related to this field.

Starting with a list of about 1,400 companies, a telephone survey was conducted to

1. determine if the services performed by the company were consistent with the information in this directory,

2. collect contact information, and

3. determine the type of business the company is involved in, their range of services, and geographic range.

All companies listed in this directory were contacted by phone and agreed to be included in the directory.

The directory includes timber-framing companies that use reclaimed lumber, as well as companies that re-mill salvaged lumber into other products, such as flooring. Demolition companies are listed if they explicitly indicate alternative services such as environmental remediation, interior and selective dismantling, salvage of wood or other materials, and in many cases where demolition services are combined with used building materials sales or brokering.

There are also listings for companies that deal in historic architectural salvage, which clearly qualifies as used building materials but is distinct from bulk used building materials that are not of high architectural or historic quality. These architectural salvage companies are listed if they appear to be broader in scope than only high-end historic building elements.

A small number of recycling companies are listed, as well as salvage brokers, dealers of equipment related to demolition, and companies that perform environmental remediation. Some large-scale industrial plant demolition companies are also listed; however, building demolition companies are included only if they either focus on or indicate the capacity and expertise to conduct dismantling of residential and commercial structures for the purpose of materials recovery for reuse. Demolition companies that indicate a focus on implosions and highly destructive methods of demolition are not included.

How to Use This Directory

For ease of use, the directory lists companies in two ways:

- Alphabetically by state and then alphabetically by company type

- Alphabetically by company type and then alphabetically by state

The directory uses a code to categorize companies by their primary activities:

Code	Description
BR	Broker of recovered materials
CN	Building contractor or trade that uses reclaimed lumber in projects
DC	Deconstruction company that practices partial or whole building disassembly for the purposes of recovering building materials for reuse
DM	Demolition company that engages in selective dismantling and deconstruction
EQ	Producer or dealer of equipment used in building deconstruction (this does not include heavy equipment)
EV	Environmental services company (such as asbestos or lead abatement)
RC	Materials recycler, and not intended to be inclusive (for example, a concrete recycler would not be listed)
UMS	Used building materials retail sales
VA	Producer/seller of value-added products

In many cases, the companies listed engage in a variety of overlapping activities. For this reason, many companies listed have more than one associated code. The most common examples of overlap include wood salvaging for the purposes of value-added product manufacturing and demolition companies that augment these services with used building materials retail sales.

If the company indicated that they primarily deal with specific species of wood, these are listed under "Species."

Directory of Wood-Framed Building Deconstruction and Reused Wood Building Materials Companies, 2005

Robert H. Falk, Research Engineer
Forest Products Laboratory, Madison, Wisconsin

G. Bradley Guy, Director of Operations
Hamer Center for Community Design Assistance
Pennsylvania State University, University Park, Pennsylvania

Wood-Framed Deconstruction and Building Materials Salvage: An Overview

Wood-framed building deconstruction is a specific approach to remove materials for reuse in such a way as to preserve their integrity and value to the greatest extent possible and as economically as possible. Deconstruction is generally perceived as manual disassembly of a building, although various combinations of manual and mechanical methods are being studied to improve cost and time performance. Solid wood recovery rates of 50% to 90% are not uncommon. Deconstruction emphasizes a hierarchy of material use; reuse first, then recycle. For example, it is deemed preferable to reuse a recovered timber beam in its whole form rather than grind it up and recycle it into mulch or boiler fuel.

The U.S. Environmental Protection Agency (EPA) estimates that the equivalent of 250,000 single-family homes is disposed of each year in the United States. This represents nearly 1 billion board feet of salvageable structural lumber per year, equivalent to about 3% of the current U.S. softwood harvest. Much of the lumber available for salvage through deconstruction is from decades of old-growth harvest and represents a resource largely unavailable from any other source. As a result, much of this wood is of higher structural and aesthetic quality (higher density, slower grown, fewer defects) than is the lumber produced today. Both reuse (as lumber or timbers) and remanufacture are options for recovered wood. Larger timbers are often used in "timber frame" construction, and if quality is high enough, adding value through remanufacture can be economical. Remilling of old lumber and timber into flooring is the most common end-use, although paneling, millwork, and siding have all been investigated.

Other aspects of deconstruction and lumber salvage should also be considered:

- Holistically, the reuse of lumber products will help conserve our natural resources and ease harvesting pressure on the existing forest resource.

- Deconstruction and material salvage can help reduce building disposal costs, both through savings from reduced landfill tipping fees (including transportation) and because the wood salvaged has resale value. Only in a very few cases will the value of the materials salvaged cover the cost of building removal; however, several case studies indicate that the net cost of deconstruction (deconstruction plus disposal minus salvage revenues) can be from $0.12 to $2.28/ft^2$ less than conventional demolition.

- Deconstruction is labor intensive and takes longer than demolition and landfill. Time can be a major factor in building removal and site renovation.

- Because many buildings slated for demolition are located in areas in need of community development (such as inner cities), many private sector organizations and government agencies view deconstruction as an opportunity for local jobs and entrepreneur training for the construction industry.

Telephone Survey Results

As part of the development of this directory, a telephone survey of more than 1,400 companies was undertaken in spring 2003. In addition to obtaining contact information for use in this directory, questions were asked related to demolition, deconstruction, used building materials, and value-adding activities using reclaimed materials. Because not every company responded to each question, and therefore the response to each question reflects a different number of companies, these results should not be considered a rigorous statistical survey of the industry. However, following are some results that provide a glimpse of the deconstruction and materials reuse industries. Due to multiple responses by individual companies, total percentages may be more or less than 100%.

Companies surveyed	Category code	Number
Total		1,078
Broker of recovered materials only	BR	15
Building contractor or trade that uses reclaimed lumber in projects only	CN	6
Deconstruction company that practices partial or whole building disassembly for the purposes of recovering building materials for reuse or a deconstruction company that also does any other activity listed above	DC	219
Demolition company that engages in selective dismantling and deconstruction that also does any other activity listed above	DM	166
Producer or dealer of equipment used in building deconstruction	EQ	3
Environmental services company, such as asbestos or lead abatement	EV	
Materials recycler only	RC	21
Used building materials retail sales, plus those that do BR, CN, or VA	UMS	534
Producer/seller of value-added products, plus those that do BR, CN, or RC	VA	114

Does your company belong to any associations?

Membership associations	Respondents (%)
National Association of Demolition Contractors	22
Used Building Materials Association	8
National Association of Homebuilders or a Local Chapter	8
National Wood Flooring Association	8
Associated Builders and Contractors	6
Timber Framers Guild	3
Associated General Contractors of America	3
Other	42

What do you think is the biggest obstacle for the deconstruction and reuse/recycling building materials industry to move forward?

Obstacle	Respondents (%)
Education of consumers	19
Markets (matching supply and demand)	14
Costs of labor	11
Environmental regulations	11
Perceptions of low quality	8
Storage needs	8
Damage to wood and contamination by nails, etc.	6
Existence of disreputable businesses and unregulated activities	6
Insurance and workman's compensation for demolition/recycling businesses	6

What steps has your company taken to overcome these obstacles?

Steps taken	Respondents (%)
Networking/education of consumers/outreach	30
Being selective of projects and types of materials salvage	12
Increased skills and safety training including OSHA regulations	11
Advertising	11
Improving costs and scheduling management practices	11
Avoiding hazardous materials handling (e.g., subcontracting where needed)	8
Adherence to regulations	4
Subsidized labor source or governmental assistance	4

Survey Questions to Deconstruction Companies (DC) Only

Smallest size lumber you salvage in width and thickness?

Smallest size (nominal in.)	Respondents (%)
2 by 4	33
1 by 4	18
2 by 6	13
1 by 6	4

Shortest length of lumber in stock?

Length (ft)	Respondents (%)
6	42.9
4	28.6

Shortest length of lumber in stock?

Length (ft)	Respondents (%)
6	38
4	31

Who are the suppliers of your used materials stock?

Supplier	Respondents (%)
Self-supply through salvage	39
General public	25
Commercial sources	21

Survey Questions to Used Materials Sales Companies (UMS) Only

Primary wood species sold?

Species	Respondents (%)
Oak	28
Pine	28
Fir	18
Chestnut	11
Heart Pine	10
Cypress	8
Maple	6
Redwood	6
Long leaf pine	4

Smallest size lumber sold in width and thickness?

Smallest size (nominal in.)	Respondents (%)
2 by 4	58
1 by 4	19
2 by 6	10
1 by 6	10

Survey Questions to Value-Adding Companies Only (VA)

Primary wood species input to your process(es)?

Species	Respondents (%)
Oak	17
Fir	14
Pine	12
Heart pine	10
Cypress	7
Chestnut	7
Long leaf pine	6
Cedar	4
Redwood	3
Walnut	3

Trade(s) of your primary construction subcontractor customers?

Subcontractor trade	Respondents (%)
Flooring/finish carpentry	50
General contracting	27
Timber framing	10

Minimum sizes and species of reclaimed lumber are important factors to the used building materials industry. It takes as much labor to salvage a 4-ft-long piece of lumber as an 8-ft piece of lumber, and the options for reuse are severely limited in the shorter piece. The industry prefers a minimum 6-ft piece of lumber at nominal 2- by 4-in. dimensions. The desirable species of wood for reuse are oak; pine and its variant, heart pine; and Douglas-fir. These are also the most prevalent species used in U.S. building construction (and hence what is available), but oak and heart pine also have superior qualities for finish carpentry. Flooring is the most common value-added product from reclaimed lumber.

The most common business model for the deconstruction and reuse building materials industry is the combination of deconstruction/demolition and used building material sales within the same company. This provides the opportunity for diversity of revenues and workforce capacity through both the supply side of building deconstruction and the demand side of the retail outlet.

Further Information

Robert H. Falk, Ph.D, PE
Team Leader, Building Products & Systems
Advanced Housing Research Center
USDA Forest Products Laboratory
One Gifford Pinchot Drive
Madison, Wisconsin 53726-2398
Tel: (608) 231–9255
Fax: (608) 231–9303
e-mail: rhfalk@fs.fed.us
www.fpl fs.fed.us

Brad Guy
Director of Operations
Hamer Center for Community Design Assistance
The Pennsylvania State University
227 East Calder Way
University Park, PA 16801
Tel: (814) 865–5733
Fax: (814) 865–1378
e-mail: Gbg2@psu.edu
www.hamercenter.psu.edu

Information Update Sheet

This directory was compiled Spring through Fall, 2003, and amended Fall 2005. It is a best faith attempt to provide a robust national directory. Naturally, some companies may have been overlooked. If you are a company that is not listed or if you know of a company not listed, please fill out this form and fax, mail, or email to

Reclaimed Wood Directory
USDA Forest Products Laboratory
One Gifford Pinchot Drive
Madison, Wisconsin. 53726–2398
FAX: (608) 231–9592
Email: rhfalk@fs.fed.us

Company Name: _____

Primary Activity(s) Code: _____ (see choices below)

Address: _____

Phone: _____

Email address: _____

Website address: _____

Primary Wood Species: (if applicable): _____

Primary Activity Code:

BR = broker of recovered materials (mainly wholesale)

CN = building contractor or trade

DC = deconstruction company

DM = demolition company

EQ = producer or dealer of equipment used in building deconstruction

EV = environmental services company

RC = materials recycler

UMS = used building materials retail sales

VA = producer/seller of value-added products

Companies Listed by State

Alabama

A.L. Roy Lumber Co. Inc.
1405 1st Avenue N
Bessemer, AL 35020
Phone: 800-476-8169
Fax: 205-425-2139
Email: david@roylumber.com
Website: www roylumber.com
Type: VA

Dixie Salvage
3630 Gault Avenue N
Fort Payne, AL 35967
Phone: 256-845-5475
Type: UMS

Elrod's Building Material and Salvage
430 4th Avenue N
Bessemer, AL 35020
Phone: 205-426-8788
Type: UMS

Fuller Surplus and Supply
3101 Jeff Davis Avenue
Selma, AL 36703
Phone: 334-872-7409
Type: UMS

James and Company Antique
Timbers and Flooring
482 County Road 209
Collinsville, AL 35961
Phone: 256-997-0703
Fax: 256-997-0773
Email: jamesandcompany@cs.com
Website: www.jamesandcompany.com
Type: UMS
Species: White Oak, Longleaf pine, Chest-
nut

Old South Wrecking Co.
400 Paul Road
Montgomery, AL 36108
Phone: 334-264-6744
Type: DM

Reaves Wrecking Co. Inc.
201 A Boulevard
Valley, AL 36854
Phone: 334-756-3237
Email: reaveswrecking@mindspring.com
Type: DC/UMS
Species: Pine

Shiver's Wrecking Company
3895 Old Seale Highway
Phoenix City, AL 36869
Phone: 334-297-2044
Type: DC
Species: Heartpine

Southern Accents Architectural Antiques
308 2nd Avenue SE
Cullman, AL 35055
Phone: 205-737-0554
Type: UMS

Southern Timberwrights
77 Baushore Place
Guntersville, AL 35976
Phone: 256-582-9299
Email: lrm@localaccess net
Website: www.southerntimberwrights.com
Type: CN/VA

Surplus and Salvage Sales
910 40th Street N
Birmingham, AL 35222
Phone: 205-592-8306
Type: UMS

Alaska

Alaska Materials Exchange
555 Cordova Street
Anchorage, AK 99501
Phone: 907-269-7586
Type: UMS

Hartvigson's Fine Furniture
and Woodworking
7133 Arctic Boulevard, Suite 8
Anchorage, AK 99518
Phone: 907-344-6612
Website: www hartvigsons.com
Type: VA

Second Chance
3106 Spenard Road
Anchorage, AK 99503
Phone: 902-277-2748
Type: UMS

Valley Materials Exchange
Big Lake Road
Big Lake, AK 99652
Phone: 907-892-7188
Type: UMS

Arizona

A-Cal Wrecking Company
13443 N 20th Street
Phoenix, AZ 85022
Phone: 602-247-2650
Type: DM/EV

Al's Building Materials and Supplies
9733 E Main Street
Mesa, AZ 85207
Phone: 480-986-4909
Type: UMS

Atwell Salvage & Demolition
3001 W Pima Street
Phoenix, AZ 85009
Phone: 602-484-7301
Fax: 602-484-0132
Type: DM/UMS

Avitia Demolition
1321 N Camino De Juan
Tuscon, AZ 85745
Phone: 520-622-3366
Email: avitiainc@aol.com
Type: DM

B&C Contractors Inc.
1324 W El Caminito Place
Tucson, AZ 85705
Phone: 520-888-2681
Fax: 520-292-3173
Email: alyweber@worldnet.att net
Type: DM

B.C.S. Enterprises, Inc.
1275 W Houston Avenue
Gilbert, AZ 85233
Phone: 480-633-8300
Fax: 480-633-8309
Website: www.bcsdemo.com
Type: DM

Barnett & Shore Contractors
819 W Silverlake Road
Tucson, AZ 85713
Phone: 520-791-0286
Type: DC/UMS

Bowen Poles and Lumber
22402 N Black Canyon Highway
Phoenix, AZ 85080
Phone: 602-993-6350
Fax: 602-516-8172
Type: VA

Breinholt Contracting
2915 W Pima Street
Phoenix, AZ 85009
Phone: 602-322-1100
Type: DM

Catclaw Contractors
10519 E Tanque Verde Road
Tucson, AZ 85749
Phone: 520-760-0185
Type: DM/EV

Dickens Quality Demolition, LLC.
1146 N 19th Avenue
Phoenix, AZ 85009
Phone: 602-206-9979
Website: www.dickensquality.com
Type: DC

Eric Building Supply
2112 N West Street
Flagstaff, AZ 86004
Phone: 928-774-3732
Type: UMS

Gerson's Used Building Materials
1811 S Park Avenue
Tucson, AZ 85713
Phone: 520-624-8585
Email: dgerson@aol.com
Type: UMS

Habitat Home Supply
215 W Leroux Street
Prescott, AZ 86303
Phone: 928-771-1777
Type: UMS

Kuhles Services LLC
219 E Navajo Drive
Prescott, AZ 86301
Phone: 928-445-8446
Type: DM/RC

Old Pueblo Adobe
9353 N Casa Grande Highway
Tucson, AZ 85713
Phone: 520-744-9268
Website: www.oldpuebloadobe.com
Type: UMS

Old Pueblo Remodelers
1700 South 4th Avenue
Tucson, AZ 85713
Phone: 520-884-8685
Type: DC/UMS

ReStore/Community Closet
2958 E 22nd Street
Tucson, AZ 85713
Phone: 520-326-1936
Website: www.tmmfs.org/
Type: UMS

Salvage Depot Inc.
5701 W San Miguel
Glendale, AZ 85301
Phone: 623-680-4874
Fax: 623-972-1341
Email: daveschueller@worldnet.att net
Type: DC/UMS
Species: Fir

Stardust Building Supplies
1720 W Broadway Road
Phoenix, AZ 85202
Phone: 602-604-0605
Fax: 602-604-0207
Email: ala@stardustbuilding.org
Website: www.stardustbuilding.org
Type: DC/UMS

Taylor Demolition and Recycling
2140 S Freeway
Tucson, AZ 85713
Phone: 520-623-0410
Fax: 520-623-0399
Type: DM

Valley of the Sun HFH ReStore
P.O. Box 20186
Phoenix, AZ 85036
Phone: 602-268-9022
Type: UMS

Arkansas

Architectural Salvage by Ri-Jo
2309 Highway 71 S
Mena, AR 71953
Phone: 479-394-2438
Email: salvage@arkansas net
Type: DC/UMS

Bear's Building Salvage
510 Huntsville Road
Fayetteville, AR 72701
Phone: 501-443-2327
Fax: 501-442-4279
Email: bear1942@nwark.com
Type: UMS

Dore & Associates Contracting, Inc.
1400 Brookwood
Little Rock, AR 72202
Phone: 800-344-7876
Email: dore@concentric.net
Website: www.doreandassociates.com
Type: DC/DM

PattonWrecking, Inc.
8222 Stagecoach Road
Little Rock, AR 72210
Phone: 501-455-2833
Fax: 501-455-4083
Email: pwi@cei med
Type: DC

California

ABDO S. Allen Co
718 Douglas Avenue
Oakland, CA 94603
Phone: 510-569-2070
Type: UMS

A.E. Schmidt Co.
14212 Lang Station Road
Canyon Country, CA 91387
Phone: 800-479-2901; 661-251-2901
Fax: 661-251-3130
Website: www.aeschmidt.com
Type: DM

Ace Recycling & Scrap Metal
21252 Nordhoff Street
Chatsworth, CA 91311
Phone: 818-772-4891
Type: RC

Adams Steel
3200 E Frontera
Anaheim, CA 92806
Phone: 714-630-6523
Website: www.adamssteel.com
Type: RC

Albion Doors & Windows
P.O. Box 220
Albion, CA 95410
Phone: 707-937-0078
Email: bysawyer@knobsession.com
Website: www.knobsession.com
Type: UMS

Almquist Lumber
P.O. Box 875
Blue Lake, CA 95525
Phone: 707-668-5652
Fax: 707-668-5454
Email: almquist@tidepool.com
Website: www.almquistlumber.com
Type: UMS

American Constructors California
16351 Gothard Street #A
Huntington Beach, CA 92647
Phone: 714-377-1414
Type: DC

Antique Building Material Co.
3707 5th Avenue
San Diego, CA 92101
Phone: 619-233-1144
Type: UMS

Antique Building Materials
6152 Wenrich Drive
San Diego, CA 92120
Phone: 619-583-3791
Fax: 619-583-9087
Email: ancientmaterials@cox net
Website: www.ancientarchitecture.com
Type: UMS

Antique Building Materials
3175 17th Street
San Francisco, CA 94110
Phone: 415-565-0287
Type: UMS

Arcadia Demolition Services
785 Walsh Avenue
Santa Clara, CA 95050
Phone: 408-248-0505
Fax: 408-248-2664
Email: info@arcadiademo.com
Website: www.arcadiademo.com
Type: DC

Architectural Antique and
Salvage Company of Santa Barbara
726 Anacapa Street
Santa Barbara, CA 93101
Phone: 805-965-2446
Type: UMS

Architectural Detail
299 N Altadena Drive
Pasadena, CA 91107
Phone: 626-844-6604
Fax: 626-844-6651
Website: www.pasadenasalvage.com
Type: UMS

Architectural Salvage of San Diego
1971 India Street
San Diego, CA 92101
Phone: 619-696-1313
Type: UMS

Armstrong Antique Plumbing & Lighting
2820 W Orange Avenue
Anaheim, CA 92804
Phone: 714-761-1320
Fax: 714-761-1320
Email: jarmst2534@aol.com
Type: UMS

AWS Construction Services, Inc.
6621 E Pacific Coast Highway #130
Long Beach, CA 90803
Phone: 562-799-4436
Email: aws@awsconstruction.com
Website: www. awsconstruction.com
Type: DC/DM

Baka Production
1785 Egbert Avenue
San Francisco, CA 94124
Phone: 415-468-8090
Type: VA

Battle Lumber & Hardware
2605 Imperial Avenue
San Diego, CA 92102
Phone: 619-234-5118
Type: UMS

Bayshore Materials
512 Solano Avenue
Vallejo, CA 94590
Phone: 707-644-0859
Type: UMS

Berkeley Architectural Salvage
1167 65th Street
Oakland, CA 94608
Phone: 510-655-2270
Type: UMS

Best New and Used Building Materials
1129 E 6th Street
Corona, CA 92879
Phone: 909-279-5079
Type: UMS

Beyond Waste
607 W Sierra
Cotati, CA 94952
Phone: 707-792-2555
Fax: 707-792-2565
Email: precycle@sonic.net
Website: www.beyondwaste.com
Type: DC/UMS
Species: Redwood, Fir

Big Ten Building Materials
757 W Woodbury Road
Altadena, CA 91001
Phone: 626-791-9747
Type: UMS

Black's Farmwood
7 Mount Lassen Road, Suite C-125
San Rafael, CA 94912
Phone: 415-499-8300
Fax: 415-499-8309
Website: www.blacksfarmwood.com
Type: UMS

Blue Diamond Materials
1245 Arrow Highway
Baldwin Park, CA 91706
Phone: 626-303-2623
Type: UMS

Blue Log Lumber
P.O. Box 804
Mendocino, CA 95460
Phone: 707-937-1735
Website: www.goodwood.org
Type: DC/VA
Species: redwood

BOSS Enterprises
2065 Kittredge Street, Suite E
Berkeley, CA 94704
Phone: 510-841-9675
Email: bossmail@self-sufficiency.org
Website: www.self-sufficiency.org
Type: DC

Bourget Brothers Building Materials
1636 11th Street
Santa Monica, CA 90404
Phone: 310-450-6556
Type: UMS

Bright Ideas
P.O. Box 586
Brookdale, CA 9507
Phone: 831-338-2522
Email: dondowell@yahoo.com
Type: DC/UMS
Species: Oak, Maple, Redwood

Building Materials Distributors
1708 Cactus Road
San Diego, CA 92173
Phone: 619-661-7181
Type: UMS

Building Materials Recycling
6467 Datsun Street
San Diego, CA 92173
Phone: 619-661-8155
Type: UMS

Building Resources
701 Amador Street
San Francisco, CA 94124
Phone: 415-285-7814
Fax: 415-285-4689
Email: brsfcr@yahoo.com
Website: www.bulidingresources.org
Type: UMS

C & K Salvage
718 Douglas Avenue
Oakland, CA 94603
Phone: 510-569-2070
Fax: 510-569-2074
Email: cksalvage@aol.com
Type: DC/UMS
Species: Fir

C&M Diversified
330 N Montgomery
San Jose, CA 94124
Phone: 408-294-5185
Type: UMS

Cal-Demo Inc.
9515 Soquel Drive # 212
Aptos, CA 95003
Phone: 877-460-DEMO
Website: www.cal-demo.com
Type: DC/DM

Caldwell's Building Salvage
Resource/Wreckers
195 Bayshore Boulevard
San Francisco, CA 94124
Phone: 415-550-6777
Fax: 415-550-0349
Website: http://caldwell-bldg-salvage.com/
Type: DC/UMS

California Hardwood Producers
1980 Grass Valley Highway
Auburn, CA 95603
Phone: 916-888-8191
Email: dave@californiahardwood.com
Website: www.californiahardwood.com
Type: VA

California Wood Recycling Inc
2950 Johnson Drive
Ventura, CA 93003
Phone: 805-650-1616
Type: RC

Calshores Deconstruction
1861-B Main Street
San Diego, CA 92113
Phone: 619-239-7636
Fax: 619-239-7633
Website: www.vintagearchitectural.com
Type: DC

Campanella Corporation
Building Demolition
494 McCormick
San Leandro, CA 94577
Phone: 510-536-4800
Type: DC

Casper Company
3825 Bancroft Drive
Spring Valley, CA 91977
Phone: 619-589-6001
Fax: 619-589-7158
Website: www.caspercompany.com
Type: DC/DM

Castroville Used Building Materials
10900 Merritt Street
Castroville, CA 95012
Phone: 831-633-0369
Type: UMS

Circosta Iron and Metal
1801 Evan Avenue
San Francisco, CA 94124
Phone: 415-282-8568
Fax: 415-641-7804
Type: RC

Clauss Construction
8956 Winter Garden Boulevard
Lakeside, CA 92040
Phone: 888-463-2291; 619-390-4944
Fax: 619-390-4944
Email: bernard@claussconstruction.com
Website: www.claussconstruction.com
Type: DM

Cleveland Wrecking Company
628 E Edna Place
Covina, CA 91723
Phone: 626-967-9799
Fax: 626-967-1479
Website: ww.clevelandwrecking.com
Type: DM

Cleveland Wrecking Company
2833 Leonis Boulevard # 210
Vernon, CA 90058
Phone: 213-269-0633
Type: DM

Community Woodworks
2420 Ukraine Street Oakland Army Base
Building 823
Oakland, CA 94607
Phone: 510-835-7690
Fax: 510-835-7691
Website: www.communitywoodworks.org/
Type: VA/UMS

Cornerstone Salvage Company
40927 Airport Road
Littleriver, CA 95456
Phone: 707-937-5011
Type: DC/UMS
Species: Redwood

Crossroads Recycled Lumber
P.O. Box 928, 57839 Road 225
North Fork, CA 93643
Phone: 888-842-3201
Fax: 559-877-3646
Email: crlumber@netptc net
Website: www.crossroadslumber.com
Type: VA

CST Environmental Inc.
404 N Berry Street
Brea, CA 92821
Phone: 714-672-3500
Fax: 714-672-3501
Email: demolition@cstenv.com
Website: cstenvironmental.com
Type: DM

Daley Marketing Corporation
151 Kalmus Drive
Costa Mesa, CA 92626
Phone: 714-662-0755
Email: daleydmc@sprintmail.com
Type: UMS

Dan Copp Crushing Corp
1300B North Hancock Street
Anaheim, CA 92807-1921
Phone: 714-777-6400
Fax: 714-777-6410
Type: RC

Delta Scrap and Salvage
1371 Main Street
Oakley, CA 94561
Phone: 925-754-1474
Website: www.deltademo.com
Type: DC/RC

Earth Source Forest Products
1618 28th Street
Oakland, CA 94608
Phone: 510-208-7257
Fax: 510-547-7252
Email: selluwood@yahoo.com
Website: www.earthsourcewood.com
Type: UMS

EcoTimber
1611 4th Street
San Rafael, CA 94901
Phone: 415-258-8454
Fax: 415-258-8455
Email: ecotimber@ecotimber.com
Website: www.ecotimber.com
Type: UMS

El Dorado County Habitat for Humanity
5781 Pleasant Valley Road
El Dorado, CA 95623
Phone: 530-621-3972
Fax: 530-295-8972
Email: drisso@edchabitat.org
Website: www.edchabitat.org
Type: DC/UMS

El Toro Materials Co.
20851 El Toro Road
Lake Forest, CA 92630
Phone: 949-458-7993
Fax: 949-859-5138
Type: UMS

Elmers Salvage & Sales
12280 Quartz Hill Road
Redding, CA 96003
Phone: 916-243-4356
Type: DC

European Reclamation
4520 Brazil Street
Los Angeles, CA 90039
Phone: 818-241-2152
Fax: 818-547-2734
Email: htc@wgn.net
Website: www.historictile.com
Type: UMS

Evans Brothers, Inc.
7589 National Drive
Livermore, CA 94550
Phone: 925-443-0225
Fax: 925-443-0229
Email: info@evansbrothers.com
Website: www.evansbrothers.com
Type: DC/DM

Ewles Materials
16081 Construction Circle W
Irvine, CA 92606
Phone: 949-552-6008
Fax: 949-552-7084
Type: UMS

Ferma Corporation
1265 Montecito Avenue, Suite 200
Mountain View, CA 94043
Phone: 650-961-2742
Fax: 650-968-3945
Type: DC

Freeway Building Materials
1124 S Boyle Avenue
Los Angeles, CA 90023
Phone: 323-261-8904
Type: UMS

Fresno House Movers
701 Pleasant Way
Felton, CA 95018
Phone: 831-335-4557
Type: DC

Garbage Reincarnation, Inc.
500 Mecham Road
Santa Rosa, CA 95402
Phone: 707-584-8666
Fax: 707-584-8291
Email: brecycle@pacbell.net
Website: www.garbage.org
Type: UMS

Gator Crushing and Recycling
2363 Willow Road
Arroyo Grande, CA 93420
Phone: 805-343-6277
Fax: 805-995-3281
Type: RC

Gilman Street Salvage
808 Gilman Street
Berkeley, CA 94710
Phone: 510-524-5500
Fax: 510-524-5192
Email: info@gilmansalvage.com
Website:
www.gilmansalvage.com/welcome html
Type: UMS

Habitat for Humanity
P.O. Box 770
Fort Bragg, CA 95437
Phone: 707-964-0942
Type: UMS

Habitat for Humanity
2219 San Joaquin Street
Fresno, CA 93721
Phone: 559-237-4102
Type: UMS

Habitat for Humanity
6414 Brace Road
Loomis, CA 95650
Phone: 916-652-1045
Type: UMS

Habitat for Humanity
1010 Doyle Street
Menlo Park, CA 94025
Phone: 650-324-2266
Type: UMS

Habitat for Humanity
2301-B Woodland Avenue
Modesto, CA 95358
Phone: 209-575-4585
Type: UMS

Habitat for Humanity
San Fernando/Santa Clarita Valleys
Pacoima, CA 91331
Phone: 818-897-0940
Type: UMS

Habitat for Humanity El Dorado County,
Inc.
180 Industrial Drive #E
Placerville, CA 95667-6803
Phone: 530-621-3972
Type: UMS

Habitat for Humanity
851 Commerce Street
Redding, CA 96002
Phone: 530-224-9684
Type: UMS

Habitat for Humanity
P.O. Box 1834
San Andreas, CA 95249
Phone: 209-754-5331
Type: UMS

Habitat for Humanity
888 N First Street
San Jose, CA 94124
Phone: 408-294-6464
Type: UMS

Habitat for Humanity
1543 Sunnyvale Avenue # 101
Walnut Creek, CA 94596
Phone: 925-933-1296
Type: UMS

Habitat for Humanity–East Bay
2619 Broadway
Oakland, CA 94612
Phone: 510-251-6303
Type: UMS

Habitat for Humanity of Ventura County
167 Lambert Street
Oxnard, CA 93030
Phone: 805-485-6065
Email: info@habitatventura.org
Website: www habitatventura.org
Type: UMS

Habitat for Humanity Orabge County
2165 S Grand Avenue
Santa Ana, CA 92705
Phone: 714-434-6202
Fax: 714-434-1222
Email: manager@restoreoc.org
Website: www restoreoc.org
Type: UMS

Habitat for Humanity Pomona Valley
2111 Bonita Avenue
La Verne, CA 91750
Phone: 909-596-7098
Fax: 909-596-2279
Email: pvhab@juno.com
Website: http://pomvalhabitat.org
Type: UMS

Habitat for Humanity ReStore
426 N 7th Street
Sacramento, CA 95814
Phone: 916-440-1215
Email: info@shfh.org
Website: www.shfh.org
Type: UMS

Habitat for Humanity Orange County
13925 Edwards
Westminster, CA 92683
Phone: 714-891-6998
Type: UMS

Hayward Lumber
10 Ragsdale Drive, Suite 100
Monterey, CA 93940
Phone: 831-643-1900
Website: www.haywardlumber.com
Type: UMS

Heim Bros. Inc.
375 Arthur Road
Martinez, CA 94553
Phone: 925-229-1610
Fax: 925-229-0447
Website: www.heimbros.com
Type: DC/DM

Hennington Construction Co.
12 Spreckels Lane
Salinas, CA 93908
Phone: 831-455-2377
Fax: 831-455-2434
Type: DC

Hexagram Antiques
426 3rd Street
Eureka, CA 95501
Phone: 707-443-4334
Type: UMS

Holmes Wilson Furniture
30361 Seaview Road
Cazadero, CA 95421
Phone: 707-847-3747
Type: VA

House Demolition & Land Clearing
2817 Ostrom Road
Marysville, CA 95901
Phone: 916-743-9305
Type: DM

Iconco, Inc.
303 Derby Avenue
Oakland, CA 94601
Phone: 510-261-1900
Fax: 510-261-2459
Email: iconco@pacbell net
Website: www.iconco-inc.com
Type: DM/UMS

Interior Demolition Inc.
6841 Foothill Boulevard
Tujunga, CA 91042
Phone: 818-353-4804
Type: DM

Into the Woods
1205 N McDowell
Petaluma, CA 94954
Phone: 707-763-0159
Type: UMS

J P Dolan Lumber
1701 Rumrill Boulevard
Richmond, CA 94806
Phone: 510-232-1273
Type: UMS

Jackel Enterpise Inc.
347 Locust Street
Watsonville, CA 95076
Phone: 831-768-3880
Fax: 831-768-3883
Email: jackel@cruzil.com
Website: www.jackelenterprises.com
Type: UMS
Species: Fir, Redwood

Jefferson Recycled Woodworks
1104 Firenzi Street
McCloud, CA 96057
Phone: 800-220-9062
Fax: 530-964-2745
Email: goodwood@snowcrest.net
Website: www.ecowood.com
Type: BR
Species: Redwood, Fir, Hardwoods

Jessie's Lumber
3609 Britton Avenue
Chula Vista, CA 91911
Phone: 619-426-3574
Type: UMS

Jim State Forest Products
Highway 3
Hayfork, CA 96041
Phone: 503-628-1101
Type: VA

Joe's Building Service
1924 1/2 35th Avenue
Oakland, CA 94601
Phone: 510-436-5617
Type: DC

Kroeker Demolition &
Recycling Contractors Inc.
4627 S Chestnut Avenue
Fresno, CA 93725
Phone: 559-237-3764
Fax: 559-268-3366
Email: rodneya@kroekerinc.com
Website: www kroekerinc.com
Type: DM

Legacy Builders
2243 Nordyke Avenue
Santa Rosa, CA 95403
Phone: 707-526-0800
Fax: 707-526-9072
Email: astanley@sonic.net
Website: www.alegacybuilt.com
Type: DC

Liz's Antique Hardware
453 S La Brea
Los Angeles, CA 90036
Phone: 323-939-4403
Website: www.lahardware.com
Type: UMS

M. Maselli & Sons, Inc.
519 Lakeville Street
Petaluma, CA 94952
Phone: 707-763-1562
Fax: 707-763-6964
Email: info@m-maselliandsons.com
Website: www m-maselliandsons.com
Type: UMS

Mad River Woodworks
P.O. Box 1067
Blue Lake, CA 95525
Phone: 707-668-5671
Fax: 707-668-5673
Email: info@madriverwoodworks.com
Website: www.madriverwoodworks.com
Type: VA

Marrone Construction
1037 Lassen Lane
Mt. Shasta, CA 96067
Phone: 530-926-1048
Type: DC

Maxwell Pacific
P.O. Box 4127
Malibu, CA 90264
Phone: 310-457-4533
Type: UMS/VA

Mendocino Specialty Lumber Company
P.O. Box 519
Hydesville, CA 95547
Phone: 707-726-0339
Fax: 707-726-0319
Email: wood@oldgrowth.com
Website: www2@oldgrowth.com
Type: VA

Michael Evenson Natural Resources
P.O. Box 157
Petrolia, CA 95558
Phone: 707-629-3679
Fax: 707-629-3679
Website: www.oldgrowthtimbers.com
Type: DC/VA

Nunez and Sons Used Building Material
4024 E Chavez Avenue
Los Angeles, CA 90063
Phone: 323-266-0518
Type: UMS

Off the Wall
P.O. Box 4561
Carmel, CA 93923
Phone: 831-624-6165
Type: UMS

Ohmega Salvage
2407 San Pablo Avenue
Berkeley, CA 94702
Phone: 510-843-7368
Fax: 510-843-7123
Email: ohmegasalvage@earhtlink net
Website: www.ohmegasalvage.com
Type: UMS

Olympic Used Building Material
2860 E Olympic Boulevard
Los Angeles, CA 90023
Phone: 323-780-9163
Type: UMS

Omega Too
2204 San Pablo Avenue
Berkeley, CA 94702
Phone: 510-843-3636
Fax: 510-843-0666
Type: UMS

Pacific Coast Lumber
225 Tank Farm Road #D4
San Luis Obispo, CA 93401
Phone: 805-543-5533
Fax: 805-543-1601
Type: VA

Pacific Heritage Wood Supply Co.
P.O. Box 1329
El Granada, CA 94018
Phone: 877-728-9231
Fax: 650-728-9231
Email: sales@phwood.com
Website: www.phwood.com
Type: UMS/VA

Pacific Post and Beam
P.O. Box 13708
San Luis Obispo, CA 93406
Phone: 805-543-7565
Fax: 805-543-1287
Type: UMS/VA

Pinocchio's
18651 Hare Creek Terrace
Fort Bragg, CA 95437
Phone: 707-964-6272
Fax: 707-964-0458
Website: www mcn.org/b/rmoore
Type: UMS/VA

Plant Reclamation
912 Harbour Way S
Richmond, CA 94804
Phone: 510-233-6552
Fax: 510-237-6739
Website: www.plantreclamation.com
Type: DC/EV

Premier Architectural Materials
P.O. Box 22667
Carmel, CA 93923
Phone: 831-662-3450
Type: UMS

Presco Building Materials
291 S Waterman Avenue
San Bernardino, CA 92408
Phone: 909-889-0084
Fax: 909-889-0085
Type: DM/UMS

Ralph's Used Building Material
1444 Island Avenue
San Diego, CA 92101
Phone: 619-232-2633
Type: UMS

Randazzo Enterprises Inc.
13550 Blackie Road
Castroville, CA 95012
Phone: 831-384-7644
Email: jrandazzo@sol.com
Type: DM

Recycle Construction Company
1575 38th Avenue
Santa Cruz, CA 95062
Phone: 408-462-4491
Type: DC

Recycled Lumberworks
1825 Airport Park Boulevard
Ukiah, CA 95482
Phone: 707-462-2567
Fax: 707-462-6122
Website: www.oldwoodguy.com
Type: VA
Species: Fir

Recycletown-Reuse-Recycling
403 Meacham Road
Petaluma, CA 94952
Phone: 707-795-3660
Type: UMS

Resale Lumber Products
4056 N Highway 101
Eureka, CA 95501
Phone: 707-822-5705
Fax: 707-822-3074
Email: konicke@urchin.net
Type: UMS

Re-Sets
12215 Montague Avenue
Pacoima, CA 91331
Phone: 818-890-6499
Type: UMS

Reusable Lumber Company
895 La Honda Road
Woodside, CA 94062
Phone: 650-529-9122
Fax: 650-529-3082
Email: info@reusablelumber.com
Website: www reusablelumber.com
Type: UMS

Reuse People
15165 Golden Gate Drive
San Leandro, CA 94579
Phone: 510-351-5628
Type: UMS

Rossel Lumber Recycling
1960 Laredo Lane
Fontana, CA 92337
Phone: 909-371-3255
Fax: 909-361-3255
Email: rosselp@yahoo.com
Type: RC

Ruiz Antique Lighting
2333 Clement Avenue
Alameda, CA 94501
Phone: 510-769-6082
Fax: 510-769-1374
Type: UMS

RWH Construction
12722 Carmenita Road
Santa Fe Springs, CA 90670
Phone: 562-407-0694
Fax: 562-407-0696
Type: DM/UMS

San Diego Habitat ReStore
3653 Costa Bella Street
Lemon Grove, CA 92101
Phone: 619-463-0464
Fax: 619-668-2149
Email: johnl@habiatatsdiego.org
Website: www habitatsdiego.org
Type: UMS

San Francisco Community Recyclers
701 Amador Street
San Francisco, CA 94124
Phone: 415-731-6720
Fax: 415-566-0102
Type: RC

SANDecon of Oceanside
242 Clementine S
Oceanside, CA 92054
Phone: 760-231-6358
Fax: 760-231-6387
Email: info@sandecon.org
Website: www.sandecon.org
Type: DC

Santa Fe Wrecking Company
1600 S Santa Fe Avenue
Los Angeles, CA 90021
Phone: 213-623-3119
Fax: 213-623-3119
Website: www.santafewrecking.com
Type: UMS

Savvy Salvage
4385 Piedmont Avenue
Oakland, CA 94611
Phone: 510-655-8877
Type: UMS

Sepulveda Building Materials
359 E Gardena Boulevard
Gardena, CA 90248
Phone: 310-217-0134
Type: UMS

Sierra Timber Framers
P.O. Box 595
Nevada City, CA 95959
Phone: 530-292-9449
Fax: 530-292-9460
Website: www.sierratimberframers.com
Type: CN/VA

SIM J. Harris Company
9229 Harris Plant Road
San Diego, CA 92145
Phone: 619-277-5481
Fax: 619-277-4517
Email: simjharris@aol.com
Type: DM

Sink Factory
2140 San Pablo Avenue
Berkeley, CA 94702
Phone: 510-540-8193
Fax: 510-540-8212
Website: www.sinkfactory.com
Type: UMS

Stockton Recycling
1533 Waterloo Road
Stockton, CA 95205
Phone: 209-942-2267
Fax: 209-942-2289
Type: DM

Studio eg
442 Rich Street
Oakland, CA 94609
Phone: 510-596-8945
Email: info@studioeg.com
Website: www.studioeg.com
Type: VA

Surplus City of Oroville
4514 Pacific Heights Road
Oroville, CA 95965
Phone: 530-534-9956
Type: DC/UMS

Terra Mai
P.O. Box 696
McCloud, CA 96057
Phone: 800-220-9062
Email: info@terramai.com
Website: www.terramai.com
Type: UMS

The Old Wood Mill
P.O. Box 1077
Willits, CA 95490
Phone: 707-459-6294
Type: DC

The Reuse People
2100 Ferry Point #150
Alameda, CA 94501
Phone: 510-522-2722
Email: info@TheReusePeople.org
Website: www.thereusepeople.com
Type: DC/UMS

The Reuse People
23010 Lake Forest Drive, Suite D-302
Laguna Hills, CA 92653
Phone: 888-588-9490
Email: info@TheReusePeople.org
Website: www.thereusepeople.com
Type: DC/UMS

The Wooden Duck
2919 7th Street
Berkeley, CA 94710
Phone: 510-848-3575
Email: info@thewoodenduck.com
Website: www.thewoodenduck.com
Type: VA

This & That
1701 Rumrill Boulevard
San Pablo, CA 94806
Phone: 510-232-1273
Type: UMS

Tony's Architectural Salvage
123 N Olive
Orange, CA 92866
Phone: 714-538-1900
Fax: 714-538-1966
Email:
webmaster@tonysarchitecturalsalvage.com
Website:
www.tonysarchitecturalsalvage.com
Type: UMS

Urban Ore
900 Murray Street
Berkeley, CA 94710
Phone: 510-841-7283
Type: UMS

Urban Ore Inc.
6082 Ralston Avenue
Richmond, CA 94805-1202
Phone: 510-232-7724
Fax: 510-235-0198
Email: marylouvan@aol.com
Type: UMS

USA Recovered Wood Resources
308 Fountain Avenue
Pacific Grove, CA 93950
Phone: 831-809-2627
Fax: 831-372-2766
Email: jbsfortord@aol.com
Type: VA

Valley Base Materials
9050 Norris Avenue
Sun Valley, CA 91352
Phone: 818-767-3088
Type: UMS

Vintage Architectural
1861-B Main Street
San Diego, CA 92113
Phone: 619-239-7636
Email: vintage@vintagearchitectural.com
Website: www.vintagearchitectural.com
Type: DC/UMS

Vintage Timberworks
1155 Industrial Avenue
Escondido, CA 92029
Phone: 760-743-0744
Fax: 760-743-5714
Website: www.vintagetimber.com
Type: DC/VA

Vintage Timberworks
47100 Rainbow Canyon Road
Temecula, CA 92592
Phone: 909-695-1003
Type: UMS

Wesco Used Lumber
910 Ohio Avenue
Richmond, CA 94804
Phone: 510-235-9995
Fax: 510-236-2863
Type: UMS

West Coast Land Clearing
P.O. Box 90126
Long Beach, CA 90803
Phone: 562-599-2882
Fax: 562-599-2787
Email: rthomas@westcoastlc.com
Website: www.westcoastlc.com
Type: DM

Westco Used Lumber
P.O. Box 1136
El Centro, CA 94530
Phone: 510-235-9995
Fax: 510-236-2863
Type: UMS

Whole House Building Supplies
1955 Pulgas Avenue
East Palo Alto, CA 94303
Phone: 650-328-8731
Fax: 650-327-1933
Email: gardner@.net.com
Website: www.driftwoodsalvage.com
Type: DC/UMS
Species: Redwood, Oak, Pine

Whole House Building Supply
731-D Loma Verde Avenue
Palo Alto, CA 94303
Phone: 650-856-0634
Fax: 650-856-0634
Email: pgard0634@aol.com
Website: www.driftwoodsalvage.com
Type: DC/UMS

Youth Employment Partnership
2300 International Bvld
Oakland, CA 94601
Phone: 510-533-3447
Website: www.yep.org
Type: DC/UMS

Colorado

A Garrett Lumber and Wrecking Company
7360 Grape Street
Commerce City, CO 80022
Phone: 303-288-4946
Fax: 303-843-9682
Type: DC/UMS

Allied Demolition, Inc.
7901 Highway 85
Commerce City, CO 80037
Phone: 303-289-3366
Fax: 303-289-3543
Website:
www.barnettlumber.com/demo htm
Type: DM/UMS

Alpine Bargain Center
3915 N Garfield Avenue
Loveland, CO 80538
Phone: 970-622-8307
Fax: 970-669-9667
Website: www.alpinebargaincenter.com
Type: UMS

Architectural Antiques
2669 Larimer Street
Denver, CO 80205
Phone: 303-297-9722
Fax: 303-297-9290
Website: www.archantiques.com
Type: UMS

Architectural Salvage
504 E Pikes Peak Avenue
Colorado Springs, CO 80903
Phone: 719-633-9294
Type: UMS

Architectural Salvage, Inc.
1215 Delaware Street
Denver, CO 80204
Phone: 303-615-5432
Type: UMS

Building for Health Materials Center
P.O. Box 113
Carbondale, CO 81623
Phone: 970-963-0437
Fax: 970-963-3318
Email: contactus@buildingforhealth.com
Website: http://buildingforhealth.com
Type: UMS

Carlisle Restoration Lumber
1445 Market Street
Denver, CO 80202
Phone: 303-893-3937
Type: UMS

Construction Junction
695 Buggy Circle
Carbondale, CO 81623
Phone: 970-963-1016
Fax: 970-963-4913
Email: staff@constructionjunction1.com
Type: UMS

Do-It-Ur-Self Plumbing
3120 Brighton Boulevard
Denver, CO 80216
Phone: 303-297-0455
Fax: 303-295-0147
Type: UMS

Habitat for Humanity Home Supply Store
4001 S Taft Hill Road
Ft. Collins, CO
Phone: 970-223-9909
Email: www habitatstore.org
Type: UMS

Habitat for Humanity Thrift Store
5250 N Highway 287
Loveland, CO 80537
Phone: 970-669-7343
Fax: 970-461-0303
Type: UMS

Mastercrafted Specialty Woods
P.O. Box 741
Edwards, CO 81632
Phone: 970-926-4552
Fax: 970-926-4574
Email: info@craftedwoods.com
Website: www.craftedwoods.com
Type: VA

Mendoza Used Brick
701 W 64th Avenue #B
Denver, CO 80221
Phone: 303-427-5675
Type: DM/UMS

Old Grain Reclaimed Wood Specialists
P.O. Box 854
Carbondale, CO 81623
Phone: 970-704-9745
Fax: 970-704-9745
Email: info@oldgrain.com
Website: www.oldgrain.com
Type: UMS/VA

Oxford Recycling
2400 W Oxford Avenue
Englewood, CO 80110
Phone: 303-762-1160
Fax: 303-762-1746
Email: info@oxfordrecycling.com
Website: www.oxfordrecycling.com
Type: RC

Queen City Architectural Salvage
4750 Brighton Boulevard
Denver, CO 80216
Phone: 303-296-0925
Type: UMS

ReConnX, Inc.
P.O. Box 3009
Boulder, CO 80307
Phone: 303-554-8554
Fax: 303-554-8556
Email: jxg@reconnx.com
Website: www.reconnx.com/
Type: EQ

Recycle Materials
6385 W 53rd Avenue
Arvada, CO 80002
Phone: 303-431-3701
Email: rmc@rmci-usa.com
Website: www.rmci-usa.com
Type: RC

ReSource 2000
1702 Walnut Street
Boulder, CO 80302
Phone: 303-441-3278
Fax: 303-441-4367
Email: mmckinne@earthnet.net
Website: www.resource2k.org
Type: DC/UMS
Species: Oak, Fir, Pine

Resource Wood Products, Inc.
7800 Hwy 82 Ste 102
Glenwood Springs, CO 81601
Phone: 970-945-5939
Email: rwtimber@aol.com
Website: www.rw-timber.com
Type: VA

San Juan Timberwrights
60 Barton Circle
Arboles, CO 81121
Phone: 970-883-2291
Website: www.sandonetimber.com
Type: CN

Singing Saw Woodworks, Inc.
67 Shady Hollow
Nederland, CO 80466
Phone: 303-258-0378
Fax: 303-258-0349
Website: www.singingsaw.com/singingsaw
Type: BR/VA

Uncle Benny's Building Supplies LLP
1815 S County Road 13C
Loveland, CO 80537
Phone: 970-593-1667
Fax: 970-461-0900
Email: unclebennys@earthlink.net
Website: unclebennysonline.com
Type: UMS

Used Again Building Materials
506 W Cucharras
Colorado Springs, CO 80905
Phone: 719-473-2150
Type: DC/UMS

Waste Not Recycling
1205 Hope Avenue
Pierce, CO
Phone: 800-584-9912
Email: recycle@waste-not.com
Website: www.waste-not.com
Type: RC

Wind River Collections,
Antique Wood Flooring
7500 E Arapahoe Road #335
Englewood, CO 80112
Phone: 720-493-5572
Fax: 720-493-5626
Email: info@windrivercollections.com
Website: www.windrivercollections.com
Type: VA

Wind River Timber Frames
14374 County Road 35.6
Mancos, CO 81328
Phone: 970-882-2112
Email: timberframes@frontier.net
Website:
www.windriver-timberframes.com
Type: CN

Connecticut

A Reclaimed Lumber co.
9 Old Post Road
Madison, CT 06443
Phone: 203-214-9705
Email: info@whitecedar.com
Website: www.reclaimedlumberco.com
Type: UMS/VA
Species: Pine, Fir, Cypress

Acadia Services, LLC.
937 Post Road, Suite 134
Fairfield, CT 06430
Phone: 203-259-8860
Fax: 203-254-9930
Email: info@acadiademolition.com
Website: www.acadiademolition.com
Type: DC

American Timbers LLC
P.O. Box 430
Canterbury, CT 06331
Phone: 800-461-8660
Fax: 860-546-9334
Email: sales@americantimbers.com
Website: www.americantimbers.com
email:amtimbers@compol.net
Type: UMS

Antique Specialty Flooring
100 W Main Street
Plantsville, CT 06479
Phone: 860-621-6787
Fax: 860-276-0704
Type: VA

Board and Beam
P.O. Box 1235
Washington, CT 06793
Phone: 860-868-6789
Fax: 860-868-0721
Email: bbeams@rcn.com
Website: www.boardandbeam.com
Type: DC/UMS
Species: Pine, Oak, Chestnut

Chestnut Oak Company
3810 Old Mountain Road
West Suffield, CT 06093
Phone: 860-668-0382
Email: info@chestnutoakcompany.com
Website: www.chestnutoakcompany.com
Type: CN/DC/VA

Chestnut Specialists, Inc.
365 Harwinton Avenue
Plymouth, CT 06782
Phone: 860-283-4209
Fax: 860-283-4209
Website: www.chestnutspec.com
Type: VA

Chestnut Woodworking and
Antique Flooring
P.O. Box 204
West Cornwall, CT 06796
Phone: 860-672-4300
Fax: 860-672-2441
Email: info@chestnutwoodworking.com
Website: www.chestnutwoodworking.com
Type: VA

Earth Technology, Inc.
250 Sackett Point Road
North Haven, CT 06473
Phone: 203-230-2040
Fax: 203-230-0302
Website: www.earthtechnology.com
Type: DM

Horse Drawn Pine
273 Pendleton Hill Road
North Stonington, CT 06359
Phone: 860-599-4493
Fax: 860-599-4403
Type: VA

Manafort Brothers, Inc.
414 New Britain Avenue
Plainville, CT 06062
Phone: 860-229-4853
Fax: 860-747-4861
Website: www.manafortbrothers.com
Type: DM

Material Exchange
62 Cherry Street
Bridgeport, CT 06605
Phone: 203-335-3452
Website:
Type: UMS

Old Wood Workshop, LLC
193 Hampton Road
Pomfret Center, CT 06259
Phone: 860-655-5259
Email: Info@Oldwoodworkshop.com
Website: www.oldwoodworkshop.com
Type: UMS
Species: Chestnut, Oak, Pine

Sara E. Armster
9 Old Post Road
Madison, CT 06443
Phone: 203-245-1781
Fax: 203-245-0755
Website: www.whitecedar. com
Type: VA
Species: White Cedar, Cypress

Stamford House Wrecking
1 Barry Place
Stamford, CT 06902
Phone: 203-324-9537
Type: DM

The Meticulous House Wrecking Company
Summit Street
New Milford, CT 06776
Phone: 860-350-5000
Type: DC

United House Wrecking
535 Hope Street
Stamford, CT 06906
Phone: 203-348-5371
Fax: 203-961-9472
Website: www.united-antiques.com
Type: UMS

V and T Used Brick
254 N Hoadly
Naugatuck, CT 06770
Phone: 203-729-9436
Type: UMS

Violette Used Brick
1400 New Britain Avenue
Farmington, CT 06032
Phone: 860-676-0411
Type: UMS

Delaware

D&D Dismantling
P.O. Box 600
Milford, DE 19963
Phone: 302-422-0922
Fax: 302-422-8051
Type: DC/RC

Service Disposal of Delaware
P.O. Box 661
New Castle, DE 19720
Phone: 302-326-9155
Fax: 302-376-9882
Type: DC/RC

The Warehouse Project
500 Duncan Road
Wilmington, DE 19809
Phone: 302-477-1671
Type: UMS

Townsend Building Supply
4324 N DuPont Highway
Townsend, DE 19734
Phone: 302-378-8846
Type: UMS

District of Columbia

All Aboard Contracting Inc.
4214 Hunt Place NE
Washington, DC 20019
Phone: 202-388-4252
Fax: 202-388-3840
Type: CN/DM

Institute for Local Self-Reliance
927 15th Street, NW 4th Floor
Washington, DC 20005
Phone: 202-898-1610
Email: nseldman@ilsr.oreg
Website: www.ilsr.org
Type: DC/RC

The Brass Knob
2329 Champlain Street NW
Washington, DC 20009
Phone: 202-265-0587
Email: bd@thebrassknob.com
Website: www.thebrassknob.com
Type: UMS

The Brass Knob
2311 18th Street NW
Washington, DC 20009
Phone: 202-265-0587
Fax: 202-332-5594
Type: UMS

Florida

A Action Recycling Corporation
1405 CR 210 W
Jacksonville, FL 32259
Phone: 904-356-8869
Type: DC/DM

A Rainbow Lumber
450 Canaveral Groves Boulevard
Cocoa, FL 32926
Phone: 321-638-3800
Type: UMS

A Thrift Store Habitat for Humanity
3962 Central Avenue
St. Petersburg, FL 33711
Phone: 727-322-9730
Type: UMS

Absolute Concrete Cutting
17265 SW 83rd CT
Miami, FL 33157
Phone: 305-969-3644
Fax: 305-969-1320
Email: absodemo@bellsouth.net
Website: www.absolute-demolition.cc
Type: DM

Adam and Eve Architectural Salvage
528 16th Street
West Pam Beach, FL 33407
Phone: 561-655-1022
Website: adamandevearchitecturalsalvage.com
Type: UMS

All Surplus Inc.
4350 NE 6th Avenue
Oakland Park, FL 33334
Phone: 954-567-0977
Fax: 954-491-8679
Email: johns567@bellsouth.net
Type: UMS

Allison's Architectural Antique
5716 Georgia Avenue
West Palm Beach, FL 33405
Phone: 561-582-2224
Type: UMS

American Salvage
7001 NW 27th Avenue
Miami, FL 33147
Phone: 305-691-7001
Fax: 305-691-0001
Email: trw@americansalvage.com
Website: www.americansalvage.com
Type: UMS

Architectural Artifacts
1900 N Miami Avenue
Miami, FL 33136
Phone: 305-573-4169
Type: DC/UMS

Architectural Design and Artifacts
515 N Andrews Avenue
Ft. Lauderdale, FL 33301
Phone: 954-525-1212
Type: UMS

Arwood Wrecking
13255 Lanier Road
Jacksonville, FL 32226
Phone: 904-751-1628
Type: DM/RC

Atlantic Building Salvage
7526 NW 7th Avenue
Miami, FL 33150
Phone: 305-693-2910
Type: UMS

Beasley & Son Inc.
4922 N 56th Street
Tampa, FL 33610
Phone: 813-626-0978
Type: DM

Builders Bargain Surplus Inc.
3045 NE 12th Terrace
Ft. Lauderdale, FL 33334
Phone: 954-564-7375
Type: UMS

Burkhalter Wrecking, Inc.
P.O. Box 2407
Jacksonville, FL 32203
Phone: 904-354-7813
Fax: 904-354-7815
Email: pjb@burkhalters.com
Website: www.burkhalters.com
Type: DC/DM

Cash & Carry Surplus Building Supply
718 Farmer's Market Road
Fort Pierce, FL 34982
Phone: 561-461-3999
Type: UMS

Central Environmental Services Inc.
3210 Friendly Avenue
Orlando, FL 32808
Phone: 407-295-7005
Fax: 407-295-7004
Website: www.centralenvironmental.com
Type: DC/UMS
Species: Heartpine, Oak, Maple

Charlotte County HFH ReStore
P.O. Box 6028
Port Charlott, FL 33949
Phone: 941-639-1261
Type: UMS

D.H. Griffin Wrecking Co., Inc.
1312 West Nine Mile Road
Pensacola, FL 32534
Phone: 850-478-1262
Type: DC/DM

Discount Building Materials
735 Carswell Avenue
Daytona Beach, FL 32117
Phone: 386-255-0002
Type: UMS

Dore & Associates Contracting, Inc.
1715 E Fowler, Suite 217
Tampa, FL 33612
Phone: 800-344-7876
Email: dore@concentric.net
Website: www.doreandassociates.com
Type: DC/DM

Florida Dismantling
7520 NW 7th Avenue
Miami, FL 33150
Phone: 305-696-8855
Type: DM

Florida Victorian Architectural Antiques
112 W Georgia Avenue
DeLand, FL 32720
Phone: 904-734-9300
Fax: 904-734-1150
Website: www floridavictorian.com
Type: UMS

Florida Wrecking and Salvage
8814 Honeywell Road
Gibsonton, FL 33534
Phone: 813-741-0405
Type: DC/DM

Forristall Enterprises, Inc.
3404 17th Street E
Palmetto, FL 34221
Phone: 941-729-8150
Fax: 941-729-7345
Website: www forristall.com
Type: DC

Giant Mart
5485 Haines Road N
St. Petersburg, FL 33714
Phone: 727-526-1494
Fax: 727-526-1494
Type: UMS

Globe Demolition and Recycling
2225 Hazelhurst Drive
Orlando, FL 32801
Phone: 407-422-4768
Fax: 407-228-0062
Email: globedemolition@yahoo.com
Type: DC

Goodwin Heart Pine Company
106 SW 109th Place
Micanopy, FL 32667
Phone: 800-336-3118
Fax: 352-466-0339
Email: goodwin@heartpine.com
Website: www.heartpine.com
Type: VA

Government Sales Associates
4972 N Orange Avenue
Winter Park, FL 32792
Phone: 407-679-1759
Fax: 407-679-1567
Email: govsls@magicnet net
Type: UMS

Habitat for Humanity Inc. (Tampa)
8100 N Florida Avenue
Tampa, FL 33604
Phone: 813-935-8805
Type: UMS

Handyman's Dreamland Inc.
18522 U.S. Highway 19
Hudson, FL 34667
Phone: 813-869-2588
Email: jjexport@gte net
Type: UMS

Insul-Coat
2049 W Central Boulevard
Orlando, FL 32805
Phone: 407-447-1684
Fax: 407-447-1679
Email: kklein@cleanbuilding.com
Website: www.cleanbuilding.com
Type: DM

L&L Demolition and Salvage
5500 Old Winter Garden Road
Orlando, FL 32811
Phone: 407-295-0875
Fax: 407-296-9855
Type: DC

Layman's Used Merchandise
12190 U.S. Highway 19 N
Clearwater, FL 33764
Phone: 727-531-3801
Type: UMS

Michael Murphy
3503 W San Juan Street
Tampa, FL 33629
Phone: 813-902-1480
Fax: 813-727-6222
Email: murphym@gte net
Type: BR

Norwood Surplus Plywood
6200 Norwood Avenue
Jacksonville, FL 32208
Phone: 904-768-6818
Type: UMS

Orange County Community
Distribution Center
2000 Lucerne Terrace
Orlando, FL 32806
Phone: 407-836-4680
Type: UMS

Pensacola Salvage 7
1245 N Warrington Road
Pensacola, FL 32506
Phone: 850-455-7000
Type: UMS

Pinellas Habitat for Humanity ReStore
3962 Central Avenue
St. Petersburg, FL 32608
Phone: 727-322-9730
Type: UMS

Pinetree Builders
814 SE 23rd Street
Ft. Lauderdale, FL 33316
Phone: 954-760-5800
Fax: 954-760-5833
Email: info@pinetreebuilders.com
Website: www.pinetreebuilders.com
Type: UMS/ CN/VA
Species: Heartpine, Cypress

Raider Demolition
4970 SW 52nd Street
Davie, FL 33063
Phone: 954-791-9913
Fax: 954-791-1435
Email: info@raiderdemo.com
Website: www raiderdemo.com
Type: DC/DM

Reilly Bros Inc.
3026 E Riverside Drive
Fort Myers, FL 33916
Phone: 239-334-1567
Type: UMS

Resources Limited
3100 Woodville Highway
Tallahassee, FL 32305
Phone: 850-878-5450
Email: lwelbon@comcast net
Type: UMS

ReUser Building Products
622 SE 2nd Street
Gainesville, FL 32601
Phone: 352-379-4600
Fax: 352-377-0037
Email: pollyodel@gru net
Type: UMS

Roz's Reusable Building Materials
18260 Paulson Drive
Port Charlotte, FL 33954
Phone: 941-766-0004
Type: UMS

S&M Used Building Materials
5275 Haines Road N
St. Petersburg, FL 33714
Phone: 727-526-8888
Fax: 727-522-8800
Email: custsvc@salvageitems.com
Website: www.salvageitems.com
Type: UMS

Sarasota Architectural Salvage
1143 Central Avenue
Sarasota, FL 34236
Phone: 941-358-7730
Email: info@sarasotasalvage.com
Type: UMS

Southland Demolition
8619 Western Way
Jacksonville, FL 32256
Phone: 904-731-1232
Email: tuengef@southland-enviro.com
Website: www.suthland-enviro.com
Type: DC

Standard Demolition Corporation
1607 43rd Street
Tampa, FL 33605
Phone: 813-626-6552
Fax: 813-626-0840
Email: info@standarddemo.com
Website: www.standarddemo.com
Type: DM

Surplus Shop Inc.
10121 SE Highway 441
Belleview, FL 34420
Phone: 352-245-4640
Fax: 352-245-6172
Website:
Type: UMS

Svinga Brothers Corp.
206 NE 9th Street
Ocala, FL 34470
Phone: 352-351-2841
Fax: 352-351-3560
Type: DC/UMS

Used Stuff Inc.
1404 Central Avenue
Sarasota, FL 34236
Phone: 941-953-5100
Email: usedstuff@comcast net
Type: UMS

WR Townsend Contracting
1465 CR 210 W
Jacksonville, FL 32259
Phone: 904-354-9202
Type: DC/DM

Georgia

AMC Demolition Specialists, Inc.
1525 Northridge Road
Atlanta, GA 30338
Phone: 770-395-1400
Fax: 770-395-0222
Email: amcdemo@mindspring.com
Website: www.amcdemolition.com
Type: DM

America Demolition Contractors
1906 Ford Avenue
Savannah, GA 31405
Phone: 912-232-0053
Type: DM

Architectural Accents
2711 Piedmont Road
Atlanta, GA 30305
Phone: 404-266-8700
Fax: 404-266-0074
Email: archaccent@aol.com
Type: UMS

Atlanta Salvage Outlet
1034 Howell Mill Road
Atlanta, GA 30318
Phone: 404-873-4416
Type: UMS

Authentic Pine Floors
4042 Highway 42
Locust Grove, GA 30248
Phone: 770-957-6038
Fax: 770-914-2925
Email: info@authenticpinefloors.com
Website: www.authenticpinefloors.com
Type: VA

Builder's Salvage
109 Addington Drive NW
Rome, GA 30165
Phone: 706-232-8869
Type: UMS

Cooper Equipment Contracting
301 Miller Street
Valdosta, GA 31601
Phone: 229-244-7696
Type: DM/UMS

DBM Imports Exports
2905 Amwiler Road
Atlanta, GA 30360
Phone: 770-729-0159
Type: UMS

EnviroShare Materials Exchange
Gainesville, GA 30503
Phone: 770-535-8284
Website: www.enviroshare.org
Type: BR

Flint River HFH ReStore
P.O. Box 710
Albany, GA 31702
Phone: 912-430-7942
Type: UMS

Georgia Heart Pine
1130 Sarracenia
Moultrie, GA 31768
Phone: 229-985-4100
Type: VA

Great Gatsby's
5070 Peachtree Ind Boulevard
Atlanta, GA 30341
Phone: 770-457-1905
Type: UMS

H.F. Bloodworth, Inc.
Route 1 / P.O. Box 1975
McIntyre, GA 31054
Phone: 912-628-5218
Type: RC

Habitat for Humanity
723 Spring Street
Americus, GA 31709
Phone: 229-931-9899
Fax: 229-931-6188
Email: restore@newhorizonshabitat.org
Website: www newhorizonshabitat.org
Type: UMS

Home Resource Interchange
750 Glenwood Avenue SE
Atlanta, GA 30316
Phone: 404-624-4434
Fax: 404-624-5299
Type: UMS

Hudgins & Company, Inc.
640 North Avenue NW
Atlanta, GA 30318
Phone: 404-523-2791
Type: UMS

Industrial Metals & Surplus
1635 Marietta Road NW
Atlanta, GA 30318
Phone: 404-355-0486
Website: www.steel-cheap.com
Type: RC

Metropolitan Artifacts
4783 Peachtree Road
Atlanta, GA 30341
Phone: 707-986-0007
Type: UMS

Northside Material Brokers
1020 Huff Road
Atlanta, GA 30318
Phone: 404-609-9900
Fax: 404-609-9964
Email: northsidematials@msn.com
Type: BR
Species: Fir, Oak, Mahogany

Owltown Recycling
4012 Sudderth Road
Buford, GA 30518
Phone: 770-271-3366
Type: RC

Pinch of the Past
109 W Broughton Street
Savannah, GA 31401
Phone: 912-232-5563
Email: pinchopast@aol.com
Website: www.pinchofthepast.com
Type: UMS

Raze Demolition and Contractors, Inc.
1605 Whitaker Street
Savannah, GA 31401
Phone: 912-201-9440
Fax: 912-447-6888
Type: DM
Species: Heartpine

Re Use the Past, Inc.
98 Moreland Street
Grantville, GA 30220
Phone: 770-583-3111
Email: bocastle@mindspring.com
Type: DC/UMS

Reaves Wrecking Co. Inc.
701 10th Street
Columbus, GA 31901
Phone: 706-322-8923
Fax: 706-322-1182
Email: billreaves@reaveswrecking.com
Website: www.reaveswrecking.com
Type: DC

Restorations & Antiques Supplies
of Savannah
600 W 51st Street
Savannah, GA 31405
Phone: 912-236-7724
Type: UMS

Restorations and Antique Supplies
600 W 51st Street
Savannah, GA 31405
Phone: 912-236-7724
Type: UMS

Sawmill Treasures
Highway 57
Irwinton, GA 31042
Phone: 478-946-2510
Email: guerryholder@hotmail.com
Website: www.sawmilltreasures.com
Type: UMS/VA

Second Chance
230 7th Street
Macon, GA 31201
Phone: 478-742-7874
Type: UMS

Southern Pine Company of Georgia
P.O. Box 2152
Savannah, GA 31402
Phone: 912-236-4112
Email: info@southernpinecompany.com
Website: www.southernpinecompany.com
Type: DC/VA
Species: Heart pine, cypress

Southern Wood Floors
472A-1 Flowing Wells Road
Augusta, GA 30907
Phone: 706-855-0779
Email: info@southernwoodfloors.com
Website: www.southernwoodfloors.com
Type: VA

Vintage Lumber Products
325 Swift Street
Toccoa, GA 30577
Phone: 706-282-0077
Type: UMS

Vintage Lumber Sales
18757 Highway 85
Gay, GA 30218
Phone: 706-538-0180
Fax: 706-538-6558
Website: www.vintagelumbersales.com
Type: UMS
Species: Heartpine, Cypress, Oak

Wrecking Barn
292 Mooreland Avenue
Atlanta, GA 30307
Phone: 404-525-0468
Type: UMS

Hawaii

Island Demo, Inc.
2769 Kilihau Street
Honolulu, HI 96819
Phone: 808-839-5522
Fax: 808-839-5515
Email: islanddemo@yahoo.com
www.gtesupersite.com/islanddemo
Type: DM

Idaho

Alternative Timber Structures
1054 Rammel Mountain Road
Tetonia, ID 83452
Phone: 208-456-2711
www.alternativetimberstructures.com
Type: VA

Bell Hardwood Floor Inc.
325 N Holmes Avenue
Idaho Falls, ID 83401
Phone: 208-522-9694
Type: VA

Building Material Thrift Store
3990 Woodside Boulevard
Hailey, ID 83333
Phone: 208-788-0014
Fax: 208-788-0816
Email: bmtbruce@earthlink net
Website:
www.woodriverlandtrust.org/store/store.html
Type: DC/UMS

Engineered Demolition Inc.
3901 N Schreiber Way
Coeur D'Alene, ID 83815
Phone: 208-676-9900
Fax: 208-676-9800
Email: bwelch@bigblast.com
Website: www.bigblast.com
Type: DC

Ross Lumber
391 Highway 75 Box 519
Shoshone, ID 83352
Phone: 208-886-7778
Fax: 208-886-7779
Email: rosslumber.com
     rickross@micron.com
Type: UMS

Salavatori's Cut and Run
1006 Elk Grove Road
Sandpoint, ID 83864
Phone: 208-265-7843
Email: tonto@coldreams.com
Type: DC

Stein and Collett, Inc.
P.O. Box 4065
McCall, ID 83638
Phone: 208-634-8228
Fax: 208-634-8228
Type: VA

Trestlewood
933 South Frontage Road
Blackfoot, ID 83221
Phone: 208-785-1151
Fax: 208-785-0458
Email: info@trestlewood.com
Website: www.Trestlewood.com
Type: DC/UMS/VA
Species: Fir, Pine, Oak

Wasankari Construction
2730 Highway 95 S
Moscow, ID 83843
Phone: 208-883-4362
Type: CN/UMS

Illinois

A & T Wrecking and Lumber
1550 W 88th Street
Chicago, IL 60636
Phone: 773-445-3100
Type: DM/UMS

A & T Wrecking & Lumber Co.
16461 Wood Street
Markham, IL 60426-5824
Phone: 708-333-4700
Type: DC/UMS

American Barn Company
3808 N Clark Street
Chicago, IL 60613
Phone: 773-327-1560
Type: UMS

American Demolition Corp.
305 Ramona Avenue
Elgin, IL 60120
Phone: 847-608-0010
Fax: 847-608-0060
Website:
www.americandemolitioncorp.com
Type: DM

Archaic Architectural
4304 S Michigan Avenue
Chicago, IL 60653
Phone: 773-268-0100
Type: DM/UMS

Architectural Artifacts
4325 N Ravenswood Avenue
Chicago, IL 60613
Phone: 773-348-0622
Fax: 773-348-6118
Type: UMS

Asset Recovery Contracting
5441 Fargo Avenue
Skokie, IL 60077
Phone: 847-674-3366
Fax: 847-674-8660
Email: jim@arcdem.com
Website: www.arcdemo.com
Type: UMS

Brandenburg Industrial Service Company
2625 S Loomis Street
Chicago, IL 60608
Phone: 312-326-5800
Fax: 312-326-5065
Email: moowila@brandenburg.info
Website: www.brandenburg.info
Type: DC

Builders Salvage
30347 U.S.150 Highway
Farmer City, IL 61842
Phone: 309-928-2344
Type: UMS

Carlson's Barnwood Company
8066 N 1200 Avenue
Cambridge, IL 61238
Phone: 309-522-5550
Fax: 309-522-5123
Email: info@carlsonsbarnwood.com
Website: www.carlsonsbarnwood.com
Type: UMS

Colonial Brick Inc.
2222 S Halstead Street
Chicago, IL 60608
Phone: 312-733-2600
Website: www.colonialbrickchicago.com
Type: UMS

Darrah–Barns
104 N Prairie Street
Rockton, IL 61072
Phone: 815-624-4434
Fax: 815-624-4547
Email: darrahbarns@hotmail.com
Type: DC/UMS

Delta Demolition, Inc.
1230 N Kostner
Chicago, IL 60651
Phone: 773-252-6370
Fax: 773-252-8263
Type: DM

Dix Lumber and Recycling
202 E Washington Street
Dix, IL 62830
Phone: 618-266-7665
Type: UMS

Ecologic, Inc.
1140 Elizabeth Avenue
Waukegan, IL 60085
Phone: 800-899-8004
Fax: 847-244-5977
Type: VA

Environmental Cleansing Corporation
16602 S Crawford Avenue
Markham, IL 60426
Phone: 708-532-7000
Fax: 708-636-3996
Email: envirocleansing@aol.com
Website:
www.environmentalcleansing.com
Type: DC

Heneghan Wrecking Co. Inc.
1321 W Concord Place
Chicago, IL 60622
Phone: 773-342-9009
Fax: 773-342-6123
Website: www.heneghanwrecking.com
Type: DC/DM

HFH of McLean County
P.O. Box 3432
Bloomington, IL 61702
Phone: 309-827-3931
Type: UMS

J Stuart Corsa–Purveyors
of Salvage Material
6528 Charles Street
Rockford, IL 61108
Phone: 815-229-0377
Email: stuart51@aol.com
Type: BR/UMS

J. Hoffman Co.
1919 Cherry Hill Road
Joilet, IL 60433
Phone: 630-513-6680
Fax: 630-513-6687
Type: VA

Jan's Antiques
225 N Racine Avenue
Chicago, Il 60607
Phone: 312-563-0275
Type: UMS

Lockett's Lumber & Salvage
2104 Baker Avenue
East St Louis, IL 62207
Phone: 618-274-1884
Type: UMS

Lowder Construction Architectural Salvage
116 E State Street
Waverly, IL 62692
Phone: 217-435-9618
Type: UMS

Mid-America Architectural Salvage
P.O. Box 926
Grayslake, IL 60030
Phone: 847-223-5772
Fax: 847-223-5775
Website: www.architectural-antqs.com
Type: UMS

Murco Recycling Enterprises Inc.
347 N Kensington Street
LaGrange Park, IL 60526
Phone: 708-352-4111
Fax: 708-352-4189
Email: jodi@murco net
Website: www murco net
Type: BR

N.F. Demolition
4333 S Knox Avenue
Chicago, IL 60632
Phone: 773-284-8300
Fax: 773-284-9316
Email: nfdemo@NFDemolition.com
Website: www nfdemolition.com
Type: DM

Old House Heaven
602 E State Street
Jacksonville, IL 62650
Phone: 217-479-8020
Fax: 217-479-8332
Email: oldhouse@csi.net
Website: www.oldhouseheaven.com
Type: UMS

Omega Demolition Corporation
1536 Brandy Parkway
Stearmwood, IL 60107
Phone: 630-837-3000
Fax: 630-837-2300
Email: chuckg@omega-demolition.com
Website: www.omega-demolition.com
Type: DM

River City Demolition
P.O. Box 726
Peoria, IL 61602
Phone: 309-655-0447
Fax: 309-767-1415
Email: rivercitydemo@aol.com
Website: www rivercitydemolition.com
Type: DC/UMS

Robinette Demolition, Inc.
0 S. 560 Highway 83
Oakbrook Terrace, IL 60181
Phone: 630-833-7997
Fax: 630-833-8047
Email: info@rdidemolition.com
Website: www rdidemolition.com
Type: DM

Salvage One
1524 S Sangamon Street
Chicago, IL 60608
Phone: 312-733-0098
Email: salvoone@aol.com
Website: www.salvageone.com
Type: UMS

Spiess Architectural Antiques
230 E Washington Street
Joliet, IL 60433
Phone: 815-722-5639
Fax: 815-722-0171
Email: SPIESSANTQ@AOL.COM
Type: UMS

The Renovation Source Inc.
3512 N Southport Avenue
Chicago, IL 60657
Phone: 773-327-1250
Fax: 773-327-1250
Type: UMS
Species: Oak, Pine, Poplar

The Restoration Place
305 20th Street
Rock Island, IL 61201
Phone: 309-786-0004
Fax: 309-786-5834
Type: UMS

The Storehouse of Vision
5001 W Harrison
Chicago, IL 60644
Phone: 773-921-3900 ext. 315
Fax: 773-921-3953
Email: sjpincham@thestorehouse.org
Website: www.thestorehouse.org
Type: UMS

United Demolition Inc.
2123 Oxford Road
Des Plaines, IL 60018
Phone: 847-296-2600
Fax: 847-816-4718
Type: DM

Indiana

Bringing It Back
5726 University Avenue
Indianapolis, IN 46219
Phone: 317-322-8388
Email: housesalvager@aol.com
Type: BR/DC

Capellier Salvage and Wrecking
11640 N East Drive
Camby, IN 46113
Phone: 317-831-4533
Fax: 317-834-3057
Email: sjack1306@aol.com
Type: DC/UMS

Crowe Wrecking Co.
2400 Grove Street
Evansville, IN 47710
Phone: 812-425-6511
Type: DM/UMS

Edgewood Building Supply
1580 E Epler Avenue
Indianapolis, IN 46227
Phone: 317-786-9208
Fax: 317-788-4023
Type: UMS

First Saturday Construction Salvage
Route 3 Box 405
Spencer, IN 47460
Phone: 812-876-6347
Fax: 812-876-6347
Email: construcsalvage@smithville net
Website: www.constructionsalvage.com
Type: DC/UMS
Species: Pine, Oak, Walnut

Foursquare Antiques and Architectural
Salvage
727 W 5th Street
Bloomington, IN 47404
Phone: 812-337-8577
Type: UMS

Hannells Wrecking Co.
3118 W U.S. Highway 40
Clayton, IN 46118
Phone: 317-539-6464
Fax: 317-539-2246
Type: DC/UMS
Species: Pine

Harris Building and Salvage
2027 West 500 S
Morocco, IN 47963
Phone: 219-285-6029
Type: UMS

Northlake Excavation & Demolition
1332 Grant Street
Gary, IN 46404
Phone: 219-886-9368
Fax: 219-886-9603
Website: www northlakegary.com
Type: DM

Rehab Resource, Inc.
3029 E Washington Street
Indianapolis, IN 46205
Phone: 800-685-4686
Email: rresource@iquest net
Website: www rehabresource.org/
Type: UMS

Richey Salvage and Demolition
5782 N CR 420 W
Greensburg, IN 47240
Phone: 812-663-6512
Type: DM

Searcy Antique Woods
Cedar Grove, IN 47016
Phone: 812-926-9775
Fax: 765-647-6454
Email: sales@searcyantiquewoods.com
Website: www.searcyantiquewoods.com
Type: DC/VA

The Reuse Development Organization
P.O. Box 47454
Indianapolis, IN 46227
Phone: 317-780-1503
Email: info@redo.org
Website: www.redo.org
Type: BR

Tim & Billy's Salvage Store
970 Fort Wayne Avenue
Indianapolis, IN 46202
Phone: 317-632-7161
Fax: 317-632-0047
Website: www.architecturalantiques net
Type: UMS

Tim and Avi's Salvage Store
2442 Central Avenue
Indianapolis, IN 46205
Phone: 317-925-6071
Type: UMS

White River Architectural Salvage
1325 W 30th Street
Indianapolis, IN 46208
Phone: 317-924-4000
Email: whiteriversal-
vage@whiteriversalvage.com
Website: www.whiteriversalvage.com
Type: DC/UMS

Iowa

Building Savers
3301 Main Street
Emmetsburg, IA 50536
Phone: 712-852-3057
Type: UMS

Cedar Valley Recovery and Demolition
553 Reed Street
Waterloo, IA 50703
Phone: 319-234-3075
Type: DM

Central C&D Recycling
1300 Lincoln Street
Des Moines, IA 50265
Phone: 515-243-6402
Type: RC

Concrete Recyclers Ltd
110 Main Street
Ossian, IA 52161
Phone: 583-532-9215
Type: RC

Eco-Youth
3351 Square D Drive SW
Cedar Rapids, IA 52404
Phone: 319-365-3501
Fax: 319-365-0104
Website: www nahp net
Type: UMS

Fuller Salvage and Wrecking
2113 E Mitchell Avenue
Waterloo, IA 50702
Phone: 391-233-2546
Type: DM

Gavin Historical Bricks
2050 Glendale Road
Iowa City, IA 52245
Phone: 319-354-5251
Email: info@historicalbricks.com
Website: www historicalbricks.com
Type: UMS

Home Recycling Exchange
805 SE 14th Court
Des Moines, IA 50317
Phone: 515-282-9296
Email: lballhre@aol.com
Type: UMS

House and Garden Restoration Specialties
1410 19th Street
Des Moines, IA 50314
Phone: 515-243-3985
Fax: 515-282-3892
Type: UMS

Iowa Demolition and Recycling Services
6400 Seminole Court NE
Cedar Rapids, IA 52411
Phone: 319-393-9013
Type: DM/RC

J. Myron Olson & Son Inc.
1718 18th Street
Sioux City, IA 51105
Phone: 712-258-5615
Type: DM

Jim's Small Demolition
P.O. Box 1235
Dubuque, IA 52004
Phone: 563-583-8673
Type: DC

Ken Hunt Building Supply & Salvage
2050 E Army Post Road
Des Moines, IA 50320
Phone: 515-287-0007
Fax: 515-287-0007
Type: UMS

ReStore HfH Quad Cities
2235 Grant Street
Bettendorf, IA 52722
Phone: 563-359-9066
Email: dancin@mcleodusa net
Website: www restoreqc.org
Type: UMS

Rock Creek Tree and Building Salvage
1538 325th Street
Osage, IA 50461
Phone: 641-732-4025
Type: DC

The Salvage Barn
1147 S Riverside Drive
Iowa City, IA 52246
Phone: 800-541-8656
Email: salvagebarn@ic-fhp.org
Website: www.ic-fhp.org/salvagebarn html
Type: DC/UMS

Kansas

Bahm Demolition
3840 NW Hodges Road
Silver Lake, KS 66539
Phone: 785-582-5190
Fax: 582-412-8785
Email: djb977@aol.com
Website: www.bahmdemolition.com
Type: DC/UMS
Species: Pine, Oak

Bill Porter Wrecking
4949 E 63rd Street S
Derby, KS 67037
Phone: 316-788-7300
Type: DM/UMS

Bob Smith Salvage
4999 E Old Highway 40
New Cambria, KS 67470
Phone: 785-823-8877
Type: DM/UMS

BOGE Iron and Metal Company Inc.
800 S Saint Francis Street
Wichita, KS 67211
Phone: 316-263-8241
Type: UMS

McPherson Wrecking Inc.
2333 Barton Road
Grantville, KS 66429
Phone: 785-246-3012
Fax: 785-246-3014
Type: DM/UMS

Novick Iron & Metal
1997 E 21st Street N
Wichita, KS 67214
Phone: 316-265-6661
Fax: 316-265-6677
Type: UMS

Reeves Lumber & Surplus
2800 E Macarthur Road
Wichita, KS 67216
Phone: 316-524-0730
Type: UMS

Wise Buys
RR 2 Box 33A
Beloit, KS 67420
Phone: 785-738-4333
Type: UMS

Kentucky

City Salvage and Recycling
2495 Greenville Road
Hopkinsville, KY
Phone: 270-886-5606
Type: UMS/RC

Heartwood Industries
3658 State Road 1414
Hartford, KY 42347
Phone: 800-318-9439
Fax: 270-298-7755
Website: www.whiskeywood.com
Type: BR

Hedges Demolition
3201 W Highway 146
LaGrange, KY 40031
Phone: 502-222-0779
Fax: 502-222-7258
Type: DM/UMS

Joe Ley Antiques, Inc.
615 Market Street
Louisville, KY 40202
Phone: 502-583-4041
Type: UMS

Longwood Antique Woods
330 Midland Place #3
Lexington, KY 40505
Phone: 869-233-2268
Email: longwood-inc@msn.com
Website: www.longwoodantiquewoods.com
Type: VA

Salvage Building Materials of Lexington
573 Angliana Avenue
Lexington, KY 40508
Phone: 859-255-4700
Type: UMS

WD Architectural Salvage
618 E Broadway Street
Louisville, KY 40202
Phone: 502-589-0670
Type: UMS

Whiskey Wood
3658 State Road 1414
Hartford, KY 42347
Phone: 270-298-0084
Fax: 270-298-7755
Website: www.whiskeywood.com
Type: VA

Louisiana

Albany Woodworks, Inc.
P.O. Box 729
Albany, LA 70711
Phone: 225-567-1155
Fax: 225-567-5150
Website: www.albanywoodworks.com
Type: VA

Antique Lumber Millwork
1920 Ridge Road
Duson, LA 70529
Phone: 800-381-9585
Fax: 318-988-2703
Type: VA

Antique Woods and Architecturals
113 Heymann Boulevard
Lafayette, LA 70503
Phone: 337-291-1139
Type: UMS

Architectural Antiques Materials Company
871 Polk Street
New Orleans, LA 70124
Phone: 504-942-7000
Type: UMS

Armadillo South Architectural
4801 Washington Avenue
New Orleans, LA 70125
Phone: 504-486-1150
Type: UMS

Builders Antique Menagerie Co.
7925 Tom Drive
Baton Rouge, LA 70806
Phone: 225-925-9582
Fax: 225-925-9506
Type: UMS

Carrollton Brick Co.
535 Iris Avenue
New Orleans, LA 70121
Phone: 504-835-0074
Type: UMS

Carrollton Lumber and Wrecking Company
2938 Leonidas Street
New Orleans, LA 70118
Phone: 504-861-3681
Fax: 504-861-2681
Email: ContactUs@CarrolltonLumber.com
Website: www.carrolltonlumber.com
Type: UMS

Crescent City Architectural
3101 Tchoupitoulas Street
New Orleans, LA 70115
Phone: 504-891-0500
Fax: 504-891-1895
Email: cca@architectural-salvage.com
Website: www.architectural-salvage.com
Type: DC/VA

Discount Building Materials and Salvage
905 N Lee Road
Covington, LA 70433
Phone: 985-898-2164
Type: UMS

Green Project
520 S Alexander Street
New Orleans, LA 70119
Phone: 504-488-6853
Type: UMS

Gulf Coast Dismantling and Salvage
P.O. Box 628
Oakdale, LA 71463
Phone: 318-335-9944
Type: DM

Habitat ReStore New Orleans
2830 Royal Street
New Orleans, LA 70117
Phone: 504-943-2240
Fax: 504-943-2214
Email: restore@habitat-nola.org
Website: www.habitat-nola.org/restore
Type: UMS

HFH St. Tammany West
P.O. Box 3082
Covington, LA 70434
Phone: 504-893-3172
Type: UMS

Louisiana\Chemical Dismantling Co., Inc.
24 27th Street
Kenner, LA 70062
Phone: 504-464-0770
Fax: 504-464-4419
Email: LaChem@aol.com
Website: www.lcdc-invirex.com
Type: DM

Louisiana Antique Woods
101 Templeton Drive
Lafayette, LA 70508
Phone: 337-269-1933
Type: UMS

New Orleans Cypressworks
3110 Magazine Street
New Orleans, LA 70115
Phone: 504-891-0001
Type: VA

Ole Fashion Things
402 SW Evangeline Trailway
Lafayette, LA 70501
Phone: 337-234-4800
Type: UMS

Ricca & Puderer Demolishing
& Building Materials
2645 Toulouse Street
New Orleans, LA 70119
Phone: 504-822-8200
Type: UMS

Second Chance Construction Salvage
403 Richard Street
Gretna, LA 70053
Phone: 504-367-7717
Type: UMS

Southern Specialty Contractors
210 Baronne Street
New Orleans, LA 70118
Phone: 504-525-4911
Type: UMS

The Architectural Antiques Bank
1824 Felicity Street
New Orleans, LA 70113
Phone: 504-523-2702
Fax: 504-523-6055
Type: UMS

The Wreckers Warehouse
401 Short Street
New Orleans, LA 70118
Phone: 504-525-4911
Type: UMS

Tiger Antique Woods
12539 S Choctaw Drive
Baton Rouge, LA 70815
Phone: 225-275-9132
Type: UMS

Vintage Woods
301 Pecan Drive
Denham Springs, LA 70726
Phone: 225-665-0017
Type: UMS

What It's Worth
11550 N Harrells Ferry
Baton Rouge, LA 70816
Phone: 504-275-1867
Type: VA

White Lumber and Architectural
Demolition
950 S Genois Street
New Orleans, LA 70112
Phone: 504-486-7576
Email: whitelumber@hotmail.com
Type: UMS
Species: Longleaf pine, Oak, Cypress

Will Branch Antique Lumber
60407 Spring Valley Road
Bogalusa, LA 70427
Phone: 985-732-3798
Fax: 985-732-5555
Email: wse@willbranch net
Website: www.willbranch net
Type: VA

Maine

Aroostock Building Materials Bank
4 Lombard Road P.O. Box 748
Caribou, ME 04736
Phone: 207-498-2575
Website: www.ccmaine.org/building-
materials html
Type: UMS

Auburn Enterprises
P.O.Box 3065
Auburn, ME 04212-3065
Phone: 207-784-4244
Email: tlabrie@auburnmachinery.com
Type: EQ/VA

Building Materials Exchange
169 Lewiston Road
Gray, ME 04039
Phone: 207-657-2957
Fax: 209-657-5910
Type: UMS

Decorum
231 Commercial Street
Portland, ME 04101
Phone: 207-775-3346
Website: www.decorumonesource.com
Type: UMS

Frederick Non-Profit Building Supply, Inc.
5813 Buckeystown Pike
Frederick, ME 21701
Phone: 301-662-2988
Type: UMS

Interstate Building Salvage
307 Stanley Road
New Vineyard, ME 04956
Phone: 207-778-9340
Type: DC/UMS

Maine Antique Structures
Salvage Company
280 Rockland Street
Rockport, ME 04856
Phone: 207-594-0607
Type: UMS

Maine Housing & Building
Materials Exchange
169 Lewiston Road
Gray, ME 04039
Phone: 207-657-2957
Fax: 207-657-5910
Email: MHBME169@yahoo.com
Website: www mainebme.org
Type: UMS

Mid Coast HFH ReStore
93 Chestnut Street
Camden, ME 04843
Phone: 207-236-4974
Type: UMS

Old House Parts Co.
24 Blue Wave Mall
Kennebunk, ME 04043
Phone: 207-985-1999
Fax: 207-985-1911
Email: restoration@oldhouseparts.com
Website: www.oldhouseparts.com
Type: UMS

Penney Pincher Discount
24 Hartland Avenue
Pittsfield, ME 04967
Phone: 207-487-3696
Type: UMS

Portland Architectural Salvage
919 Congress Street
Portland, ME 04101
Phone: 207-780-0634
Website: www.portlandsalvage.com
Type: UMS

Seacoast Architectural Salvage
5 Lime
Rockport, ME 04856
Phone: 207-594-4836
Type: UMS

The Green Store
71 Main Street
Belfast, ME 04915
Phone: 207-338-4045
Fax: 207-338-5988
Type: RC/VA

Maryland

Colonial Lumber
207 W Ashby Ellis Road
Oakland, MD 21550
Phone: 301-334-3189
Email: coloniallmbr@gcnetmail net
Website: www.coloniallumber.com
Type: VA

Craftwright Timberframe Co.
100 Railroad Avenue 105
Westminster, MD 21157
Phone: 410-876-0999
Fax: 410-876-0999
Email: greyoak1@aol.com
Website:
www.craftwrighttimberframes.com
Type: VA
Species: Oak, Chestnut, Heartpine

Custom Demolition
3208 Kimberly Drive
Mount Airy, MD 21771
Phone: 410-635-3144
Type: DM

International Wood Products
32203 Park Avenue
Queen Anne, MD 21657
Phone: 410-364-5031
Fax: 410-364-5905
Type: VA

Newel Post
7600 Jefferson Avenue
Landover, MD 20785
Phone: 301-627-4499
Website: www.pghct.org/newelpost html
Type: UMS

Old Line Timberframes
400 Dilks Lane
Elkton, MD 21921
Phone: 410-287-1545
Fax: 410-287-1545
Email: joe@oldlinetimberframes.com
Website: www.oldlinetimberframes.com
Type: CN/VA

Old Wood & Co.
1013 S Talbot Street
Saint Michaels, MD 21663
Phone: 410-745-0035
Type: VA

Power Component Systems Inc.
7526-R Connelley Drive
Hanover, MD 21076
Phone: 410-760-0022
Fax: 410-760-0028
Email: toby@powercomponentsystems.com
Website:
www.powercomponentsystems.com
Type: DC

Second Chance
1645 Warner Street
Baltimore, MD 21230
Phone: 410-385-1101
Email: info@secondchanceinc.org
Website: www.secondchanceinc.org
Type: DC/UMS

The Loading Dock
2523 Gwynns Falls Parkway
Baltimore, MD 21216
Phone: 410-728-3625
Fax: 410-728-3633
Email: stafford@loadingdock.org
Website: www.loadingdock.org
Type: DC/UMS

The Woods Co. Inc.
2357 Bottler Road
Brownsville, MD 21715
Phone: 301-432-8419
Type: VA

Tri-State Reuse Centre
225 W Main Street
Hancock, MD 21750
Phone: 301-678-6160
Fax: 301-678-7841
Type: RC

Vintage Lumber Company
1 Council Drive
Woodsboro, MD 21798
Phone: 301-845-2500
Fax: 301-845-6475
Email: woodfloors@vintagelumber.com
Website: www.vintagelumber.com
Type: VA
Species: Oak, Chestnut, Pine

Massachusetts

A Shapiro & Sons Inc.
341 Ashland Street
North Adams, MA 01247
Phone: 413-663-6525
Type: UMS

Power Component Systems Inc.

Architectural Timber and Millwork
49 Mount Warner Road
Hadley, MA 01035
Phone: 413-586-3045
Fax: 413-586-3046
Email: tmh@atimber.com
Website: www.atimber.com
Type: DC/UMS

Associated Building Wreckers Inc.
352 Albany Street
Springfield, MA 01105
Phone: 413-732-3179
Fax: 413-734-6224
Type: DM/UMS

Atlantic Building Salvage
178 E Union Street
Ashland, MA 01721
Phone: 508-231-1473
Type: DM

Boston's ReStore inc.
P.O. Box 240881
Dorchester, MA 02124
Phone: 617-288-8400
Email: bperkins@bostonrestore.org
Website: www.bostonrestore.org
Type: DC/UMS

Building Materials Resource Center
100 Terrace Street
Boston, MA 02120
Phone: 617-442-8917
Fax: 617-427-2491
Email: info@bbmc.com
Website: www.bostonbmrc.org
Type: UMS

Cataumet Saw Mill
494 Thomas Landers Road
East Falmoth, MA 02536
Phone: 508-457-9239
Fax: 508-540-7974
Website: www.cataumet.com
Type: VA
Species: Heartpine, Fir, Oak

Central Building Salvage Corp.
141 Boston Street
Everett, MA 02149
Phone: 617-387-3700
Type: UMS

Colonial Barn Restoration
269 Old Bay Road
Bolton, MA 01740
Phone: 978-779-9865
Email: Tim@ColonialBarn.com
Website: www.colonialbarn.com
Type: CN/DC/UMS

Costello Dismantling
2 Rocky Gutter Street
Middleborough, MA 02346
Phone: 508-946-0880
Fax: 508-947-3093
Email: costello99@attby.com
Website: www.costellodismantling.com
Type: DC
Species: Pine

Craftsman Lumber Company
436 Main Street P.O. Box 222
Groton, MA 01450
Phone: 978-448-5621
Email: mark@craftsmanlumber.com
Website: www.craftsmanlumber.com
Type: VA

Environmental Futures Inc.
530 Atlantic Avenue
Boston, MA 02210
Phone: 617-443-1300
Type: DC

E-wood
Wellesley, MA 02482
Phone: 877-487-6504
Website: www.e-wood.com
Type: BR

Hercules Building Wrecking
138 Wilder Street
Brockton, MA 02401
Phone: 508-588-3390
Fax: 508-580-0334
Type: DM/UMS

Jay Harding Construction
96 Brook Street
Clinton, MA 01754
Phone: 978-897-7411
Fax: 978-897-3609
Website: www.oldewood.com
Type: VA

JC Antique Boards and Beams
P.O. Box 2079
Nantucket, MA 02554
Phone: 508-325-8808
Type: UMS

Karp WoodWorks
136 Fountain Street
Ashland, MA 01721
Phone: 508-881-7000
Fax: 508-881-7084
Type: VA
Species: Oak, Maple, Heartpine

Longleaf Lumber
70 Webster Avenue
Sommerville, MA 02143
Phone: 617-625-3659
Fax: 617-625-3615
Email: info@longleaflumber.com
Website: www.longleaflumber.com
Type: DC/VA

Neptune Demolition Corporation
70 Tenney Street
Georgetown, MA 01883
Phone: 978-352-6210
Type: DM/UMS

New England Demolition & Salvage
3065 Cranberry Highway
East Wareham, MA 02538
Phone: 508-291-7258
Fax: 508-273-0274
Email: homeneds@aol.com
Website: www.nedsalvage.com
Type: DC

Nor'East Architectural Antiques
5 Market Square
Amesbury, MA 01913
Phone: 978-834-9088
Fax: 978-499-7136
Email: mail@noreast1.com
Website: www.noreast1.com
Type: UMS/VA

Old Mansions
1305 Blue Hill Avenue
Mattapan, MA 02126
Phone: 617-296-0445
Type: UMS

Old Woods Limited
202 N Spencer Road
Spencer, MA 01562
Phone: 508-885-6000
Type: UMS

Pioneer Valley Deconstruction
235 Eastern Avenue
Springfield, MA 01109
Phone: 413-827-0781
Fax: 413-827-0780
Email: johndunne.pvp@verizon net
Type: DC

Professional Engineering Co.
110 Ferry Street
Lawrence, MA 01841
Phone: 888-205-2555
Website: www.ceilingdemo.com
Type: EQ

Restoration Resources
31 Thayer Street
Boston, MA 02118
Phone: 617-542-3033
Fax: 617-542-3034
http://members.aol.com/wcrres/index htm
Type: UMS

ReStore Home Improvement Center
250 Albany Rear
Springfield, MA 01105
Phone: 413-788-6900
Fax: 413-788-6909
Email: hollym@cetonline.org
Website: www restoreonline.org
Type: UMS

RJ O'Brien Building Wrecking & Salvage
460 Forest Street
Rockland, MA 02370
Phone: 781-878-1961
Email: OBrienRJO@gateway.com
Type: DC

South Mountain Company
P.O. Box 1260
West Tisbury, MA 02575
Phone: 508-693-4850
Type: UMS

South Shore HFH ReStore
28 River Street
Braintree, MA 02184
Phone: 781-843-9080
Type: UMS

The Olde Bostonian Architectural Antiques
66 Von Hillern Street
Dorchester, MA 02125
Phone: 617-282-9300
Fax: 617-282-3565
Email: anthgr01@aol.com
Website: www.oldbostonian.com
Type: UMS

Michigan

Adamo Demolition
300 E Seven Mile Road
Detroit, MI 48203
Phone: 313-892-7330
Fax: 313-892-4656
Email: support@citrisonic.com
Website: www.adamodemolition.com
Type: DM

Architectural Salvage Wing-Grand Illusion
201 E Michigan Avenue
Grass Lake, MI 49240
Phone: 517-522-8715
Email: leede1@aol.com
Type: UMS

Best Wrecking Co.
601 Beaufait Avenue
Detroit, MI 48201
Phone: 800-820-2378
Fax: 313-259-7250
Email: best@bestwrecking.com
Type: DM

Bierlein Companies, Inc.
2000 Bay City Road
Midland, MI 48642
Phone: 800-336-6626; 989-496-0066
Email: info@bierlein.com
Website: www.bierlein.com
Type: DM

D&M Wrecking Co., Inc./Axxiom, Inc.
250 S 4th Street
Kalamazoo, MI 49009
Phone: 616-375-1313
Fax: 616-375-2767
Type: DM/UMS

Detroit Building Materials
1551 Rosa Parks Boulevard
Detroit, MI 48216
Phone: 313-965-6520
Type: UMS

Detroit Recycled Concrete Co.
14294 Myers Road
Detroit, MI 48227
Phone: 313-934-7677
Type: RC

Dore & Associates Contracting, Inc.
900 Harry S Truman Parkway
Bay City, MI 48707
Phone: 800-344-7876
Fax: 989-684-6663
Email: dore@concentric.net
Website: www.doreandassociates.com
Type: DC/DM

Dore & Associates Contracting, Inc.
1221 E McNichols
Detroit, MI 48203
Phone: 800-344-7876
Email: dore@concentric.net
Website: www.doreandassociates.com
Type: DC/DM

Habitat ReStore Detroit
2718 Rosa Parks Boulevard
Detroit, MI 48216-1213
Phone: 313-891-7867
Email: jacob@ic.org
Type: UMS

Heritage Architectural Salvage and Supply
150 N Edwards Street
Kalamazoo, MI 49009
Phone: 269-385-1004
Type: UMS

Heritage Building and Materials Co.
13136 Puritan Street
Detroit, MI 48227
Phone: 313-345-3711
Type: UMS

Home Repair Services
1100 S Division Avenue
Grand Rapids, MI 49507
Phone: 616-241-2601
Fax: 616-241-5151
Email: info@homerepairservices.org
Website: www.homerepairservices.org
Type: UMS

K D Used Brick & Building Material
10244 Harper Avenue
Detroit, MI 48213
Phone: 313-923-4129
Type: UMS

Larry's Building Materials
13855 Grand River
Detroit, MI 48227
Phone: 313-273-4699
Fax: 313-272-8090
Type: UMS

Materials Unlimited
2 W Michigan Avenue
Ypsilanti, MI 48197
Phone: 734-483-6980; 800-299-9462
Fax: 734-482-3636
Email: materials@materialsunlimted.com
Website: www.materialsunlimted.com
Type: UMS

Motorcity Building Materials Center
4485 W Jefferson Avenue
Detroit, MI 48209
Phone: 313-843-7540
Type: UMS

North American Dismantling Corp.
P.O. Box 307
Lapeer, MI 48446
Phone: 810-664-2888
Fax: 810-664-6053
Email: cshuler@nadc1.com
Website: www.nadc1.com
Type: DM

Odom Re-Use and Consulting
5555 Brentwood Avenue N
Grawn, MI 49637
Phone: 231-276-6330
Email: reusebruce@coslink.net
Website: www.odomreuse.com
Type: DC/UMS

Pitsch Wrecking
675 Richmond Street NW
Grand Rapids, MI 49504
Phone: 616-363-4895
Type: DC

Recycle Ann Arbor
2420 S Industrial
Ann Arbor, MI 48104
Phone: 734-662-6288
Fax: 734-662-6649
Email: richard@recycleannarbor.org
Website: www.recycleannarbor.org
Type: UMS

21st Century Salvage
10750 Martz Road
Ypsilanti, MI 48197
Phone: 734-485-4855
Type: DC

Upright Wrecking
P.O. Box 241580
Detroit, MI 48224
Phone: 313-331-7000
Type: DM

Minnesota

All State Salvage Inc.
1354 Jackson Street
St. Paul, MN 55101
Phone: 651-488-6675
Type: UMS

Architectural Antiques
1330 Quincy Street NE
Minneapolis, MN 55413
Phone: 612-332-8344
Fax: 612-332-8967
Email: sales@archantiques.com
Website: www.archantiques.com
Type: UMS

Bauer Brothers Salvage
2432 2nd Street N
Minneapolis, MN 55411
Phone: 612-331-9492
Fax: 612-521-0494
Type: DC/UMS

Carl Bolander & Sons Co.
251 Starkey Street
Saint Paul, MN 55107
Phone: 800-676-6504; 651-224-6299
Fax: 651-223-8197
Email: info@bolander.com
Website: www.bolander.com
Type: DC

Century Construction Co., Inc.
820 N Concord Street, Suite 101
South St. Paul, MN 55075
Phone: 651-451-1020
Fax: 651-451-2745
Email: info@centuryconstruct.com
Website: www.centuryconstruct.com
Type: CN/DC

City Salvage Antiques
505 1st Avenue NE
Minneapolis, MN 55413
Phone: 612-627-9107
Email: mail@citysalvage.com
Website: www.citysalvage.com
Type: DC/UMS

Deconstruction Services
2316 E Lake Street
Minneapolis, MN 55407
Phone: 612-728-9388
Fax: 612-724-2288
Website: www.greeninstitute.org
Type: DC

Duluth Timber Company
P.O. Box 16717
Duluth, MN 55816
Phone: 218-727-2145
Fax: 218-727-0393
Email: liz@duluthtimber.com
Website: www.duluthtimber.com
Type: BR/VA
Species: Fir, Longleaf pine, Cypress

F.M. Frattalone Excavating
3066 Spruce Street
St. Paul, MN 55117
Phone: 651-484-0448
Fax: 651-484-7839
Email: jimw@fmfrattalone.com
Website: www.fmfrattalone.com
Type: DC/UMS
Species: Pine, Fir, Oak

Guilded Salvage Antiques
1315 Tyler Street NE
Minneapolis, MN 55413
Phone: 612-789-1680
Fax: 612-789-1688
Type: UMS

Kellington Construction Inc.
20110 Auger Ave
Corcoran, MN 55340
Phone: 612-416-3200
Fax: 612-416-3201
Email: rlewis@kellington.com
Website: www kellington.com
Type: CN/DM

Minnesota Timber Salvage
13737 100th Street
Foreston, MN 56330
Phone: 320-369-4507
Type: DC/VA

North Shore Architectural Antiques
521 7th Street
Two Harbors, MN 55616
Phone: 218-834-0018
Email: jmccarthy@frontiernet net
Website:
www.north-shore-architectural-antiques.com
Type: DC/UMS

Old Growth Woods
6456 160th Street
Rosemount, MN 55068
Phone: 651-690-3188
Fax: 651-698-6641
Email: sales@oldgrowthwoods.com
Website: www.oldgrowthwoods.com
Type: DC/VA

PPL Shop
850 15th Avenue NE
Minneapolis, MN 55413
Phone: 612-789-3322
Fax: 612-789-2319
Type: UMS

Rural Resource Recovery
1320 Jefferson Avenue
Saint Paul, MN 55105
Phone: 651-695-1732
Email: info@ruralresourcerecovery.org
Website: www ruralresourcerecovery.org
Type: BR

SKB Environmental
251 Starkey Street
St Paul, MN 55107
Phone: 651-224-6329
Fax: 651-223-5053
Email: info@skbinc.com
Website: www.skbinc.com
Type: DC/RC

The Reuse Center
2216 E Lake Street
Minneapolis, MN 55407
Phone: 612-724-2608
Fax: 612-724-2288
Email: JanetMester@Greeninstitude.org
Website:
www.greeninstitute.org/reusecenter.htm
Type: DC/UMS

Mississippi

Back Road Architectural Salvage Services
836 C Ridgewood Road Ext
Ridgeland, MS 39157
Phone: 601-957-3777
Email: cjej@a2ldial.net
Type: DC/UMS

Gibsons Demolition Inc.
52 Minor Street
Natchez, MS 39120
Phone: 601-445-2214
Type: DM/UMS

H & K Salvage
14391 Highway 49
Gulfport, MS 39503
Phone: 228-832-9499
Type: UMS

Metro Jackson HFH ReStore
P.O. Box 55634
Jackson, MS 39296-5634
Phone: 601-353-6000
Type: UMS

Old Mississippi Lumber
P.O. Box 562
Holly Springs, MS 38634
Phone: 662-252-3395
Email: broev@bellsouth net
Website: www heartpinefloors.com
Type: DC/VA

T & E Salvage-Buy & Sell
13015 Highway 67
Biloxi, MS 39532
Phone: 228-392-9814
Type: UMS

Missouri

Anderson Fine Carpentry and Salvage
228 W 4th Street
Kansas City, MO 64111
Phone: 816-531-5976
Email: TheThaine@aol.com
Type: DC/UMS

Ben Tarbe Used Brick Inc.
1202 Genessee Street
Kansas City, MO 66102
Phone: 913-432-9726
Type: UMS

Century Used Brick
12982 Maurer Industrial Drive
Sappington, MO 63127
Phone: 314-843-1213
Fax: 314-843-9203
Type: UMS

Chuck's Stone and Brick Co.
2955 S Brentwood
St Louis, MO 63144
Phone: 314-968-2230
Fax: 314-968-7591
Email: cbrickston@aol.com
Type: UMS

Deco Companies
2101 Manchester Traffic Way
Kansas City, MO 64126
Phone: 816-483-5656
Fax: 816-483-51586
Email: judir@deco.com
Website: www.deco-kc.com
Type: DC

Fellenz Antiques and Architectural
Artifacts
439 N Euclid Avenue
St. Louis, MO 63108
Phone: 314-367-0214
Type: UMS

Habitat for Humanity ReStore
4535 W Chestnut Expressway
Springfield, MO 65802
Phone: 417-829-4001
Fax: 417-829-4003
Email: restore@drury.edu
Website: www.habitatrestore.com
Type: DC/UMS

Habitat ReStore
4701 Deramus
Kansas City, MO 64120
Phone: 816-231-6889
Type: DC/UMS

Hardico
Suite 130, 112 W Jefferson
Kirkwood, MO 63122
Phone: 314-965-3535
Fax: 314-965-7333
Email: hardico@swbell net
Type: UMS

Heartwood Associates Int'l.
5068 Tholozan Avenue
St. Louis, MO 63109
Phone: 314-352-9242
Fax: 314-752-2152
Email: longleaf1@prodigy net
Website: www heartwoodassociates.com
Type: DC/VA

Mack Circle Used Brick and Wrecking
1414 Marcus Avenue
St. Louis, MO 63113
Phone: 314-531-2997
Type: UMS

Madget & Griffin Inc.
2425 S 6th Street
St. Joseph, MO 64501
Phone: 816-232-6210
Fax: 816-232-8573
Type: DM

Perhat Lumber Co.
6023 S Broadway
St Louis, MO 63111
Phone: 314-481-9302
Type: UMS

Peterson Wrecking Used Lumber
2008 Aull Lane
Lexington, MO 64067
Phone: 660-259-6500
Type: UMS

Pitchpine Lumber
19864 Gore Drive
Sainte Genevieve, MO 63670
Phone: 573-747-1733
Fax: 573-747-1680
Email: lloyd@pitchpine.com
Website: www.pitchpine.com
Type: DC/VA
Species: Heartpine, Oak, Cypress

Sanders Enterprise, Inc.
3019 Nash Road
Scott City, MO 63780
Phone: 314-334-9600
Fax: 314-334-2077
Type: VA

Spirtas Wrecking Company
951 Skinker Parkway
St. Louis, MO 63112
Phone: 314-862-9800
Fax: 314-862-9802
Email: info@spirtas.com
www.spirtas.com
Website: www.spiritas.com
Type: DM

St. Louis HFH ReStore
3763 Forest Park Avenue
St. Louis, MO 63108
Phone: 314-531-4155
Type: UMS

Stockton Heartwoods Limited
624 Holly Hills Avenue
St. Louis, MO 63101
Phone: 800-788-4828
Fax: 314-352-6110
Email: heartwoods@earthlink net
Website: www heartwoods.com
Type: VA
Species: Heartpine, Oak, Fir

Montana

ANS Metals
2100 Meadowlark Lane
Butte, MT 59701
Phone: 406-494-1661
Fax: 406-494-1607
Type: RC

Big Timberworks Inc.
P.O. Box 368
Gallatin Gateway, MT 59730
Phone: 406-763-4639
Fax: 406-763-4818
Email: bigtimberworks.com
Type: DC/VA

Envirocon, Inc.
101 International Way
Missoula, MT 59808
Phone: 406-523-1150
Fax: 406-543-7987
Email: Market@envirocon.com
Website: www.envirocon.com
Type: DM

Industrial Salvage and Demolition
P.O. Box 17767
Missoula, MT 59808
Phone: 406-543-8893
Type: DM/UMS

Nellis Custom Woodworks
4470 Amsterdam Road
Manhattan, MT 59741
Phone: 406-282-9049
Fax: 406-282-9050
Email: eric@nelliscustomwoodworks.com
Website:
www.nelliscustomwoodworks.com/aboutus.html
Type: CN/VA

Superior Hardwoods and Millwork
P.O. Box 4731/5120 Highway 93 S
(show room)
Missoula, MT 59801
Phone: 406-251-2272
Fax: 406-251-2520
Email: superhrdwds@blackfoot.net
Website: www.superior'hardwoods.com
Type: VA
Species: Fir, Oak

Nebraska
MT Salvage
3717 S 66th Street
Omaha, NE 68106
Phone: 402-391-5315
Type: UMS

RPM Salvage
1109 Bellevue Boulevard
Omaha, NE 68005
Phone: 402-346-4470
Type: UMS

Nevada
Arcadia Demolition Services
2620 S Maryland Parkway
Las Vegas, NV 89109
Phone: 702-388-4498
Fax: 702-388-4473
Email: info@arcadiademo.com
Website: www.arcadiademo.com
Type: DC

Phil's Salvage Emporium
1131 S Main Street
Las Vegas, NV 89104
Phone: 702-382-7528
Type: UMS

Roldan Construction, Inc.
3280 W Hacienda Avenue
Las Vegas, NV 89118
Phone: 702-739-DEMO
Fax: 702-739-6909
Email: Jerry@roldaninc.com
Website: www.roldaninc.com
Type: DC/UMS

New Hampshire
Admac Salvage
111 Saranac Street
Littleton, NH 03561
Phone: 603-444-1200
Website: www.musar.com/trader/admac.html
Type: DC/UMS

Architectural Salvage
3 Mill Street
Exeter, NH 03833
Phone: 603-773-5635
Email: arch@ttlc net
Website: www.oldhousesalvage.com
Type: UMS

Benson Woodworking Co. Inc.
6 Blackjack Crossing
Walpole, NH 03608
Phone: 603-756-3600
Email: info@bensonwood.com
Website: www.bensonwood.com
Type: CN/VA

Carlisle Restoration Lumber
1676 Route 9
Stoddard, NH 03464
Phone: 800-595-9663
Fax: 603-446-3540
Email: info@wideplankflooring.com
Website: www.wideplankflooring.com
Type: VA
Species: Pine, Heartpine, Oak

Great Northern Barns
182 Grafton Tpk
Canaan, NH 03741
Phone: 603-523-7134
Fax: 603-523-8248
Email: info@greatnorthernbarns.com
Website: greatnorthernbarns.com
Type: DC

Institution Recycling Network
7 South State Street
Concord, NH 03301
Phone: 603-229-1962
Email: mmckinney@ir-network.com
Website: www.wastemiser.com

Lead Source
23 Horne Street
Dover, NH 03820
Phone: 603-749-9274
Fax: 603-742-5044
Email: curtk@lead-source net
Website: www.lead-source net
Type: DM/EV

LL&S Wood Recycling
87 Lowell Road
Salem, NH 03079
Phone: 603-898-4098
Type: RC

Northfield Restoration
10 Kensington Road
Hampton Falls, NH 03844
Phone: 603-926-5383
Fax: 603-926-5383
Email: northfields@neaccess net
Website: www northfield.com
Type: VA
Species: Pine, Oak, Chestnut

Renovators Supply
P.O. Box 2515
Conway, NH 03818
Phone: 413-423-3737
Type: UMS

T-REX Corporation
532 Mammoth Road
Londonderry, NH 03053
Phone: 603-425-6660
Website: www.trexcorporation.com
Type: DC

Vermont Salvage
2 Lumber Lane
Manchester, NH 03102
Phone: 603-624-0868
Type: UMS

New Jersey
American Antique and Specialty Woods
51 Mt. Bethel Road
Warren, NJ 07059
Phone: 908-822-0006
Fax: 908-822-7111
Website: www.americanwoodsnj.com
Type: VA

American Demolition Corp.
2 English Lane
Egg Harbor Township, NJ 08234
Phone: 609-926-7373
Type: DM

American Wrecking Corporation of NJ
P.O. Box 29
Perth Amboy, NJ 08862
Phone: 732-442-6990
Fax: 732-442-0036
Email: info@awcnj.com
Website: www.awcnj.com
Type: DM

ATS Wood Recycling
15 Polhemus Lane
Bridgewater, NJ 08807
Phone: 908-725-8484
Type: RC

Bace Demolition, Inc.
135 Columbia Turnpike
Florham Park, NJ 07932
Phone: 973-822-3322
Type: DM/RC

Blue Skys Auction Co.
218 Blue Ridge Road
Voorhees, NJ 08043
Phone: 856-354-0199
Type: BR

Contractors Surplus
931 Asbury Avenue
Asbury Park, NJ 07712
Phone: 732-974-2871
Type: UMS

Joseph Fazzio Inc.
2760 Glassboro Cross Keys Road
Glassboro, NJ 08028
Phone: 856-881-3185
Type: UMS

Mazzocchi Wrecking
32 Williams Parkway
East Hanover, NJ 07940
Phone: 973-884-8682
Fax: 973-337-7464
Email: grace@mazzocchiwrecking.com
Website: www.mazzocchiwrecking.com
Type: DM

MW Wood Enterprises
6 Bywood Lane
Ewing, NJ 08628
Phone: 609-538-8680
Fax: 609-530-1922
Type: VA

R. Baker & Son All Industrial Services, Inc.
1 Globe Court
Red Bank, NJ 07701
Phone: 732-222-3553
Email: info@RBaker.com
Website: www.rbaker.com
Type: DC/DM

Recmediation Inc.
396 Whitehead Avenue
South River, NJ 08882
Phone: 732-698-9699
Fax: 732-698-0991
Email: info@recmediation.com
Website: www.recmediation.com
Type: DM

Recycling the Past
381 N Main Street
Barnegat, NJ 08005
Phone: 609-660-9790
Fax: 800-878-3251
Email: whitey99@cybercomm net
Website: www.recyclingthepast.com
Type: UMS

Relics Reconstruction: Architectural
Salvage
201 Church Street
Millburn, NJ 07041
Phone: 201-376-4745
Type: DC/UMS

Restoration Materials Company
1260 New Market Avenue
South Plainfield, NJ 07080
Phone: 800-336-6548
Type: DC/UMS

Trenton Materials Exchange
800 New York Avenue
Trenton, NJ 08638
Phone: 609-278-0033
Type: UMS

Willard Brothers Saw Mill
300 Basin Road
Trenton, NJ 08619
Phone: 609-890-1990
Fax: 609-587-6750
Type: VA

Yannuzzi Demolition and Recycling
563 White Street
Orange, NJ 07050
Phone: 973-672-8333
Fax: 973-672-5523
Website: www.yannuzi net
Type: DM

New Mexico

Coronado Wrecking & Salvage Co.
4200 Broadway Boulevard SW
Albuquerque, NM 87105
Phone: 505-877-2821
Type: DM/UMS

Frontier Wood
4523 State Highway 14
Sante Fe, NM 87508
Phone: 505-474-9663
Type: UMS

Habitat for Humanity
5 Roberts Circle
Los Lunas, NM 87031
Phone: 505-747-7200
Type: UMS

Habitat for Humanity ReStore
P.O. Box 238
Espanola, NM 87532
Phone: 505-747-2690
Type: UMS

Habitat for Humanity ReStore
1143 Siler Park Lane
Sante Fe, NM 87507
Phone: 505-473-1114
Type: UMS

La Puerta
1302 Cerrillos Road
Santa Fe, NM 87505
Phone: 505-984-8164
Fax: 505-986-5838
Type: UMS

Plaza Hardwood, Inc.
219 W Manhattan Street
Santa Fe, NM 87501
Phone: 505-992-3260
Fax: 505-992-8766
Email: paulfuge@certifiedwood.com
Website: www.plzfloor.com
Type: VA

Salvation Army Thrift Store
1202 Camino Carlos Rey
Santa Fe, NM 87507
Phone: 505-473-7735
Type: UMS

New York

A-1 Salvage
Route 26
South Otselic, NY 13155
Phone: 315-653-4409
Email: norton@ascent net
Type: DC

Accent Hardwood Flooring &
Supply Corp. (NY)
390 Route 25, P.O. Box 180
Middle Island, NY 11953
Phone: 800-545-6435
Fax: 631-924-4584
Email: sales@accentflooring.com
Website: www.accentflooring.com
Type: VA

American Architectural Salvage
and Demolition
245 S Greenfield Road
Greenfield Center, NY 12833
Phone: 518-580-1849
Type: DC

Antiques and Vintage Woods of America
Route 199
Pine Plains, NY 12567
Phone: 518-398-1797
Type: UMS

Architectural Antiques
105 Anderson Avenue
Rochester, NY 14607
Phone: 585-271-6290
Type: UMS

Architectural Salvage Warehouse
337 Berry Street
Brooklyn, NY 11211
Phone: 718-388-4527
Type: UMS

Arlyn Lumber and Home Center
715 E 98th Street
Brooklyn, NY 11236
Phone: 718-498-0600
Type: UMS

ARROW Reuse Center
51-02 21st Street
Long Island, NY 11101
Phone: 718-472-1180
Email: nctai@att.net
Website: www.arrowonline.org
Type: UMS

Barn Shadow Enterprises
32 Lee Place
Wellsville, NY 14895
Phone: 585-593-5075
Fax: 585-593-5075
Email: barnse@rctc.com
Website: www.barnshadow.com
Type: VA

Barnstormers Flooring
166 Malden Turnpike
Saugerties, NY 12477
Phone: 845-246-3622
Fax: 845-246-3623
Email: safesol@frontier net
Website: www.safesolutionsllc.com
Type: DC
Species: Chestnut, Maple, Oak

Bianchi-Trison Corp.
300 Long Branch Road
Syracuse, NY 13209
Phone: 800-DEMO-201
Website: www.bianchitrison.com
Type: DM

Big Wood
P.O. Box 24
East Bethany, NY 14054
Phone: 315-986-8119
Fax: 315-986-2622
Email: larry@big-wood net
Website: www.big-wood net
Type: DC/UMS
Species: Longleaf pine, Fir

BJ Corelli Inc.
1941 Jerome Avenue #A
Bronx, NY 10453
Phone: 718-731-2400
Type: UMS

BRB Contracting, Inc.
20 Denker Drive
Ballston Lake, NY 12019
Phone: 518-693-6348
Email: brbci@hotmail.com
Type: DC/DM

Breezy Point Lumber Co.
28 Market Street
Breezy Point, NY 11697
Phone: 718-634-2600
Type: UMS

Cat House Antiques
136 Bruceville Road
High Falls, NY 12440
Phone: 845-687-0790
Type: UMS

Chief's Used Brick
3221 Edson Avenue
Bronx, NY 10469
Phone: 718-379-1232
Type: UMS

Country Road Associates, Ltd
63 Front Street
Millbrook, NY 12545
Phone: 845-677-6041
Fax: 845-677-6532
Email: info@countryroadassociates.com
Website: www.countryroadassociates.com
Type: VA

Creative Look
29 W 30th Street
New York, NY 10001
Phone: 212-330-9971
Type: UMS

Demolition Depot
216 E 125th Street
New York, NY 10035
Phone: 212-860-1138
Fax: 212-860-1560
Email: info@demolitiondepot.com
Website: www.demolitiondepot.com
Type: DC/UMS

Dorp Salvage Co.
566 Broadway
Schenectady, NY 12305
Phone: 518-393-1744
Type: UMS

Environmental Construction Outfitters
901 E 134th Street
Bronx, NY 10454
Phone: 800-238-5008
Website: www.environproducts.com
Type: UMS

Frasier Wrecking Contractors
212 E State Extension
Gloversville, NY 12078
Phone: 518-725-1915
Type: DM

Full Circle, Inc.
509 Manida Street
Bronx, NY 10474
Phone: 800-775-1516
Fax: 718-328-4462
Type: RC

Gateway Demolition
134-22 32nd Avenue
Flushing, NY 11354
Phone: 718-359-1400
Fax: 718-461-6558
Email: info@gatewaydemolition.com
Website: www.gatewaydemolition.com
Type: DC/DM

Gothic City Architectural Antiques
1940 Niagra Street
Buffalo, NY 14207
Phone: 716-874-4479
Fax: 716-875-1209
Email: charley@gothiccity.com
Website: www.gothiccity.com
Type: UMS
Species: Heartpine, Oak, Walnut

Gramercy Group, Inc.
100 Grand Street
Westbury, NY 11590
Phone: 516-876-0020
Fax: 516-876-0021
Website: www.gramercygroupinc.com
Type: DM

Grossman Lumber Co.
P.O. Box 772
Manhasset, NY 11030
Phone: 718-251-1020
Type: UMS

Historic Albany Foundation
Architectural Parts
89 Lexington Avenue
Albany, NY 12206
Phone: 518-465-2987
Type: UMS

Historic Home Supply
215 River Street
Troy, NY 12180
Phone: 518-266-0675
Fax: 518-266-0810
Email: homedupply@earthlink net
Website: www homesupply.com
Type: UMS

Horsefeathers Architectual Antiques
346 Connecticut Street
Buffalo, NY 14213
Phone: 716-882-1581
Fax: 716-882-0215
Email: horsehoe@buffnet net
Website: www horsefeathers-antiques.com
Type: UMS

House Parts
540 South Avenue
Rochester, NY 14620
Phone: 716-325-2329
Fax: 716-325-3613
Email: houseparts@msn.com
Type: UMS

Hudson Valley Materials Exchange
1101 First Street
New Windsor, NY 12553
Phone: 845-567-1445
Fax: 845-567-1536
Website: www hvmaterialsexchange.com
Type: UMS

International Chimney Corp.
55 S Long Street
Williamsville, NY 14221
Phone: 716-634-3967
Fax: 716-634-3983
Website: www.internationalchimney.com
Type: DC/DM

Irreplaceable Artifacts
14 Second Avenue
New York, NY 10003
Phone: 212-777-2900
Type: UMS

Jackson Demolition Service
2754 Aqueduct Road
Schenectady, NY 12309
Phone: 800-440-2113
Fax: 518-372-1116
Email: jackdemo@capital net
Website: www.jacksondemolition.com
Type: DM

Kaywood Flooring and Supply Co.
P.O. Box 314
Eastport, NY 11941
Phone: 631-325-0666
Fax: 631-325-8955
Email: oldfloor@optonline net
Website: www.antiquebarnwood.com
Type: VA

Kleine's Antique Barnwood
Flooring & Lumber
18 River Avenue
Eastport, NY 11941
Phone: 516-325-8955
Fax: 516-325-1465
Email: info@antiquebarnwood.com
Type: VA

LaPointe Construction
P.O. Box 691
Hague, NY 12836
Phone: 518-543-6341
Fax: 518-543-6946
Type: CN

Lebis Enterprises, Inc.
P.O. Box 606 262 Woodward Avenue
Kenmore, NY 14217
Phone: 877-600-DEMO
Fax: 716-875-6252
Email: angela@lebis.com
Website: www.lebis.com
Type: DM

Legacy Antique Woods
114 Sibley Road
Honeoye Falls, NY 14472
Phone: 585-624-1011
Fax: 716-624-1094
Email: legacywood99@aol.com
Website: www.legacyantiquewoods.com
Type: DC/UMS
Species: Chestnut, Heartpine, Oak

LVI Demolition Services Inc.
80 Broad Street
New York, NY 10004
Phone: 212-951-3661
Fax: 212-481-9895
Email: corporate@lviservices.com
Website: www.lviservices.com
Type: EV/DM

M. Fine Lumber
1301 Metropolitan Avenue
Brooklyn, NY 11237
Phone: 718-381-5200
Fax: 718-366-8907
Email: rob@mfinelumber.com
Website: www mfinelumber.com
Type:BR/VA
Species: Fir, Pine

New Energy Works Timber Framers, Inc
1180 Commercial Drive
Farmington, NY 14425
Phone: 800-486-0661
Fax: 585-924-9962
Email: joinery@newenergyworks.com
Website: www newenergyworks.com
Type: CN/VA

New York Wastewatch
253 Broadway, Rm 302
New York, NY 10004
Phone: 212-942-5219
Email: jrosenfield@itac.org
Type: BR/DC

Olde Good Things
124 W 24th Street
New York, NY 10011
Phone: 212-989-8401
Fax: 212-463-8005
Email: mail@oldegoodthings.com
Website: www.oldegoodthings.com
Type: UMS

Ontario Specialty Contracting Inc.
333 Ganson Street
Buffalo, NY 14203
Phone: 716-856-3333
Fax: 716-842-1785
Email: bwegrzyn@ontariospecialty.com
Website: www.ontariospecialty.com
Type: DC/DM

Pioneer Millworks
1180 Commercial Drive
Farmington, NY 14425
Phone: 585-924-9970
Fax: 585-924-9962
Email: jonathen@pioneermillworks.com
Website: www.pioneermillworks.com
Type: DC/UMS

Pioneer Millworks
1755 Pioneer Road
Shortsville, NY 14548
Phone: 716-289-3093
Fax: 716-289-3221
Website: www newenergworks.com
Type: VA

Pittsford Lumber and Woodshop
50 State Street
Pittsford, NY 14534
Phone: 585-586-1877
Fax: 585-586-1934
Type: VA/UMS

Original Doors of Rochester
203 Milburn Street
Rochester, NY 14607
Phone: 716-271-6290
Type: DM

ReHouse Inc.
1840 Kennedy Road
Webster, NY 14580
Phone: 585-872-1450
Email: scamprath@rehouseny.com
Website: www rehouseny.com
Type: UMS

Sabre Demolition Corporation
73 Generese Street
Baldwinsville, NY 13027
Phone: 315-635-3759
Fax: 315-635-3790
Email: sabredemo@aol.com
Website: www.sabre-demolition.com
Type: DC/DM

Shaver Brothers
32 Perrine Street
Auburn, NY 13021
Phone: 800-564-7206
Email: pjguerrette@a-znet.com
Type: UMS/VA

Significant Elements / Historic Ithaca, Inc
212 Center Street
Ithaca, NY 14850
Phone: 607-277-3450
Fax: 607-273-4816
Email: elements@lightlink.com
Website: www.significantelements.org
Type: UMS

Siwek Contractors
4340 Park Avenue
Bronx, NY 10457
Phone: 718-364-1400
Type: UMS

Toddville Building Materials
2201 Crompond Road
Peekskill, NY 10566
Phone: 914-736-1117

Urban Archaeology
143 Franklin Street
New York, NY 10013
Phone: 212-431-4646
Fax: 212-343-9312
Type: UMS

Van's Demolition, Inc.
422 Magazine Street
Albany, NY 12204
Phone: 518-438-1936
Type: DM

Vintage Barns, Woods & Restoration
333 Mossy Brook Road
High Falls, NY 12440
Phone: 845-340-9870
Fax: 845-339-4573
Email: info@vintagewoods.com
Website: www.vintagewoods.com
Type: UMS
Species: Pine–white, Cypress, Oak

Zaborski Emporium
27 Hoffman Street
Kingston, NY 12401
Phone: 845-338-6465
Fax: 845-338-6465
Email: ZaborskiEmporium@aol.com
Website: www.stanthejunkman.com
Type: UMS

North Carolina

Airedale Woodworks LLC
P.O. Box 307
Murfreesboro, NC 27855
Phone: 800-489-0639
Fax: 252-398-8429
Email: sales@airedalewoodworks.com
Website: www.airedalewoodworks.com
Type: DC/UMS

Architectural Salvage
P.O. Box 220193
Charlotte, NC 28222
Phone: 704-552-7560
Type: UMS

Architectural Salvage of Greensboro
300 W Bellemeade Street
Greensboro, NC 27402
Phone: 336-389-9118
Email: asg@blandwood.org
Type: DC/UMS

Artisan Woodworks
10837 Liberty Road
Liberty, NC 27298
Phone: 336-622-5441
Email: artisanwoodworks@intrex.net
Website: www.artisanwoodworks.com
Type: VA

Asheville Architectural Salvage
23 Rankin Avenue
Asheville, NC 28801
Phone: 828-281-2600
Type: UMS

Asheville Recyclers
19 Biltmore Avenue
Asheville, NC 28801
Phone: 828-254-5700
Type: UMS

Axel Demolition & Salvage
253 A S Churton Street
Hillsborough, NC 27278
Phone: 919-644-8244
Type: BR

Building Supply Recycling Center
302 E Pettigrew Street
Durham, NC 27701
Phone: 919-490-0414
Fax:
Email: renovatenc@aol.com
Type: UMS

Building Supply Salvage, Inc.
2207 English Road
High Point, NC 27262
Phone: 336-889-2207
Type: UMS

Clark Woodworking
P.O. Box 53210
Fayetteville, NC 28305
Phone: 910-678-0899
Type: VA

Classic Antique Wood
12431 Walkers Meadow Lane
Charlotte, NC 28273
Phone: 704-506-1955
Website: www.classicantiquewood.com
Type: UMS
Species: Pine

D.H. Griffin Wrecking Co.
1600 North Graham Street
Charlotte, NC 28206-3024
Phone: 704-331-9400
Fax: 704-336-6860
Type: DC/DM

D.H. Griffin Wrecking Co., Inc.
4700 Hilltop Road
Greensboro, NC 27407
Phone: 888-336-DEMO
Email: elwalker@dhgriffin.com
Website: www.dhgriffin.com
Type: DC/DM

D.H. Griffin Wrecking Company
304 N 3rd Street
Smithfield, NC 27577
Phone: 919-989-7564
Email: dhgwc@constructionnet net
Website: www.dhgriffin.com
Type: DM/RC

Ed Knapp
782 Beech Tree Road
Whittier, NC 28789
Phone: 828-586-0755
Fax: 828-586-4647
Email: vintageb@gte net
Website:
www.vintagebeamsandtimbers.com
Type: BR
Species: Pine, Others

Fayetteville ReStore
443 Franklin Street
Fayetteville, NC 28301
Phone: 910-322-9822
Type: UMS/DC

Gideons Home Building
Materials and Salvage
1700 W Lee Street
Greensboro, NC 27403
Phone: 336-294-0789
Type: UMS

Habitat for Humanity of
Greater New Bern Inc.
1249 Pollack Street
New Bern, NC 28560
Phone: 252-633-9599
Fax: 252-633-4632
Type: UMS

Habitat for Humanity ReStore
P.O. Box 34397
Charlotte, NC 28234
Phone: 704-376-2054
Type: UMS

Habitat for Humanity Reuse Center
2400 Alwin Ct
Raleigh, NC 27604
Phone: 919-833-6768
Fax: 919-833-8256
Website: www habitatwake.org
Type: UMS

Harmony Exchange
2700 Big Hill Road
Boone, NC 28607
Phone: 828-264-2314
Fax: 828-264-4770
Website: www harmonyexchange.com
Type: VA

Hawk Creek Hollow Timber Products
P.O. Box 147
Tryon, NC 28782
Phone: 828-859-5180
Fax: 828-859-5108
Email: ann@annielauries.com
Type: VA

Heartwood Pine Floors
P.O. Box 187 Highway 87 S
Pittsboro, NC 27312
Phone: 800-524-7463
Email: email@heartwoodpine.com
Website: www heartwoodpine.com
Type: VA

J. L. Powell & Co., Inc.
723 Pine Log Road
Whiteville, NC 28472
Phone: 800-227-2007
Fax: 910-642-3164
Email: heather@palnkfloors.com
Website: www.plankfloors.com
Type: VA
Species: Longleaf pine, Pine

Material Salvage and Recycling
1521 Huffman Mill Road
Burlington, NC 27215
Phone: 336-584-1193
Type: UMS

Miller C&D Recycling
131 Rowan Street
Salisbury, NC 28146
Phone: 704-279-2012
Fax: 704-279-2015
Type: RC

Natural Wood Flooring
119 Gail Drive
Roanoke Rapids, NC 27870
Phone: 800-726-PINE
Type: VA

Pete Hendricks
1414 Jenkins Road
Wake Forest, NC 27587
Phone: 919-556-2284
Type: DC

Piedmont Grading & Wrecking Co., Inc.
3652 Beatties Ford Road
Charlotte, NC 28216
Phone: 800-968-2374
Email: Piedmontgrading@aol.com
Type: DM

Piedmont Salvage and Equipment
4620 Hilltop Road
Greensboro, NC 27407
Phone: 336-510-6905
Email: jdsmith510@triad rr.com
Type: UMS

Preservation Hall
55 N Main Street
Weaverville, NC 28787
Phone: 828-645-1047
Website: www.preservation-hall.com
Type: UMS

Renovator Supply of NC
302 E Pettigrew Street
Durham, NC 27701
Phone: 919-490-0414
Email: rensup@aol.com
Website: www renovator-nc.com
Type: UMS

ReStore
443 Franklin Street
Fayetteville, NC 28301
Phone: 910-321-0780
Type: UMS

Rike Wrecking Co. Inc.
1005 Rundell Street
Winston Salem, NC 27105
Phone: 336-725-8789
Fax: 336-725-8789
Type: DC/UMS
Species: Oak, Pine

Rocky's Material and Salvage
409 Dover Road
Kinston, NC 28501
Phone: 252-522-2424
Type: UMS

Salvage Building Materials
951 N Liberty Street
Winston Salem, NC 27101
Phone: 336-724-1739
Type: UMS

Salvage King
204 Cooper Road
Staley, NC 27355
Phone: 336-622-1595
Fax: 336-622-3883
Email: salvageking@msn.com
Website: www.salvageking.com
Type: DC/RC

Scotland Neck Heartpine
105 Creek Street
Tarboro, NC 27886
Phone: 252-826-2755
Email: wburgwyn@yahoo.com
Type: DC/UMS

The Joinery
P.O. Box 518
Tarboro, NC 27886
Phone: 919-823-3306
Fax: 919-823-0818
Type: VA

The Salvage House
22-24 Bonlee-Bennett Road
Bonlee, NC 27213
Phone: 919-837-2376
Email: jeff@thesalvagehouse.com
Website: www.thesalvagehouse.com
Type: UMS

Third Creek Salvage Company
2067 Shelton Avenue
Statesville, NC 28677
Phone: 704-872-7502
Fax: 704-872-9247
Email: wes@thirdcreeksalvage.com
Website: www.thirdcreeksalvage.com
Type: UMS

Vintage Beams and Timbers
Architectural Salvage
P.O. Box 548
Sylva, NC 28779
Phone: 828-586-0755
Fax: 828-586-4647
Email: info@vintagebeamsandtimbers.com
Website:
www.vintagebeamsandtimbers.com
Type: UMS/VA

Waughton Millwork and Salvage
Building Material
215 Cassell Street
Winston Salem, NC 27127
Phone: 336-788-0990
Type: UMS

Wilmington Architectural Salvage
20 Brunswick Street
Wilmington, NC
Phone: 910-762-2511
Type: UMS

Woodhouse
P.O. Box 7336
Rocky Mount, NC 27801
Phone: 252-977-7336
Fax: 252-641-4477
Type: VA

Yesterday's Windows
327 Haywood Road
Asheville, NC 28806
Phone: 828-259-9936
Fax: 828-259-9936
Type: UMS

North Dakota

Carlisle Restoration Lumber
NCR 32
Stoddard, ND 03464
Phone: 603-446-3937
Fax: 603-446-3540
Type: VA

Ohio

Acme Construction Services
3104 Syracuse Street
Cincinnati, OH 45206
Phone: 513-281-5151
Type: UMS

Allied Erecting and Dismantling
2100 Poland Av
Youngstown, OH 44502
Phone: 330-744-0808
Fax: 330-7443218
Email: info@aed.cc
Website: www.aed.cc
Type: DC/UMS

American Services Group, Inc.
5695 State Route 128
Cleves, OH 45002
Phone: 800-498-2450
Website: www.amersvs.com
Type: DM

Amish Timber Framers
11627 Hametown Road
Doylestown, OH 44230
Phone: 800-392-8789
Email: info@amishtimberframers.com
Website: www.amishtimberframers.com
Type: CN

Angelo Building Wreckers
375 W Park Avenue
Columbus, OH 43223
Phone: 614-279-9700
Type: DM/UMS

Architectural Artifacts
20 S Ontario Street
Toledo, OH 43602
Phone: 419-243-6916
Fax: 419-243-0094
Email: architectural@speedvox net
Type: UMS

B and B Wrecking and Excavating Inc.
5801 Train Avenue
Cleveland, OH 44102
Phone: 216-651-9090
Fax: 216-651-9095
Email: bandbwrecking@ameritech.net
Website: www.bbwrecking.com
Type: DC/UMS

Barnwares
1888 Jacoby Road
Copley, OH 44321
Phone: 330-335-9907
Fax: 330-334-2097
Email: info@barnwares.com
Website: www.barnwares.com
Type: DC/VA

Broadway Contracting Inc.
3950 E 89th Street
Cleveland, OH 44105
Phone: 800-709-4129
Fax: 216-271-3944
Email: ger1056@aol.com
Website: www.broad3939.com
Type: DC/UMS

Buckeye Wrecking
1800 19th Street NE
Canton, OH 44714
Phone: 330-445-0088
Type: DM/UMS

Build It Again Center
3529 Cleveland Avenue
Columbus, OH 43224
Phone: 614-267-7778
Fax: 614-267-6655
Email: biac@habitat-columbus.org
Website: www.habitat-columbus.org
Type: DC/UMS

Cleveland Deconstructors Inc.
6270 Greenwood Pkwy #305
Sagamore Hills, OH 44067
Phone: 330-467-7595
Email: nickkack@bright net
Website:
Type: DC

Complete Resources Co.
3483 E Fulton Street
Columbus, OH 43219
Phone: 614-445-9485
Website: www.complete-resources.com
Type: RC

Dayton Demolition & Contracting Inc.
222 Washington Street
Dayton, OH 45402
Phone: 937-228-3525
Fax: 937-228-1516
Type: DM

Eagle Creek Designs, Inc.
6025 Schustrich P.O. Box 163
Mantua, OH 44255
Phone: 330-274-2041
Fax: 330-274-3370
Email: hfs1917@aol.com
Type: DC/VA

Habitat for Humanity ReStore
3529 Cleveland Avenue
Columbus, OH 43224
Phone: 614-267-7778
Type: UMS

Habitat for Humanity ReStore
1041 S Patterson Boulevard
Dayton, OH 45402
Phone: 937-586-0860
Type: UMS

J and J Barnwood
36019 Glasgow Road
Salineville, OH 43945
Phone: 330-424-4977
Type: VA

Kent Demolition Tool
711 Lake Street
Kent, OH 44240
Phone: 800-527-2282
Email: sales@kenttool.com
Website: www kentdemolition.com
Type: EQ

King Wrecking Co., Inc.
5038 Beech Street
Cincinnati, OH 45212
Phone: 513-241-1116
Email: kingwrecking@fuse net
Website: www kingwrecking.com
Type: DM

L & L Demolition Excavating Inc.
715 Dayton Road
Springfield, OH 45506
Phone: 937-324-0122
Type: DM/UMS

Lincoln Street Salvage
14657 Lincoln Street SE
Minerva, OH 44657
Phone: 330-868-1375
Type: UMS

Loewendick's
4248 Linnville Road
Health, OH 43056
Phone: 740-323-3127
Type: UMS

Mays Wrecking Co.
1031 Hanson Street
Toledo, OH 43605
Phone: 419-693-6783

Murphy's Plumbing Supplies
1927 Dryden Road
Dayton, OH 45439
Phone: 937-293-1142
Type: UMS

National Salvage Supply, Inc.
1668 Copley Road
Akron, OH 44320
Phone: 330-922-9844
Type: UMS

North Hill Salvage Store
813 Elma Street
Akron, OH 44310
Phone: 330-762-4509
Type: UMS

O'Rourke Wrecking Company
660 Lunken Park Drive
Cincinnati, OH 45226
Phone: 800-354-9850
Fax: 513-871-1313
Email: info@orourkewrecking.com
Website: www.orourkewrecking.com
Type: DM

Precision Environmental
5722 Schaaf Road
Independence, OH 44131
Phone: 216-642-6040
Email: inquiries@precision-env.com
Website: www.precision-env.com
Type: DM/EV

Raisch John P Contractor
1312 Fairway Court
Miamisburg, OH 45342
Phone: 937-866-3094
Type: DM

Rex Salvage Store
1201 S Arlington Street
Akron, OH 44306
Phone: 330-773-8605
Type: UMS

Salvage II
22045 Bates Road
Minerva, OH 44567
Phone: 330-868-3137
Type: UMS

Salvage Masters
445 Fairport Nursery Road
Painesville, OH 44077
Phone: 440-942-8769
Email: salvagemasters@roundOhio
Website: http://webpost net/te/teammaker/
Salvage/quicktakes htm
Type: UMS

Stark Wrecking Company
7081 Germantown Pike
Miamisburg, OH 45342
Phone: 937-866-5032
Type: DM/UMS

Stock Pile The
1387 Claredon Avenue SW
Canton, OH 44710
Phone: 330-455-4585
Type: UMS

The Rose Group Ltd
778 Winding River Boulevard
New Lebanon, OH 45065
Phone: 513-494-9444
Fax: 810-963-2625
Email: webmaster@rose-grp.com
Website: www rose-grp.com
Type: DC

The Stone Salvage Company
Cleveland, OH 44077
Phone: 440-352-7686
Fax: 440-357-7076
Email: stonemaon@stonemason.com
Website: www.stonesalvage.com
Type: DM/UMS

United Salvage Co.
921 Hazel Street
Akron, OH 44305
Phone: 330-253-2403
Type: RC/UMS

Valley Building Materials The
2000 State Avenue
Cincinnati, OH 45214
Phone: 513-921-2822
Type: UMS

Oklahoma

Apache Lumber Co.
2703 E Apache Street
Tulsa, OK 74110
Phone: 918-425-0295
Type: UMS

Architectural Antiques
1900 Linwood Boulevard
Oklahoma City, OK 73106
Phone: 405-232-0759
Type: UMS

Ark Wrecking Co. of OKLA Inc.
1800 S 49th W Avenue
Tulsa, OK 74103
Phone: 918-583-0488
Type: DM

Bibler Brothers Lumber Co.
5500 NW Texas
Idabel, OK 74745
Phone: 580-286-9470
Type: UMS

Central Oklahoma HFH ReStore
1025 N Broadway Avenue
Oklahoma City, OK 73102
Phone: 405-524-7151
Type: UMS

Cherry Trucking and Wrecking
13336 NW Expressway Street
Piedmont, OK 73078
Phone: 405-373-2555
Type: UMS

Cleveland County HfH
1835 Industrial Boulevard
Norman, OK 73069
Phone: 405-360-7868
Type: UMS

Dawson Building Supply
5519 E Tecumseh Street
Tulsa, OK 74115
Phone: 918-832-0071
Fax: 918-835-4788
Type: UMS
Species: Pine, Fir

Friendly Plumbing
15 SE 23rd Street
Oklahoma City, OK 73129
Phone: 405-236-1151
Type: UMS

Habitat Renovation Station
1800 Broadway Avenue
Oklahoma City, OK 73103
Phone: 405-232-5592
Type: UMS

Midwest Wrecking Company
P.O. Box 3757
Edmond, OK 73083
Phone: 405-478-8833
Type: DM/UMS

Shanbour Lindy
530 S Broadway Avenue
Oklahoma City, OK 73109
Phone: 405-239-7749
Type: UMS

Tulsa Metro Area HFH ReStore
P.O. Box 1357
Tulsa, OK 74101
Phone: 918-592-4224
Type: UMS

Oregon

1874 House Antiques
8070 SE 13th Avenue
Portland, OR 97202
Phone: 503-233-1874
Email: 1874store@aol.com
Type: UMS

Asher Traditional Homes
15795 SW Serena Ct
Portland, OR 97224
Phone: 503-620-6163
Type: CN/UMS

Aurora Mills Architectural Salvage
14971 1st Street NE
Aurora, OR 97002
Phone: 503-678-6083
Type: UMS

Bend Area Habitat ReStore
540 NE 1st Street
Bend, OR 97702
Phone: 541-312-6709
Fax: 541-749-2553
Website: www.bendhabitat.org
Type: UMS

BioReclaim
P.O. Box 246
Sheridan, OR 97378
Phone: 503-843-6262
Fax: 503-843-7717
Email: mgilham@onlinemac.com
Website:
http://sites onlinemac com/bioreclaim/contacts htm
Type: RC

Brady Peeks Enterprises
P.O. Box 101
Curtin, OR 97428
Phone: 541-942-2079
Type: UMS

BRING Recycling
86641 Franklin Boulevard
Eugene, OR 97403
Phone: 541-746-3023
Fax: 541-746-3023
Email: davidw@bringrecycling.org
Website: www.bringrecycling.org
Type: DC/UMS

Builders City
8905 N Vancouver Avenue
Portland, OR 97217
Phone: 503-285-0546
Fax: 503-240-1691
Type: BR/UMS

Capital Products
P.O. Box 719
Philomath, OR 97370
Phone: 541-929-5308
Type: DC/UMS

Craftmark Reclaimed Wood
P.O. Box 237
McMinnville, OR 97128
Phone: 503-472-6929
Fax: 503-472-5150
Website: www.craftmarkinc.com
Type: UMS/VA

Crosscut Hardwoods
3065 NW Front Avenue
Portland, OR 97210
Phone: 503-224-9663
Fax: 503-227-4670
Type: UMS

Deconstruction Management Group
12345 NW Harborton Drive
Portland, OR 97231
Phone: 503-341-3050
Email: jprimdahl@ilsr.org
Type: BR/DC

Dillon & Associates inc
2545 SW Spring Garden Street
Portland, OR 97219
Phone: 503-244-2822
Type: UMS

Elder Demolition
5635 SE 111th Avenue
Portland, OR 97266
Phone: 503-760-6330
Fax: 503-497-3115
Email: kdriver@viser.net
Type: DM

Endura Wood Products
1303 SE 6th Avenue
Portland, OR 97214
Phone: 503-233-7090
Fax: 503-233-7091
Email: EdM@EnduraWood.com
Website: www.endurawood.com
Type: VA

Environmental Building Supplies
819 SE Taylor Street
Portland, OR 97214
Phone: 503-222-3881
Fax: 503-222-3756
Email: ebs@ecohaus.com
Website: www.ecohaus.com
Type: UMS/VA

Gilmer Wood Company
2211 NW St. Helens Road
Portland, OR 97210
Phone: 503-274-1271
Fax: 503-274-9839
Email: gilmerwood@aol.com
Website: www.gilmerwood.com
Type: UMS

Grand & Benedicts Annex
111 SE Belmont Street
Portland, OR 97214
Phone: 503-234-3792
Type: UMS

Green Mountain Woodworks
P.O. Box 1433
Phoenix, OR 97535
Phone: 541-535-5880
Fax: 514-535-5331
Email: mstella@mind net
Website:
www.greenmountainwoodworks.com
Type: VA

Heartwood ReSources
355 Atlanta Street
Roseburg, OR 97470
Phone: 541-673-4070
Fax: 541-673-4223
Email: heartwoodre-
sources@umpquacdc.org
Website: www.heartwoodresources.com
Type: DC/UMS

HfH ReStore
740 NE 1st Street
Bend, OR 97701
Phone: 541-312-6709
Type: UMS

HfH ReStore
141 S Wasson Street
Coos Bay, OR 97420
Phone: 541-888-1103
Type: UMS

HfH Restore
Box 11527
Portland, OR 97211
Phone: 503-283-6247
Type: UMS

Hippo Hardware and Trading Company
1040 E Burnside Street
Portland, OR 97214
Phone: 503-231-1444
Fax: 503-201-5078
Website: www hipponet.com
Type: UMS

J & J Property Investments Corp.
Portland, OR 97223
Phone: 503-639-9584
Type: UMS

Jefferson Smurfit Recycling Company
1330 NW 14th Avenue
Portland, OR 97209
Phone: 503-294-1560
Fax: 503-742-9113
Type: VA

Knez Building Materials
12301 SE Highway 212
Clacmus, OR 97223
Phone: 503-655-1991
Type: UMS

Konell Construction & Demolition
36000 Industrial Way
Portland, OR 97055
Phone: 503-668-3516

Leslie Larry Lewisburg
Auction & Gen Store
5830 NW Highway 99
Corvallis, OR 97330
Phone: 541-745-5373
Type: UMS

Morrow's Used Building Materials
2784 Jacksonville Highway # B
Medford, OR 97401
Phone: 541-770-6867
Type: UMS

Northwest Demolition
8200 Hunziker SW
Tigard, OR 97223
Phone: 503-638-6900
Type: DC/DM

Northwest Demolition & Dismantle
P.O. Box 930
Wilsonville, OR 97070
Phone: 503-638-6900
Fax: 503-638-1019
Email: m.smith6273@aol.com
Type: DM

Oregon Breakers Inc. Wholesale
1926 SE 10th Avenue
Portland, OR 97214
Phone: 503-736-0921
Type: UMS

Oregon Lumber Company
543 3rd Street #81
Lake Oswego, OR 97034
Phone: 503-636-8191
Fax: 503-635-6140
Type: VA

Pakit Liquidators
903 SE Armour Drive
Bend, OR 97702
Phone: 541-389-7047
Type: UMS

Peddle'n Pete Secondhand Store
& Used Lumber
212 W Front
Merrill, OR 97633
Phone: 541-798-1037
Type: UMS

Products Corporation of North America,
Inc.
6726 SW Burlingame Avenue
Portland, OR 97219-2126
Phone: 503-244-0701
Fax: 503-244-0589
Email: askfred@productscorp.com
Type: BR

Rejuvenation House Parts
1100 SE Grand Avenue
Portland, OR 97214
Phone: 503-238-1900
Email: www rejuvenation.com
Type: UMS

Storie Steel and Wood Products Co.
P.O. Box 12490
Portland, OR 97212
Phone: 503-287-1775
Fax: 503-282-9884
Email: clearcut@earthlink.net
Type: DC/UMS

The ReBuilding Center
3625 N Mississippi Avenue
Portland, OR 97227
Phone: 503-331-1877
Fax: 503-331-1873
Website: www.rebuildingcenter.org
Type: DC/UMS

The Timber Recycler
188 HWY99 N
Eugene, OR 97405
Phone: 541-687-0817
Fax: 541-485-0996
Email: ttrzirg@aol.com
Type: VA
Species: Fir

Pennsylvania

A-1 New & Used Plumbing & Heating
30 Prospect Street
Somerville, PA 02143
Phone: 617-625-6140
Fax: 617-718-0827
Email: a-1plumbimg@rcn.com
Website:
www.antiqueplumbingandradiators.com
Type: UMS

Aged Woods
2331 E Market Street, Suite 6
York, PA 17402
Phone: 800-233-9307
Fax: 717-840-1468
Email: INFO@AGEDWOODS.COM
Website: WWW.AGEDWOODS.COM
Type: CN/UMS

Antique Wood and Colonial Restoration
1273 Redding Avenue
Boyer Town, PA 19512
Phone: 610-367-8193
Fax: 610-367-6911
Email: antiquewds@aol.com
Website: vintagewoods.com
Type: UMS
Species: Cypress, Hemlock, Pine

Antique Woods
1600 Chestnut Tree Road
Elverson, PA 19520
Phone: 610-942-0973
Type: UMS

Architectual Antiques Exchange
715 N 2nd Street
Philadelphia, PA 19123
Phone: 215-922-3669
Fax: 215-922-3680
Email: aaexchange@aol.com
Website: www.architectualantiques.com
Type: UMS

Architectural Emporium
207 Adams Avenue
Canonsburg, PA 15317
Phone: 724-746-4301
Type: UMS

Authentic Wood Floors
2301 N Cameron Street
Harrisburg, PA 17110
Phone: 717-234-0812
Type: UMS/VA

Bambi Used Brick
520 E Fornance Street
Norristown, PA 19401
Phone: 610-275-5777
Type: UMS

Brian Murphy Barn Restoration, Inc.
8 Anna Wanda Road
Oxville, PA 18942
Phone: 610-847-2616
Email: thebarnguy@aol.com
Website: www.barnguys.com
Type: DC/UMS/VA

Barnwood Connection (The)
91 Bull Road
Barto, PA 19504
Phone: 610-845-3101
Fax: 610-845-3167
Email: info@barnwoodconnection.com
Website: www.barnwoodconnection.com
Type: DC/UMS

Bucks County TimberCraft Inc.
P.O. Box 4
Carversville, PA 18938
Phone: 610-737-2481
Fax: 215-249-3916
Email: batnguy1@aol.com
Type: CN

Central Salvage
124 N Narbeth Avenue
Narbeth, PA 19072
Phone: 610-667-1186
Fax: 610-667-1920
Email: adam@centralsalvagepa.com
Type: DC

Centre Mills Antique Floors
P.O. Box 16
Aspers, PA 17304
Phone: 717-334-0249
Fax: 717-334-6223
Website: www.igateway.com/mall/
homeimp/wood/index htm
Type: DC/VA

Conklin's Authentic Antique Barnwood
RD 1 Box 70
Susquehanna, PA 18847
Phone: 717-465-3832
Fax: 717-465-3832
Website: www.conklinsbarnwood.com
Type: UMS/VA

Construction Junction
214 N Lexington Avenue
Pittsburgh, PA 15201
Phone: 412-243-5025
Fax: 412-243-5026
Website: www.constructionjunction.org
Type: UMS
Species: Oak, Pine, Cherry

Cronin Builders And Supply
11106 Terry HWY P.O. 436
Meadville, PA 16335
Phone: 814-336-4523
Type: DC/UMS

Delaware Valley Recycling
3107 S 61st Street
Philadelphia, PA 19153
Phone: 215-724-2244
Type: UMS

Empire Services
1420 Clarion Street
Reading, PA 19601
Phone: 610-372-6511
Fax: 610-372-3402
Website: www.empireservicesberks.com
Type: DC/DM

ERA, Inc.
68 Eisenhour Road
Myerstown, PA 17067
Phone: 231-768-5827
Type: VA

Habitat ReStore of Lancaster County
1520 Lincoln Highway E
Lancaster, PA 17602
Phone: 717-293-0250
Type: UMS

Hess Christopher D Inc.
3931 Cedar Drive
Walnut Port, PA 18088
Phone: 610-760-9533
Email: chbarndawg@entermail.net
Website: www.christopherdsinc.com
Type: VA
Species: Heartpine, Chestnut, Oak

Lelinski John
729 Main Street
Bristol, PA 19007
Phone: 215-945-2475
Type: UMS

LS Sadler Inc.
150 Sadler Drive
Indiana, PA 15701
Phone: 724-463-3044
Type: UMS

Mayse Woodworking Company
319 Richardson Road
Lansdale, PA 19446
Phone: 215-822-8307
Fax: 215-822-8307
Type: VA/UMS
Species: Heartpine, Longleaf pine, Hemlock

McHugh Dismantlement Services
P.O. Box 109
Berwyn, PA 19312
Phone: 610-640-1444
Fax: 610-640-1457
Email: mchughdemo@aol.com
Type: DC

Merritt's Antiques
1860 Weaverton Road
Douglassville, PA 19518
Phone: 610-689-9541
Fax: 610-689-4538
Type: UMS

Noralco Corporation
1920 Lincoln Road
Pittsburgh, PA 15235
Phone: 412-361-6678
Fax: 412-361-6535
Email: noralco@aol.com
Website: www noralco.com
Type: DM

Olde Good Things
400 Gilligan Street
Scranton, PA 18508
Phone: 570-341-7668
Email: mail@oldegoodthings.com
Website: www.oldegoodthings.com
Type: UMS

Patina Woods
3363 New Franklin Road
Chambersburg, PA 17201
Phone: 717-264-8009
Website:
www.penmar net/patinawoods/index html
Type: DC/VA

PDG Environmental
1386 Beulah Road
Pittsburgh, PA 15235
Phone: 800-972-7341
Website: www.pdge.com
Type: DM

Recycle Shack
814 2nd Avenue
Royersford, PA 19468
Phone: 484-686-7641
Email: recycall@hotmail.com
Type: DC/UMS

ReStore
3016 E Thompson Street
Philadelphia, PA 19134
Phone: 215-634-3474
Type: UMS

Russo Demolition & Salvage
800 31st Street
Altoona, PA 16602
Phone: 814-946-3215
Fax: 814-946-3176
Type: DM/UMS

Sable Construction Inc.
1609 N Delaware Avenue
Philadelphia, PA 19125
Phone: 215-427-1462
Fax: 215-427-1796
Email: rcw@sableinc.com
Website: www.sableinc.com
Type: DC

Sahd Frank Salvage
1045 Lancaster Avenue
Columbia, PA 17512
Phone: 717-684-8506
Email: fpuzz@aol.com
Website: www.demolition-salvage.com
Type: UMS
Species: Pine

Selective Dismantlement, Inc.
998 Shavertown Road
Boothwyn, PA 19061
Phone: 610-361-8793
Fax: 610-361-8798
Type: DC

Stauffer & Sons Inc.
33 Glenola Drive
Leola, PA 17540
Phone: 717-656-2811
Type: UMS

Sylvan Brandt LLC Resawn
& Antique Floors
651 E Main Street
Lititz, PA 17543
Phone: 717-626-4520
Fax: 717-626-5867
Email: dean@sylvanbrandt.com
Type: UMS/VA

The Woods Co. Inc.
5045 Kansas Avenue
Chambersburg, PA 17201
Phone: 717-263-6524
Fax: 717-263-9346
woodfloors@thewoodscompany.com
Website: www.thewoodscompany.com
Type: VA
Species: Oak, Chestnut, Pine

Tullytown Metal & Iron Company
729 Main Street
Bristol, PA 19007
Phone: 215-945-2475
Type: UMS

U.S. Recycling and Wrecking
390 Eckman Road
Lancaster, PA 17603
Phone: 717-393-2992
Fax: 717-464-1845
Type: DC/UMS

Victorian Memories
313 13th Street
Franklin, PA 16323
Phone: 814-437-9450
Email: Vmpostman@aol.com
Type: UMS

W W Charles & Daughters Inc.
252 Hollow Road
New Providence, PA 17560
Phone: 717-786-3738
Type: UMS

Wood Natural Restorations
3038 Woodlane Avenue
Orefield, PA 18069
Phone: 610-395-6451
Email: ken@woodnatural.com
Website: www.woodnatural.com
Type: DC/VA

Woodfinder
Springtown, PA 18081
Phone: 877-933-4637
Website: www.woodfinder net
Type: BR

Yesteryear Floorworks Company
2331 E Market Street, Suite 6
York, PA 17402
Phone: 800-233-9307
Fax: 717-840-1468
Website: www.agedwoods.com
Type: VA

Zuk Lumber & Demolition
530 W Broad Street
Bethlehem, PA 18018
Phone: 610-868-7440
Type: DM

Rhode Island

AA Wrecking & Asbestos Abatement
1307 Hartford Avenue
Johnston, RI 02919
Phone: 401-351-1188
Type: DM/UMS

Atlantic Industrial Services
7 Echo Drive
Barrington, RI 02806
Phone: 401-247-2426
Type: DM

Columbus Door Co.
1884 Elmwood Avenue
Warwick, RI 02888
Phone: 401-781-7792
Fax: 408-467-3620
Type: UMS

Gladu Wrecking & Recycling
Beacon Avenue
Woonsocket, RI 02895
Phone: 401-769-9125
Type: DM

National Wrecking Company
64 Grotto Street
Pawtucket, RI 02860
Phone: 401-723-1545
Fax: 401-723-1547
Type: DC/UMS

New England Architectural Center
334 Knight Street
Warwick, RI 02885
Phone: 401-732-1383
Email: ne_architectural@att net
Website: www nearchitecturalcenter.com
Type: UMS

New England Timber Frames
188 Windstone Drive
Portsmouth, RI 02871
Phone: 401-683-2541
Fax: 401-682-2142
Email: netimbrfrm@aol.com
Website:
http://members.aol.com/netimbrfrm
Type: VA

Ocean State Wrecking &
Asbestos Removal
32 Shun Pike
Johnston, RI 02919
Phone: 401-946-6131
Type: DM/EV

South Carolina

Antique Hardware and Home
19 Buckingham Plantation Drive
Buffington, SC 29910
Phone: 800-422-9982
Website: www.antiquehardware.com
Type: UMS

Big Wood
SC
Phone: 864-898-1655
Fax: 864-898-1675
Email:
Website: www.big-wood net
Type: DC/UMS

Browns Housewrecking & Salvage
609 Meeting Street
Charleston, SC 29403
Phone: 843-722-1643
Type: DM

Carolina Building Materials and Salvage
2440 Meeting Street Road
Charleston, SC 29405
Phone: 843-744-2575
Type: UMS

Charleston Wrecking Co.
Charleston, SC 29401
Phone: 843-723-1322
Type: DM/UMS

Cogan's Antiques
110 N Palmer Street
Ridgeway, SC 29130
Phone: 803-337-3939
Type: UMS

H&H Fencing and Salvage
739 Bruce Street
Columbia, SC 29223
Phone: 803-736-6631
Type: UMS

Heart Pine Lumber and Millworks
P.O. Box 1844
Orangeburg, SC 29116
Phone: 803-534-8478
Fax: 803-533-0051
Type: VA
Species: Heartpine

HFH ReStore
122 Maxwell Avenue
Greenwood, SC 29646
Phone: 864-953-9880
Type: UMS

HfH-Sumter ReStore
30 Bridge Court
Sumter, SC 29150
Phone: 803-934-9749
Type: UMS

Old House Salvage
95 Big Survey Road
Piedmont, SC 29673
Phone: 864-243-5990
Type: UMS

Sea Island HFH ReStore
3487 McGill Court
Johns Island, SC 29455-7232
Phone: 803-768-0998
Type: UMS

Wild Clover Reclamation & Lumber Co.,
Inc.
P.O. Box 101
Murrells Inlet, SC 29576
Phone: 803-237-5490
Fax: 803-237-5091
Type: UMS

Wolverine Brass Inc.
2951 Highway 501 E
Conway, SC 29526
Phone: 843-347-3122
Type: UMS

South Dakota

Architectural Elements
818 E 8th Street
Sioux Falls, SD 57103
Phone: 605-339-9646
Email: architecturalelements@mail.com
Type: UMS
Species: Fir, Oak

Keetagilly
528 Suni Avenue
Baltic, SD 57003
Phone: 605-529-6152
Email: salvage@keetagilly.com
Type: DC/VA

Materials Clearance and Salvage
1109 Creek Drive
Rapid City, SD 57701
Phone: 605-343-1993
Fax: 605-343-1993
Type: UMS

Second Chance Lumber
Viborg, SD 57070
Phone: 605-766-5145
Email: mellamy001@yahoo.com
Type: DC/UMS

Tennessee

America Heart Pine, Inc.
4626 Billy Maher Road
Memphis, TN 38135
Phone: 800-544-5765
Type: VA

American Heritage Preservation
1869 Highway 52 E
Portland, TN 37148
Phone: 888-427-2276
Fax: 615-325-2701
Email: nbced@mindspring.com
www.americanheritagepreservation.com
Type: DC/UMS
Species: Oak, Chestnut

Architectural Exchange
1300 McCallie Avenue
Chattanooga, TN 37405
Phone: 423-697-1243
Email: ACR1300@aol.com
Website: http://mywebpages.comcast.net/
tnhotairpilot/archex/index html
Type: UMS

Bob's Salvage
756 Old Hickory
Jackson, TN 38305
Phone: 731-668-9431
Type: UMS

Boyzie Turner Coal Co.
1924 Leslie Avenue
Knoxville, TN 37921
Phone: 865-522-7902
Type: DM/UMS

Burnett Demolition and Salvage
1220 Prosser Road
Knoxville, TN 37914
Phone: 865-637-3996
Type: DM/UMS

Chandler Demolition Company
1223 N Watkins Street
Memphis, TN 38108
Phone: 901-276-5459
Fax: 901-276-5450
Website: www.chandlerdemolition.com
Type: DM

Habitat for Humanity of Blount County
1620 W Broadway, S215
Maryville, TN 37801
Phone: 423-458-8950
Type: UMS

Hailey Salvage and Building Materials
1224 Dickerson Pike
Nashville, TN 37207
Phone: 615-226-0696
Type: UMS

Hailey Salvage and Building Materials
725 Lebanon Road
Nashville, TN 37210
Phone: 615-224-9050
Type: UMS

Havron Contracting
1513 Williams Street
Chattanooga, TN 37408
Phone: 423-265-8883
Fax: 423-265-3627
Email: havron@mindspring.com
Website: www.demolitionsalvage.com
Type: DC/UMS
Species: Heartpine

HFH ReStore
169 Scott Street
Memphis, TN 38112
Phone: 901-323-9250
Type: UMS

Holston HFH ReStore
P.O. Box 5265
Kingsport, TN 37663-0265
Phone: 423-239-7689
Type: UMS

Knoxville HFH ReStore
2209 N Central Avenue
Knoxville, TN 37917
Phone: 423-521-4909
Type: UMS

Loudon County HFH ReStore
204 Lakeside Plaza, Suite 115
Loudon, TN 37774
Phone: 423-458-8950
Type: UMS

Loudon County Salvage and Building
410 Magnolia Avenue
Knoxville, TN 37917
Phone: 423-525-1926
Type: UMS

Memphis Wrecking Company Inc.
2301 S 3rd Street
Memphis, TN 38109
Phone: 901-774-4011
http://yp.bellsouth.com/sites/memwreck/
Type: DM

Nashville Discount Building Materials
1400 51st Avenue N
Nashville, TN 37209
Phone: 615-292-7856
Type: UMS

North Hixson Salvage Door and Window
7505 Hixson Pike
Hixson, TN 37343
Phone: 423-847-6774
Type: UMS

Push Hard Lumber
4635 N Fairmount Road
Signal Mountain, TN 37377
Phone: 423-517-0089
Email: info@pushhardlumber.com
Website: www.pushhardlumber.com
Type: VA

Regency Reclaimed Woods
5977 Old Dayton Pike
Chattanooga, TN 37415
Phone: 423-877-0879
Type: UMS

Salvage and Building Materials
103 E Centre Stage Business
Clinton, TN 37716
Phone: 865-457-7897
Type: UMS

Salvage Lumber Co.
2711 Western Avenue
Knoxville, TN 37921
Phone: 865-525-6645
Type: UMS

Southeastern Salvage
6052 Lee Highway
Chattanooga, TN 37421
Phone: 423-892-5766
Fax: 423-899-4429
Type: UMS

The Reuse Center
3010 Ambrose Avenue
Nashville, TN 37207
Phone: 615-254-6301
Type: UMS

The Reuse Center
903 Dickerson Pike
Nashville, TN 37207
Phone: 615-650-5001
Type: UMS

Wilmot Inc.
3654 Knollwood Road
Nashville, TN 37215
Phone: 615-533-0696
Fax: 615-385-5744
Email: Tiffany_Wilmot@Yahoo.com
Website: www.Wilmotandassoc.com
Type: DC/UMS

Texas

A & R Demolition
13201 FM812
Del Valle, TX 78617
Phone: 512-243-0512
Type: UMS

A Full Service Co.
212 E Amarillo Boulevard
Amarillo, TX 79107
Phone: 806-379-6225
Type: UMS

A Pallet Co.
610 E French Avenue
Temple, TX 76501
Phone: 254-742-1231
Type: UMS

A&R Demolition Inc.
13201 FM812
Del Valle, TX 78617
Phone: 512-243-0512
Type: DM/UMS

AAA Demolishing Co. Inc.
220 S Lockwood
Houston, TX 77011
Phone: 713-926-3018
Type: DM

AAA Salvage & Demolition
200 Corinth Street
Dallas, TX 75207
Phone: 214-428-1888
Fax: 214-428-1889
Type: DM/UMS

Abe's Salvage
2108 E Rosedale Street
Fort Worth, TX 76104
Phone: 817-536-2381
Type: UMS

Acme Brick Company
11261 Harry Hines Boulevard
Dallas, TX 75229
Phone: 972-241-1400
Type: UMS

Action Lumber Salvage & Demolition
1424 S Loop Drive
Waco, TX 76704
Phone: 254-752-9759
Fax: 254-757-3103
Email: bergman@hot1 net

Adkins Architectural Antiques
3515 Fannin Street
Houston, TX 77004
Phone: 713-522-6547
Type: UMS

All Universal Service Co.
4021 Oak Lane
Bacliff, TX 77518
Phone: 281-339-1333
Type: DM/UMS

American Demolition Inc.
2318 Chavaneaux
San Antonio, TX 78214
Phone: 210-627-2377
Email: gus@americandemolition.com
Website: www.americandemolition.com
Type: DC/DM

Anderson New and Used Bricks
11126 Mesa Drive
Houston, TX 77078
Phone: 281-458-4752
Type: UMS

Antique Lumber Co.
1811 Rock Island
Dallas, TX 75207
Phone: 214-428-7774
Fax: 214-428-1889
Email: sales@antiquelumber.com
Website: www.antiquelumber.com
Type: UMS/VA

Antique Lumber Company
104 Corsicana Street
Hillsboro, TX 76645
Phone: 214-686-7400
Fax: 254-580-0944
Email: hardgrove@airmail net
Website: www.antiquelumber.com
Type: CN/UMS
Species: Heartpine, Pine, Oak

Architectural Antiques Salvage
403 Dawson Street
San Antonio, TX 78202
Phone: 210-226-6863
Fax: 210-224-4712
Email: oldhouseparts@juno.com
Website:
www.urweb net/architectural.antiques
Type: UMS

ATCO Company
2001 Moneda Street
Haltorn City, TX 76117
Phone: 817-834-2055
Type: DM

Austin Brick Company
5180 Highway 290 W
Austin, TX 78735
Phone: 512-899-1550
Type: UMS

Austin Habitat for Humanity Re-Store
310 Comal, #101
Austin, TX 78733
Phone: 512-478-2165
Fax: 512-478-9477
Email: dbmackie@aol.com
Website: www re-store.com
Type: DC/UMS

Brazoria County HFH ReStore
P.O. Box 2216C
Freeport, TX 77542
Phone: 409-823-7200
Type: UMS

Building Materials Outlet
10421 NIH35
Austin, TX 78701
Phone: 512-836-1663
Email: bm010421@smart net
Type: UMS

Cherry Demolition
6131 Selinsky
Houston, TX 77048
Phone: 713-987-0000
Fax: 713-991-6236
Email: mike@cherrydemolition.com
Website: www.cherrydomolition.com
Type: DC/UMS

Cunningham Construction
100 Private Road 331
Hillsboro, TX 76645
Phone: 254-582-3089
Fax: 254-582-3684
Email: tc45@hotmail.com
Type: UMS
Species: Longleaf pine, Cedar, Cypress

Cyborg Palace
5952 W Highway 84-67
Bangs, TX 76823
Phone: 325-752-6267
Type: UMS

Del Valley Recycling
1713 Hwy 71
Austin, TX
Phone: 512-385-4617
Type: UMS

Delta Lumber
4701 E 5th Street
Austin, TX 78702
Phone: 512-385-8522
Type: VA
Species: Longleaf Yellow Pine

Discount Home Warehouse
1750 Empire Central
Dallas, TX 75235
Phone: 214-631-2755
Email: dhw_1@msn.com
Website: www.dhwsalvage.com
Type: UMS

DYN-O-Mite Demolition
6916 CF Hawn Freeway
Dallas, TX 75217
Phone: 214-398-6496
Fax: 214-398-6497
Type: DM/UMS

Environmental Light Recyclers, Inc.
2737 Bryan Avenue
Fort Worth, TX 76104
Phone: 800-755-4117
Fax: 817-924-3692
Type: RC

Family Resale
8000 Jensen Drive
Houston, TX 77093
Phone: 713-691-0506
Type: UMS

Frenchman Lumber
206 G Street
Kerrville, TX 78028
Phone: 830-792-3381
Fax: 830-792-3381
Type: UMS

Gemini Forest Products
9104 Bellechase Road
Granbury, TX 76049
Phone: 817-573-7103
Fax: 817-713-5453
Email: greghalm@earthlink net
Type: VA
Species: Longleaf pine, Cypress

Habitat for Humanity ReStore
119 Lake Street
Bryan, TX 77801
Phone: 409-823-7200
Type: UMS

Habitat for Humanity ReStore
3020 Bryan Street
Dallas, TX 75204
Phone: 214-827-4037
Type: UMS

Habitat for Humanity ReStore
3345 S Jones Street
Fort Worth, TX 76110
Phone: 817-926-9219
Fax: 817-926-8575
Email: info@fwhabitat.org
Type: UMS

Habitat for Humanity ReStore
2910 Avenue N-R
Lubbock, TX 79405
Phone: 806-763-4663
Type: UMS

Habitat for Humanity ReStore
311 Probandt
San Antonio, TX 78204
Phone: 210-223-5203
Type: UMS

Habitat for Humanity ReStore
P.O. Box 6362
Tyler, TX 75711
Phone: 903-595-6630
Type: UMS

Habitat for Humanity ReStore
1507 N Main Street
Victoria, TX 77901
Phone: 361-570-4700
Fax: 361-570-6170
Email: restore@icsi net
Type: UMS

Heart of Texas Pine Company
4538 South IH 35
San Marcos, TX 78666
Phone: 512-392-1965
Email: texasheartpine@centurytel net
Type: VA

Heritage Restorations
Brazos de Dios
Elm Mott, TX 76640
Phone: 254-717-5531
Email: info@heritagebarns.com
Website: www heritagebarns.com
Type: DC/VA

Hill Country Woodworks of Texas
E Jackson Street
Burnet, TX 78611
Phone: 512-756-6950
Fax: 512-756-2804
Email: byron@texaswoodwork.com
Website: www.texaswoodwork.com
Type: VA
Species: Longleaf pine, Mesquite

Historic Houston
P.O. Box 130463
Houston, TX 77219
Phone: 713-522-0542
Fax: 713-522-0566
Email: info@historichouston.org
Website: www historichouston.org
Type: UMS

Ken Richter Dismantling
2203 Lillie Lane
Taylor, TX 76574
Phone: 512-924-3108
Type: DC/UMS

Landmark Brick
129 N Murphy Road
Plano, TX 75094
Phone: 972-578-8585
Type: UMS

McKinney Wrecking
18 Ruhlen Court
El Paso, TX 79925
Phone: 915-533-2006
Fax: 915-542-0032
Type: DC/UMS
Species: Pine, Oak

Midwest Steel Company, Inc.
9825 Moers Road
Houston, TX 77075
Phone: 713-991-7843
Fax: 713-992-4745
Email: chrisgiven@midwest-steel.com
Website: www midwest-steel.com
Type: DM

Miller Enterprises
136 W McLeroy
Saginaw, TX 76179
Phone: 817-626-1941
Type: DM/UMS

Moore for Less Salvage
Discount Building Materials
Highway 114
Rhome, TX 76078
Phone: 817-636-2552
Type: UMS

Old Lumber Yard Antiques
116 W Bailey Street
Ponder, TX 76259
Phone: 940-479-0203
Type: UMS

Pam Gaylor Dismantling
Route 1, Box 750-H
Elgin, TX 78621
Phone: 512-332-0819
Type: UMS

Pieces of the Past
411 W Monroe
Austin, TX 78704
Phone: 512-326-5141
Fax: 512-326-5181
Email: kathy@pieces-of-the-past.com
Website: www.pieces-of-the-past.com
Type: UMS

Pieces of the Past
3607 Broadway Street
San Antonio, TX 78209
Phone: 210-828-0757
Type: UMS

Precision Woodworks
507 E Jackson Street
Burnet, TX 78611
Phone: 512-756-6950-
Fax: 512-756-2804
Website: www.precisionwoodworks.com
Type: UMS

Precision Woodworks
417 North Briery Road
Irving, TX 75061
Phone: 972-790-8831
Fax: 512-756-6950
Type: UMS

Quality Surplus
1004 N Simmons Freeway
Lake Dallas, TX 75065
Phone: 940-497-3749
Fax: 940-494-2769
Type: UMS
Species: Pecan, Oak, Pine

Ramirez Properties
3131 Balstrop Hwy
Austin, TX
Phone: 512-385-5512
Type: UMS

Reed-Orr Wrecking Company
1903 Rock Island Street
Dallas, TX 75207
Phone: 214-428-7429
Type: UMS

Remanufactured Hardwoods
2630 Loop 35
Alvin, TX 77511
Phone: 281-331-7838
Fax: 281-331-6467
Email: recycle@poboxes.com
Website:
www.clever net/qms/hardwood htm
Type: VA

Restore
3020 Bryan Street
Dallas, TX 75204
Phone: 214-827-9083
Type: UMS

Salvage Lumber of Texas
100 S Roberts Drive
West, TX 76691
Phone: 254-826-4458
Fax: 254-757-3103
Email: bergman@hot1 net
Type: UMS

Salvage Sale, Inc.
1001 McKinney, Suite 700
Houston, TX 77002
Phone: 713-286-4601
Email: customercare@salvagesale.com
Website: www.salvagesale.com
Type: BR

Scott's Salvage
13494 Gholson Road
Waco, TX 76705
Phone: 254-829-1448
Type: UMS

Second Chance Building Components
817 Spring Street
Columbus, TX 78934
Phone: 409-732-6646
Type: UMS

Steven L. Remley
2737 Bryan Avenue
Fort Worth, TX 76104
Phone: 817-924-9300
Fax: 817-9249380
Email: elrinc@flash net
Website: www.lightrecyclers.com
Type: DC

Strickland Lumber
115 Lee Street
Wichita Falls, TX 76301
Phone: 940-322-2716
Type: UMS

Texas Woods, Inc.
1192 Highway 304
Bastrop, TX 78602
Phone: 512-303-5667
Fax: 512-303-7700
Email: mesquite@bastrop.com
Website: www.texaswoods.com
Type: VA

The Emporium
1800 Westheimer
Houston, TX 77098
Phone: 713-528-3808
Fax: 713-528-5494
Email: info@the-emporium.com
Website: www.the-emporium.com
Type: UMS

The Phoenix Commotion
2913 Montgomery Road
Huntsville, TX 77340
Phone: 936-291-1333
Email: brnsqz@txucom net
Website: www.phoenixcommotion.com
Type: CN/VA

The Woodshop of Texas
P.O. Box 202
Porter, TX 77365
Phone: 888-950-9663
Fax: 713-329-9969
Email: tlhurd@ev1.net
Website: www.antiquewoods net
Type: VA

The Wrecking Barn, Inc.
3111 Ross Avenue
Dallas, TX 75204
Phone: 214-827-7173
Fax: 214-747-4211
Type: UMS

Thomas Elisha
2108 E Rosedale Street
Fort Worth, TX 76104
Phone: 817-536-2381
Type: UMS

Town & Country Brick & Supply Inc
15711 Fm 2920 Road
Tomball, TX 77375
Phone: 281-351-6356
Type: UMS

Tuck Used Lumber
1303 Hutchins Road
Dallas, TX 75203
Phone: 214-948-7285
Type: UMS

Union Salvage
2505 South Street
Nacogdoches, TX 75964
Phone: 936-560-4534
Type: UMS

Union Salvage
104 Simonds Road
Seagoville, TX 75159
Phone: 972-287-5190
Type: UMS

W K Lumber Company
4721 Airport Freeway
Haltorn City, TX 76117
Phone: 817-831-8847
Type: UMS

Welpman & Son Door & Salvage
2200 E Maddox Avenue
Fort Worth, TX 76104
Phone: 817-535-0906
Fax: 817-535-0906
Type: UMS

What It's Worth
P.O. Box 162135
Austin, TX 78716
Phone: 512-328-8837
Fax: 512-328-8837
Type: VA

Utah

Alpine Barns
1060 Orchard Lane
Alpine, UT 84004
Phone: 801-310-5004
Email: info@alpinebarns.com
Website: www.alpinebarns.com
Type: CN/VA

Bowen Enterprises
P.O. Box 12005
Ogden, UT 84412
Phone: 801-621-3626
Type: UMS

Community Development of Utah
501 East 1700 S
Salt Lake City, UT 84105
Phone: 801-994-7222
Email: slcdc@slcdc.org
Type: UMS

Costello Co.
1240 Princeton Avenue
Salt Lake City, UT 84101
Phone: 801-581-0084
Type: UMS

Demolition Salvage Supply Company
430 Slade Place
Salt Lake City, UT 84102
Phone: 801-539-1140
Type: DM/UMS

George's Demolition & Salvage
430 East 900 S
Salt Lake City, UT 84111
Phone: 801-521-8717
Type: DM/UMS

Pappas Brick & Stone
1860 Lincoln Avenue
Ogden, UT 84401
Phone: 801-621-1613
Type: DM

Trestlewood
292 North 2000 W
Lindon, UT 84042
Phone: 801-443-4002
Email: info@trestlewood.com
Website: www.Trestlewood.com
Type: DC/UMS/VA
Species: Fir, Pine, Oak

Trestlewood Furniture
1035 South 800 W
Salt Lake City, UT 84104
Phone: 801-972-9970
Fax: 801-973-0999
Email: trestle@trestlewood.com
Type: VA

Urban Forest Woodworks
1065 West 600 N
Logan, UT 84321
Phone: 435-752-7268
Fax: 435-752-4471
Email: ufww@urbanforestww.com
Website: www.urbanforestww.com
Type: UMS/VA

Vermont

Architectural Salvage Warehouse
53 Main Street
Burlington, VT 05401
Phone: 802-658-5011
Email: salvage@together.net
Website: www.architecturalsalvagevt.com
Type: UMS
Species: www.greatsalvage.com

David D. Parker
P.O. Box 6458
Brattleboro, VT 05302
Phone: 802-251-0000
Fax: 802-251-0001
Website: www.parkerrestoration.com
Type: VA

David D. Parker Structural Restoration
P.O. Box 6458
Brattleboro, VT 05302
Phone: 802-251-0000
Fax: 802-251-0001
Website: www.parkerrestoration.com
Type: DC/VA

J H Lumber & Wood Products
R D 2 Box 5320
Montpelier, VT 05602
Phone: 802-229-4148
Website: www.jhlumber.com
Type: VA

Mason Brothers Architectural Salvage
11 Maple Street
Essex Junction, VT 05452
Phone: 802-879-4221
Type: DC/UMS
Species: Pine, Fir

ReCycle North
266 Pine Street
Burlington, VT 05401
Phone: 802-658-4143
info@recyclenorth.org
Website: www recyclenorth.org
Type: DC/UMS

Re-New Building Materials & Salvage
Wellington Road
22 Browne Court, Unit 185
Brattleboro, VT 05301-4428
Phone: 802-246-2400
Email: renew@sover net
Website: www renewsalvage.org

Second Harvest Antique Lumbers
Box 240 Willson Road
Jeffersonville, VT 05464
Phone: 802-644-8169
Fax: 802-644-8005
Type: DC/UMS
Species: Pine, Spruce, Hemlock

Shiningwater Enterprises
484 Mill Road
Lincoln, VT 05443
Phone: 802-453-2825
Email: jaxfam@sover.net
Website: www.traditional-building.com/
brochure/members/1architecturalsalvage.shtml
Type: DC/VA

The Barn People
2218 U.S. Route 5
Windsor, VT 05089
Phone: 802-674-5898
Fax: 802-674-6310
Email: barnman@sover.net
Website: www.thebarnpeople.com
Type: CN/DC

Vermont Salvage Exchange
2-4 Gates Street
White River Junction, VT 05001
Phone: 802-295-7616
Fax: 802-295-5744
Email: help@vermontsalvage.com
Website: www.vermontsalvage.com
Type: DC

Virginia

Ahoora, Inc.
P.O. Box 826
Merrifield, VA 22116
Phone: 703-438-0957
Fax: 703-438-1726
Email: ahoora@aol.com
Type: UMS

Antique Building Products
P.O. Box 206
Amherst, VA 24521
Phone: 804-946-0634
Fax: 804-946-0835
Website:
www.antiquebuildingproducts.com
Type: UMS/VA

Appalachian Woods
1240 Cold Springs Road
Stuarts Draft, VA 24477
Phone: 540-337-1801
Fax: 540-337-1030
Email: jonas@appalachianwoods.com
Website: www.appalachianwoods.com
Type: DC/UMS
Species: Heartpine, Oak, Fir

Bargain Village
12197 Jefferson Davis Highway
Woodford, VA 22580
Phone: 804-448-0059
Type: UMS

Big Wood
Afton, VA 22920
Phone: 434-361-9300
Fax: 434-361-1873
Website: www.big-wood net
Type: DC/UMS

Black Dog Salvage
902 13th Street SW
Roanoke, VA 24016
Phone: 540-343-6200
Fax: 540-343-6295
Email: info@blackdogsalvage.com
Website: www.blackdogsalvage.com
Type: UMS

Blue Ridge Timberwrights
P.O. Box 30
Christiansburg, VA 24068
Phone: 540-382-1102
Fax: 540-382-8039
Email:
questions@blueridgetimberwrights.com
Website: www.blueridgetimberwrights.com
Type: CN
Species: Fir, Oak

Caravati's Architectural Antiques
104 E 2nd Street
Richmond, VA 23224
Phone: 804-232-4175
Fax: 804-233-7109
Email: webmaster@recentruins.com
Website: www.recentruins.com
Type: UMS

Cmc
4509 Pouncey Tract Road
Glen Allen, VA 23059
Phone: 804-369-2120
Type: DM/UMS

Cochran's Lumber and Millwork
33735 Snickersville Turnpike
Bluemont, VA 20135
Phone: 540-554-8274
Website: www.lumberandmillwork.com
Type: VA

Dwight Snead Construction
11255 Washington Highway
Glen Allen, VA 23059
Phone: 804-798-1611
Fax: 804-798-8224
Email: dwight@sneadconstruction.com
Website: www.sneadconstruction.com
Type: DM

Empire Salvage & Recycling, Inc.
200 Thistle Street
Bluefield, VA 24605
Phone: 276-322-3554
Type: UMS

E.T. Moore Manufacturing
3100 N Hopkins Road, Suite 101
Richmond, VA 23224
Phone: 804-231-1823
Fax: 804-231-0759
Email: orders@etmoore.com
Website: www.etmoore.com
Type: DC/UMS/VA
Species: Longleaf pine, Cypress

Governors Antiques and Architectural
Supply
8000 Antique Lane
Mechanicsville, VA 23116
Phone: 804-746-1030
Fax: 804-730-8308
Email: governorsantiques@earthlink.net
Website: governorsantiques.net
Type: UMS

Hamilton Salvage Building Materials
3201 Dwina Road
Coeburn, VA 24230
Phone: 276-762-5140
Type: UMS

Heartwood International
141 Heartwood Circle
Afton, VA 22920
Phone: 804-361-1323
Fax: 804-361-1873
contact@heartwoodinternational.com
Website: www heartwoodinternational.com
Type: VA

Imperial Building Supply
856 W 45th Street
Norfolk, VA 23508
Phone: 757-489-4254
Type: UMS

Kings Arrow Antiques Lumber
11175 Tattersall Trail
Oakton, VA 22124
Phone: 703-4075912
Email: kingsarrow@prodigy net
Type: DC/UMS
Species: Chestnut, Longleaf pine

Lantz Building Supply
138 Linville Avenue
Broadway, VA 22815
Phone: 540-896-7048
Type: UMS

Mountain Lumber
P.O. Box 289
Ruckersville, VA 22968
Phone: 800-445-2671
Fax: 804-985-4105
Email: sales@mountainlumber.com
Website: www mountainlumber.com
Type: DC/UMS

Old Wood
4501 Liberty Hall Court
Quinton, VA 23141
Phone: 804-932-8013
Fax: 804-642-2532
Email: will@3bubbas.com
Type: VA
Species: Pine, Oak, Cypress

Pryor's Hauling Company
4509 Pouncey Tract Road
Glen Allen, VA 23059
Phone: 804-360-2120
Type: DM/UMS

Shenandoah Valley Reclaimed Lumber
3586 Horizons Way
Harrisonburg, VA 22801
Phone: 540-896-7600
Fax: 540-896-5455
Email: butlerj@horizonsva.com
Website: svreclaimedlumber.com
Type: DC/UMS
Species: Pine, Oak, Chestnut

Showcase
1657 W Broad Street
Richmond, VA 23220
Phone: 804-340-1900
Type: UMS

The Housewright Shop
187 Pine Tree Lane
Fort Valley, VA 22652
Phone: 540-933-6458
Email: pwcj@yahoo.com
Type: DC/UMS

Vintage Pine Company
P.O. Box 85
Pamplin, VA 23958
Phone: 434-248-9000
Type: VA

Virginia Antique Building Materials
600 Greenview Court
Pulaski, VA 24301
Phone: 540-980-4232
Fax: 540-980-4338
Email: tdalton@i-plus.net
Type: DC/UMS
Species: Heartpine, Oak, Chestnut

Washington

BCR Barn Dismantling
734 Harrison Avenue
Beloit, WA 53511
Phone: 608-363-0012
Type: DC

Bear Creek Lumber
P.O. Box 669
Winthrop, WA 98862
Phone: 509-997-3110
Fax: 509-997-2040
Email: customerservice@bearcreeklumber.com
Website: www.bearcreeklumber.com
Type: UMS

Brown's Lumber Yard
112 N Erie Street
Spokane, WA 99202
Phone: 509-535-0112
Type: UMS

Centralia Perks
113 N Tower Avenue
Centralia, WA 98531
Phone: 360-330-2882
Type: UMS

Chuckanut Log Design
1421 N State Street
Bellingham, WA 98225
Phone: 360-647-2633
Fax: 360-647-3342
Type: VA

Duluth Timber Co.
5715 Gilkey Avenue
Bow, WA 98232
Phone: 360-766-6253
Type: UMS

Earthwise, Inc.
2462 1st Avenue S
Seattle, WA 98134
Phone: 206-624-4510
Email: earthwise@qwest net
Website: www.earthwise-salvage.com
Type: RC/UMS

Earthworks Recycling Inc.
1904 E Broadway Avenue
Spokane, WA 99202
Phone: 509-534-1638
Website: www.earthworksrecycling.com
Type: UMS

Eco-Woodworks
3016 Sapp Road
Tumwater, WA 98512
Phone: 360-943-3808
Fax: 360-943-4217
Type: VA

Environmental Home Center
1724 4th Avenue S
Seattle, WA 98134
Phone: 206-682-7332
Fax: 682-206-8275
Email: pattis@environmentalhomecenter.com
Website: www.environmentalhomecenter.com
Type: UMS

G.R. Plume Co.
1373 W Smith Road, Suite A1
Ferndale, WA 98248
Phone: 360-384-2800
Fax: 360-384-0035
Email: plumegr@plumes.com
Website: www.grplume.com
Type: VA

Grand and Benedicts
3825 1st Avenue S
Seattle, WA 98134
Phone: 206-223-1988
Type: UMS

Habitat for Humanity–Builders
Surplus Store
E 850 Trent Avenue
Spokane, WA 99202
Phone: 509-535-9517
Type: UMS

J Squared Timbers
5448 Shilshole Avenue NW
Seattle, WA 98107
Phone: 800-598-3074
Fax: 206-781-1600
Type: VA

Montana Originals
33100 114th SE
Preston, WA 98050
Phone: 425-222-6497
Fax: 425-222-4567
Type: UMS

Northwest Demolition and Dismantling
Seattle, WA 98101
Phone: 206-243-2270
Website: www nwdemolition.com
Type: DM

Northwest Salvage & Second Hand
7402 NE St. Johns Road
Vancouver, WA 98665
Phone: 360-694-0662
Type: UMS

Northwest Tub Co.
103 S Tower Avenue
Centralia, WA 98531
Phone: 360-888-8827
Type: UMS

Nuprecon
35131 SE Center Street
Snoqualmie, WA 98065
Phone: 425-881-0623
Fax: 425-881-2072
Email: sales@Nuprecon.com
Website: www.nuprecon.com
Type: DM

R.W. Rhine Inc.
1124 112th Street E
Tacoma, WA 98554
Phone: 253-531-7223
Fax: 253-531-9548
Type: DM/UMS

Rabanco Recycling
2733 3rd Avenue S
Seattle, WA 98134
Phone: 425-646-2576
Fax: 206-624-2991
Type: RC

Ray's Demolition Warehouse
2101 E Broadway Avenue
Spokane, WA 99202
Phone: 509-533-1903
Type: UMS

Recovery 1
1630 18th Street E
Tacoma, WA 98421
Phone: 206-537-5852
Type: UMS

Resource Woodworks Inc.
627 E 60th
Tacoma, WA 98404
Phone: 253-474-3757
Fax: 253-474-1139
Website: www.rw-timber.com
Type: DC/VA

Re-Tech Wood Products
1324 Russell Road
Forks, WA 98331
Phone: 360-374-4141
Fax: 360-374-4141
Email: retech@olypen.com
Website: www.retechwoodproducts.com
Type: DC/VA
Species: Fir, Cedar

Reusable Building Material Exchange
Seattle, WA 98104
Phone: 800-325-6165
Website: www.rbme.com
Type: BR

Re-Use Consulting
2421 St. Clair Street
Bellingham, WA 98229
Phone: 360-201-6977
Email: re-use@comcast net
Website: www reuseconsulting.com
Type: BR
Species: Douglas-fir

Seattle Building Salvage
2114 Hewitt Avenue
Everett, WA 98201
Phone: 425-303-8500
Type: UMS

Seattle Building Salvage
330 Westlake Avenue N
Seattle, WA 98103
Phone: 206-381-3453
Website: www.seattlebuildingsalvage.com
Type: UMS

Second Use Building Materials
7953 2nd Avenue S
Seattle, WA 98108
Phone: 206-763-0436
Fax: 206-763-6021
Website: www.seconduse.com
Type: UMS

Sound Builders Resource
210 Thurston Avenue NE
Olympia, WA 98501
Phone: 360-753-1575
Fax: 360-753-5402
Email: info@fbroly.org
Website: www.sbroly.org
Type: UMS
The ReStore
600 W Holly Street
Bellingham, WA 98225
Phone: 360-647-5921
Email: restore@re-sources.org
Website: www re-sources.org
Type: DC/UMS
Species: Fir, Oak, Maple

The ReStore
1440 NW 52nd Street
Seattle, WA 98107
Phone: 206-297-9119
Email: patfinn@Seattle@re-sources.org
Website: www re-sources.org/contact.htm
Type: DC/UMS

TreeHouse Workshop Inc.
303 NW 43 Street
Seattle, WA 98107
Phone: 206-782-0208
Website: www.treehouseworkshop.com
Type: UMS

Waste Not Want Not
724 E 1st Street
Port Angeles, WA 98362
Phone: 360-417-3016
Type: UMS

Waste Not Want Not
304 10th Street
Port Townsend, WA 98368
Phone: 360-379-6838
Fax: 360-379-6838
Email: wnwn@cablespeed.com
Website: www.wastenot-recycle.com
Type: UMS

Windfall Lumber Products
210 Thurston Avenue
Olympia, WA 98501
Phone: 360-352-2250
Fax: 603-894-5571
Website: www.windfalllumber.com
Type: UMS/VA

YV ReStore
2500 S 26th Avenue
Yakima, WA 98903
Phone: 509-576-8077
Email: Habitat@yvn net
Website: www.yakimahabitat.org
Type: UMS

West Virginia

Almost Heaven HFH ReStore
P.O. Box 98
Circleville, WV 26804
Phone: 304-567-2300
Type: UMS

Americo Inc.
One River Park 16th Street
McMechen, WV 26040
Phone: 304-232-1333
Fax: 304-233-1333
Website: www.americo.ohgolly.com
Type: UMS

Antique Cabins and Barns
106 E Washington Street
Lewisburg, WV 24901
Phone: 304-645-7612
Fax: 304-925-3303
Type: DC

Fultineers's Wood Recycling
P.O. Box 131
Lost Creek, WV 26385
Phone: 304-622-0535
Type: UMS/RC

Southland Surplus Building Materials
216 Business Street
Beckley, WV 25801
Phone: 304-252-6515
Type: UMS

Vintage Log and Lumber
P.O. Box 130 Route 219 N
Renick, WV 24966
Phone: 304-497-2700
Fax: 304-497-3651
Email: sales@vintagelog.com
Website: www.vintagelog.com
Type: DC/UMS

Wisconsin

American Resource Recovery
9168 N 124th Street
Milwaukee, WI 53224
Phone: 414-355-8500
Type: DM

Azarian, Sam Wrecking
726 Water Street
Racine, WI 53403
Phone: 262-637-4153
Fax: 262-637-7520
Type: DM

Barnwood Products
Black River Falls, WI 54615
Phone: 715-284-2469
Email: ctrywdcrft@discover-net net
Website: www.barnwoodproducts.com
Type: VA

Beaver Wrecking and Salvage
W8025 State Road 33
Beaver Dam, WI 53916
Phone: 920-887-7030
Fax: 920-887-7030
Type: DM

Coughlin Contractors, Inc.
Welch Road
Watertown, WI 53098
Phone: 920-261-7637
Fax: 920-261-7658
Email: rjcmvc@execpc.com
Type: UMS
Species: 2×4

DeConstruction Inc.
1010 Walsh Road
Madison, WI 53714
Phone: 608-244-8759
Fax: 908-244-8981
Email: deconstruct@mailbag.com
Website: www.deconstructinc.com
Type: DC/UMS

Eckert Wrecking Inc.
4743 U.S. Highway 8
Rhinelander, WI 54501
Phone: 715-362-6550
Fax: 715-362-1837
Type: DC

Gerovac Wrecking Company
11836 W Saint Martins Road
Franklin, WI 53132
Phone: 414-425-1500
Type: DM/UMS

Glenville TimberWrights
S5390 State Road 13
Baraboo, WI 53913
Phone: 608-355-9950
Fax: 608-355-2922
Email: woodshop@tds net
Website: www.glenvilletimberwrights.com
Type: VA

HfH ReStore
208 Cottage Grove Road
Madison, WI 53716
Phone: 608-661-2813
Type: UMS

Homesource Center
3701 W Lisbon Avenue
Milwaukee, WI 53208
Phone: 414-344-4142
Type: UMS

I M Salvage Company
4025 W Loomis Road
Milwaukee, WI 53221
Phone: 414-281-8733
Type: UMS

Milwaukee Timber Company
585 Kossow Road
Milwaukee, WI 53186
Phone: 262-798-8986
Email: david@reclaimed-timbers.com
Website: www reclaimed-timbers.com
Type: VA

Old House Salvage
4404 Stewart Avenue
Wausau, WI 54401
Phone: 715-849-5077
Email: delirevanceman@aol.com
Type: DC/UMS

Pagenkopf Scott
Green Bay, WI 54301
Phone: 920-498-1755
Type: DM/UMS

Reclaimed Lumber Co.
633 Ellis Avenue
Baraboo, WI 53913
Phone: 608-356-8849
Email: David@reclaimed-lumber.com
Website: www reclaimed-lumber.com
Type: DC/UMS

Reclaimed Lumber Company
585 Kossow Road
Waukesha, WI 53186
Phone: 262-798-8986
Fax: 262-798-9401
Email: david@old-barn-wood.com
Website: www.old-barn-wood.com
Type: DC/VA

Salvage Heaven Inc.
206 E Lincoln Avenue
Milwaukee, WI 53207
Phone: 414-329-7170
Type: UMS

Scarboro River Barn and Lumber
Green Bay, WI 54301
Phone: 920-498-1755
Type: DM/UMS

Schuler's Country Store and Workshop
533 N Main Street
Janesville, WI 53545
Phone: 608-754-4052
Email: info@schulercountry.com
Website: www.schulercountry.com
Type: VA

Scs of Wisconsin Inc.
4001 W Loomis Road
Milwaukee, WI 53221
Phone: 414-281-8733
Type: DM/UMS

Timeless Timber
2200 E Lake Shore Drive
Ashland, WI 54806
Phone: 888-653-5647
Fax: 715-685-9620
Email: sales@timelesstimber.com
Website: www.timelesstimber.com
Type: UMS

Traditional Woodworks and Lumber Co.
1679 38th Street
Somerset, WI 54025
Phone: 800-882-2718
Website: www.tradwood.com
Type: VA

Urban Evolutions
867 Valley Road
Menasha, WI 54952
Phone: 920-380-4149
Fax: 920-380-4184
Website: www.urbanevolutions.com
Type: DC/UMS
Species: Pine, Oak, Ash

Wyoming

Centennial Woods
7512 Ridge Road
Cheyenne, WY 82009
Phone: 307-778-8762
Fax: 307-778-8762
Type: UMS

Companies Listed by
Primary Activity

Salvage Broker (BR)

California

Jefferson Recycled Woodworks
1104 Firenzi Street
McCloud, CA 96057
Phone: 800-220-9062
Fax: 530-964-2745
Email: goodwood@snowcrest.net
Website: www.ecowood.com
Species: Redwood, Fir, Hardwoods

Colorado

Singing Saw Woodworks, Inc
67 Shady Hollow
Nederland, CO 80466
Phone: 303-258-0378
Fax: 303-258-0349
Website: www.singingsaw.com/singingsaw

Florida

Michael Murphy
3503 W San Juan Street
Tampa, FL 33629
Phone: 813-902-1480
Fax: 813-727-6222
Email: murphym@gte net

Georgia

EnviroShare Materials Exchange
Gainesville, GA 30503
Phone: 770-535-8284
Website: www.enviroshare.org

Northside Material Brokers
1020 Huff Road
Atlanta, GA 30318
Phone: 404-609-9900
Fax: 404-609-9964
Email: northsidematials@msn.com
Species: Fir, Oak, Mahogany

Illinois

J Stuart Corsa–Purveyors of
Salvage Material
6528 Charles Street
Rockford, IL 61108
Phone: 815-229-0377
Email: stuart51@aol.com

Murco Recycling Enterprises Inc.
347 N Kensington Street
LaGrange Park, IL 60526
Phone: 708-352-4111
Fax: 708-352-4189
Email: jodi@murco net
Website: www murco net

Indiana

Bringing It Back
5726 University Avenue
Indianapolis, IN 46219
Phone: 317-322-8388
Email: housesalvager@aol.com

The Reuse Development Organization
P.O. BOX 47454
Indianapolis, IN 46227
Phone: 317-780-1503
Email: info@redo.org
Website: www redo.org

Kentucky

Heartwood Industries
3658 St Road 1414
Hartford, KY 42347
Phone: 800-318-9439
Fax: 270-298-7755
Website: www.whiskeywood.com

Massachusetts

E-wood
Wellesley, MA 02482
Phone: 877-487-6504
Website: www.e-wood.com

Minnesota

Duluth Timber Company
P.O. Box 16717
Duluth, MN 55816
Phone: 218-727-2145
Fax: 218-727-0393
Email: liz@duluthtimber.com
Website: www.duluthtimber.com
Species: Fir, Longleaf pine, Cypress

Rural Resource Recovery
1320 Jefferson Avenue
Saint Paul, MN 55105
Phone: 651-695-1732
Email: info@ruralresourcerecovery.org
Website: www ruralresourcerecovery.org

New Jersey

Blue Skys Auction Co.
218 Blue Ridge Road
Voorhees, NJ 08043
Phone: 856-354-0199

New York

M. Fine Lumber
1301 Metropolitan Avenue
Brooklyn, NY 11237
Phone: 718-381-5200
Fax: 718-366-8907
Email: rob@mfinelumber.com
Website: www mfinelumber.com
Species: Fir, Pine

New York Wastewatch
253 Broadway, Rm 302
New York, NY 10004
Phone: 212-942-5219
Email: jrosenfield@itac.org

North Carolina

Axel Demolition & Salvage
253 A S Churton Street
Hillsborough, NC 27278
Phone: 919-644-8244

Ed Knapp
782 Beech Tree Road
Whittier, NC 28789
Phone: 828-586-0755
Fax: 828-586-4647
Email: vintageb@gte net
Website:
www.vintagebeamsandtimbers.com
Species: Pine, Others

Oregon

Builders City
8905 N Vancouver Avenue
Portland, OR 97217
Phone: 503-285-0546
Fax: 503-240-1691

Deconstruction Management Group
12345 NW Harborton Drive
Portland, OR 97231
Phone: 503-341-3050
Email: jprimdahl@ilsr.org

Products Corporation of North America,
Inc.
6726 SW Burlingame Avenue
Portland, OR 97219-2126
Phone: 503-244-0701
Fax: 503-244-0589
Email: askfred@productscorp.com

Pennsylvania

Woodfinder
Springtown, PA 18081
Phone: 877-933-4637
Website: www.woodfinder.net

Salvage Broker (BR)—Con.

Texas

Salvage Sale, Inc.
1001 McKinney, Suite 700
Houston, TX 77002
Phone: 713-286-4601
Email: customercare@salvagesale.com
Website: www.salvagesale.com

Washington

Reusable Building Material Exchange
Seattle, WA 98104
Phone: 800-325-6165
Website: www.rbme.com

Re-Use Consulting
2421 St. Clair Street
Bellingham, WA 98229
Phone: 360-201-6977
Email: re-use@comcast net
Website: www.reuseconsulting.com
Species: Douglas-fir

Contractor/Uses Reclaimed Lumber (CN)

Alabama

Southern Timberwrights
77 Baushore Place
Guntersville, AL 35976
Phone: 256-582-9299
Email: lrm@localaccess net
Website: www.southerntimberwrights.com

California

Sierra Timber Framers
P.O. Box 595
Nevada City, CA 95959
Phone: 530-292-9449
Fax: 530-292-9460
Website: www.sierratimberframers.com

Colorado

San Juan Timberwrights
60 Barton Circle
Arboles, CO 81121
Phone: 970-883-2291
Website: www.sandonetimber.com

Wind River Timber Frames
14374 County Road 35.6
Mancos, CO 81328
Phone: 970-882-2112
Email: timberframes@frontier.net
Website:
www.windriver-timberframes.com

Connecticut

Chestnut Oak Company
3810 Old Mountain Road
West Suffield, CT 06093
Phone: 860-668-0382
Email: info@chestnutoakcompany.com
Website: www.chestnutoakcompany.com

District of Columbia

All Aboard Contracting Inc.
4214 Hunt Place NE
Washington, DC 20019
Phone: 202-388-4252
Fax: 202-388-3840

Florida

Pinetree Builders
814 SE 23rd Street
Ft. Lauderdale, FL 33316
Phone: 954-760-5800
Fax: 954-760-5833
Email: info@pinetreebuilders.com
Website: www.pinetreebuilders.com
Species: Heartpine, Cypress

Idaho

Wasankari Construction
2730 Highway 95 S
Moscow, ID 83843
Phone: 208-883-4362

Maryland

Old Line Timberframes
400 Dilks Lane
Elkton, MD 21921
Phone: 410-287-1545
Fax: 410-287-1545
Email: joe@oldlinetimberframes.com
Website: www.oldlinetimberframes.com

Massachusetts

Colonial Barn Restoration
269 Old Bay Road
Bolton, MA 01740
Phone: 978-779-9865
Email: Tim@ColonialBarn.com
Website: www.colonialbarn.com

Minnesota

Century Construction Co., Inc.
820 N Concord Street, Suite 101
South St. Paul, MN 55075
Phone: 651-451-1020
Fax: 651-451-2745
Email: info@centuryconstruct.com
Website: www.centuryconstruct.com

Kellington Construction Inc.
20110 Auger Aev
Corcoran, MN 55340
Phone: 612-416-3200
Fax: 612-416-3201
Email: rlewis@kellington.com
Website: www.kellington.com

Montana

Nellis Custom Woodworks
4470 Amsterdam Road
Manhattan, MT 59741
Phone: 406-282-9049
Fax: 406-282-9050
Email: eric@nelliscustomwoodworks.com
Website:
www.nelliscustomwoodworks.com/aboutus.html

New Hampshire

Benson Woodworking Co. Inc
6 Blackjack Crossing
Walpole, NH 03608
Phone: 603-756-3600
Email: info@bensonwood.com
Website: www.bensonwood.com

New York

LaPointe Construction
P.O. Box 691
Hague, NY 12836
Phone: 518-543-6341
Fax: 518-543-6946

New Energy Works Timber Framers, Inc.
1180 Commercial Drive
Farmington, NY 14425
Phone: 800-486-0661
Fax: 585-924-9962
Email: joinery@newenergyworks.com
Website: www newenergyworks.com

Ohio

Amish Timber Framers
11627 Hametown Road
Doylestown, OH 44230
Phone: 800-392-8789
Email: info@amishtimberframers.com
Website: www.amishtimberframers.com

Oregon

Asher Traditional Homes
15795 SW Serena Court
Portland, OR 97224
Phone: 503-620-6163

Contractor/Uses Reclaimed Lumber—Con.

Pennsylvania

Aged Woods
2331 E Market Street, Suite 6
York, PA 17402
Phone: 800-233-9307
Fax: 717-840-1468
Email: info@agedwoods.com
Website: www.agedwoods.com

Bucks County TimberCraft Inc.
P.O. Box 4
Carversville, PA 18938
Phone: 610-737-2481
Fax: 215-249-3916
Email: batnguy1@aol.com

Texas

Antique Lumber Company
104 Corsicana Street
Hillsboro, TX 76645
Phone: 214-686-7400
Fax: 254-580-0944
Email: hardgrove@airmail net
Website: www.antiquelumber.com
Species: Heartpine, Pine, Oak

The Phoenix Commotion
2913 Montgomery Road
Huntsville, TX 77340
Phone: 936-291-1333
Email: brnsqz@txucom net
Website: www.phoenixcommotion.com

Utah

Alpine Barns
1060 Orchard Lane
Alpine, UT 84004
Phone: 801-310-5004
Email: info@alpinebarns.com
Website: www.alpinebarns.com

Vermont

The Barn People
2218 U.S. Route 5
Windsor, VT 05089
Phone: 802-674-5898
Fax: 802-674-6310
Email: barnman@sover net
Website: www.thebarnpeople.com

Virginia

Blue Ridge Timberwrights
P.O. Box 30
Christiansburg, VA 24068
Phone: 540-382-1102
Fax: 540-382-8039
Email: questions@blueridgetimberwrights.com
Website: www.blueridgetimberwrights.com
Species: Fir, Oak

Deconstruction/Soft-Stripping (DC)

Alabama

Reaves Wrecking Co. Inc.
201 A Boulevard
Valley, AL 36854
Phone: 334-756-3237
Email: reaveswrecking@mindspring.com
Species: Pine

Shiver's Wrecking Company
3895 Old Seale Highway
Phenix City, AL 36869
Phone: 334-297-2044
Species: Heartpine

Arizona

Barnett & Shore Contractors
819 W Silverlake Road
Tucson, AZ 85713
Phone: 520-791-0286

Dickens Quality Demolition, LLC.
1146 N 19th Avenue
Phoenix, AZ 85009
Phone: 602-206-9979
Website: www.dickensquality.com

Old Pueblo Remodelers
1700 South 4th Avenue
Tucson, AZ 85713
Phone: 520-884-8685

Salvage Depot Inc.
5701 W San Miguel
Glendale, AZ 85301
Phone: 623-680-4874
Fax: 623-972-1341
Email: daveschueller@worldnet.att net
Species: Fir

Stardust Building Supplies
1720 W Broadway Road
Phoenix, AZ 85202
Phone: 602-604-0605
Fax: 602-604-0207
Email: ala@stardustbuilding.org
Website: www.stardustbuilding.org

Arkansas

Architectural Salvage by Ri-Jo
2309 Highway 71 S
Mena, AR 71953
Phone: 479-394-2438
Email: salvage@arkansas net

Dore & Associates Contracting, Inc.
1400 Brookwood
Little Rock, AR 72202
Phone: 800-344-7876
Email: dore@concentric.net
Website: www.doreandassociates.com

PattonWrecking Inc.
8222 Stagecoach Road
Little Rock, AR 72210
Phone: 501-455-2833
Fax: 501-455-4083
Email: pwi@cei med

California

American Constructors California
16351 Gothard Street #A
Huntington Beach, CA 92647
Phone: 714-377-1414

Arcadia Demolition Services
785 Walsh Avenue
Santa Clara, CA 95050
Phone: 408-248-0505
Fax: 408-248-2664
Email: info@arcadiademo.com
Website: www.arcadiademo.com

AWS Construction Services, Inc.
6621 E Pacific Coast Highway #130
Long Beach, CA 90803
Phone: 562-799-4436
Email: aws@awsconstruction.com
Website: www. awsconstruction.com

Beyond Waste
607 W Sierra
Cotati, CA 94952
Phone: 707-792-2555
Fax: 707-792-2565
Email: precycle@sonic.net
Website: www.beyondwaste.com
Species: Redwood, Fir

Blue Log Lumber
P.O. Box 804
Mendocino, CA 95460
Phone: 707-937-1735
Website: www.goodwood.org
Species: redwood

Deconstruction/Soft-Stripping (DC)—Con.

BOSS Enterprises
2065 Kittredge Street, Suite E
Berkeley, CA 94704
Phone: 510-841-9675
Email: bossmail@self-sufficiency.org
Website: www.self-sufficiency.org

Bright Ideas
P.O. Box 586
Brookdale, CA 9507
Phone: 831-338-2522
Email: dondowell@yahoo.com
Species: Oak, Maple, Redwood

C & K Salvage
718 Douglas Avenue
Oakland, CA 94603
Phone: 510-569-2070
Fax: 510-569-2074
Email: cksalvage@aol.com
Species: Fir

Cal-Demo Inc.
9515 Soquel Drive # 212
Aptos, CA 95003
Phone: 877-460-DEMO
Website: www.cal-demo.com

Caldwell's Building Salvage
Resource/Wreckers
195 Bayshore Boulevard
San Francisco, CA 94124
Phone: 415-550-6777
Fax: 415-550-0349
Website: http://caldwell-bldg-salvage.com

Calshores Deconstruction
1861-B Main Street
San Diego, CA 92113
Phone: 619-239-7636
Fax: 619-239-7633
Website: www.vintagearchitectural.com

Campanella Corporation
Building Demolition
494 McCormick
San Leandro, CA 94577
Phone: 510-536-4800

Casper Company
3825 Bancroft Drive
Spring Valley, CA 91977
Phone: 619-589-6001
Fax: 619-589-7158
Website: www.caspercompany.com

Cornerstone Salvage Company
40927 Airport Road
Littleriver, CA 95456
Phone: 707-937-5011
Species: Redwood

Delta Scrap and Salvage
1371 Main Street
Oakley, CA 94561
Phone: 925-754-1474
Website: www.deltademo.com

El Dorado County Habitat for Humanity
5781 Pleasant Valley Road
El Dorado, CA 95623
Phone: 530-621-3972
Fax: 530-295-8972
Email: drisso@edchabitat.org
Website: www.edchabitat.org

Elmers Salvage & Sales
12280 Quartz Hill Road
Redding, CA 96003
Phone: 916-243-4356

Evans Brothers, Inc.
7589 National Drive
Livermore, CA 94550
Phone: 925-443-0225
Fax: 925-443-0229
Email: info@evansbrothers.com
Website: www.evansbrothers.com

Ferma Corporation
1265 Montecito Avenue, Suite200
Mountain View, CA 94043
Phone: 650-961-2742
Fax: 650-968-3945

Fresno House Movers
701 Pleasant Way
Felton, CA 95018
Phone: 831-335-4557

Heim Bros. Inc.
375 Arthur Road
Martinez, CA 94553
Phone: 925-229-1610
Fax: 925-229-0447
Website: www heimbros.com

Hennington Construction Co.
12 Spreckels Lane
Salinas, CA 93908
Phone: 831-455-2377
Fax: 831-455-2434

Joe's Building Service
1924 1/2 35th Avenue
Oakland, CA 94601
Phone: 510-436-5617

Legacy Builders
2243 Nordyke Avenue
Santa Rosa, CA 95403
Phone: 707-526-0800
Fax: 707-526-9072
Email: astanley@sonic.net
Website: www.alegacybuilt.com

Marrone Construction
1037 Lassen Lane
Mt. Shasta, CA 96067
Phone: 530-926-1048

Michael Evenson Natural Resources
P.O. Box 157
Petrolia, CA 95558
Phone: 707-629-3679
Fax: 707-629-3679
Website: www.oldgrowthtimbers.com

Plant Reclamation
912 Harbour Way S.
Richmond, CA 94804
Phone: 510-233-6552
Fax: 510-237-6739
Website: www.plantreclamation.com

Recycle Construction Company
1575 38th Avenue
Santa Cruz, CA 95062
Phone: 408-462-4491

SANDecon of Oceanside
242 Clementine S
Oceanside, CA 92054
Phone: 760-231-6358
Fax: 760-231-6387
Email: info@sandecon.org
Website: www.sandecon.org

Surplus City of Oroville
4514 Pacific Heights Road
Oroville, CA 95965
Phone: 530-534-9956

The Old Wood Mill
P.O. Box 1077
Willits, CA 95490
Phone: 707-459-6294

The Reuse People
2100 Ferry Point #150
Alameda, CA 94501
Phone: 510-522-2722
Email: info@TheReusePeople.org
Website: www.thereusepeople.com

The Reuse People
23010 Lake Forest Dr, Suite D-302
Laguna Hills, CA 92653
Phone: 888-588-9490
Email: info@TheReusePeople.org
Website: www.thereusepeople.com

Deconstruction/Soft-Stripping (DC)—Con.

Vintage Architectural
1861-B Main Street
San Diego, CA 92113
Phone: 619-239-7636
Email: vintage@vintagearchitectural.com
Website: www.vintagearchitectural.com

Vintage Timberworks
1155 Industrial Avenue
Escondido, CA 92029
Phone: 760-743-0744
Fax: 760-743-5714
Website: www.vintagetimber.com

Whole House Building Supplies
1955 Pulgas Avenue
East Palo Alto, CA 94303
Phone: 650-328-8731
Fax: 650-327-1933
Email: gardner@.net.com
Website: www.driftwoodsalvage.com
Species: Redwood, Oak, Pine

Whole House Building Supply
731-D Loma Verde Avenue
Palo Alto, CA 94303
Phone: 650-856-0634
Fax: 650-856-0634
Email: pgard0634@aol.com
Website: www.driftwoodsalvage.com

Youth Employment Partnership
2300 International Bvld
Oakland, CA 94601
Phone: 510-533-3447
Website: www.yep.org

Colorado

A Garrett Lumber and Wrecking Company
7360 Grape Street
Commerce City, CO 80022
Phone: 303-288-4946
Fax: 303-843-9682

ReSource 2000
1702 Walnut Street
Boulder, CO 80302
Phone: 303-441-3278
Fax: 303-441-4367
Email: mmckinne@earthnet net
Website: www resource2k.org
Species: Oak, Fir, Pine

Used Again Building Materials
506 W Cucharras
Colorado Springs, CO 80905
Phone: 719-473-2150

Connecticut

Acadia Services, LLC.
937 Post Road, Suite 134
Fairfield, CT 06430
Phone: 203-259-8860
Fax: 203-254-9930
Email: info@acadiademolition.com
Website: www.acadiademolition.com

Board and Beam
P.O. Box 1235
Washington, CT 06793
Phone: 860-868-6789
Fax: 860-868-0721
Email: bbeams@rcn.com
Website: www.boardandbeam.com
Species: Pine, Oak, Chestnut

Chestnut Oak Company
3810 Old Mountain Road
West Suffield, CT 06093
Phone: 860-668-0382
Email: info@chestnutoakcompany.com
Website: www.chestnutoakcompany.com

The Meticulous House Wrecking Company
Summit Street
New Milford, CT 06776
Phone: 860-350-5000

Delaware

D&D Dismantling
P.O. Box 600
Milford, DE 19963
Phone: 302-422-0922
Fax: 302-422-8051

Service Disposal of Delaware
P.O. Box 661
New Castle, DE 19720
Phone: 302-326-9155
Fax: 302-376-9882

District of Columbia

Institute for Local Self-Reliance
927 15th Street, NW 4th Floor
Washington, DC 20005
Phone: 202-898-1610
Email: nseldman@ilsr.oreg
Website: www.ilsr.org

Florida

A Action Recycling Corporation
1405 CR 210 W
Jacksonville, FL 32259
Phone: 904-356-8869

Architectural Artifacts
1900 N Miami Avenue
Miami, FL 33136
Phone: 305-573-4169

Burkhalter Wrecking, Inc.
P.O. Box 2407
Jacksonville, FL 32203
Phone: 904-354-7813
Fax: 904-354-7815
Email: pjb@burkhalters.com
Website: www.burkhalters.com

Central Environmental Services Inc.
3210 Friendly Avenue
Orlando, FL 32808
Phone: 407-295-7005
Fax: 407-295-7004
Website: www.centralenvironmental.com
Species: Heartpine, Oak, Maple

D.H. Griffin Wrecking Co., Inc.
1312 West Nine Mile Road
Pensacola, FL 32534
Phone: 850-478-1262

Dore & Associates Contracting, Inc.
1715 E Fowler, Suite 217
Tampa, FL 33612
Phone: 800-344-7876
Email: dore@concentric.net
Website: www.doreandassociates.com

Florida Wrecking and Salvage
8814 Honeywell Road
Gibsonton, FL 33534
Phone: 813-741-0405

Forristall Enterprises, Inc.
3404 17th Street E
Palmetto, FL 34221
Phone: 941-729-8150
Fax: 941-729-7345
Website: www forristall.com

Globe Demolition and Recycling
2225 Hazelhurst Dr
Orlando, FL 32801
Phone: 407-422-4768
Fax: 407-228-0062
Email: globedemolition@yahoo.com

L&L Demolition and Salvage
5500 Old Winter Garden Road
Orlando, FL 32811
Phone: 407-295-0875
Fax: 407-296-9855

Deconstruction/Soft-Stripping (DC)—Con.

Raider Demolition
4970 SW 52nd Street
Davie, FL 33063
Phone: 954-791-9913
Fax: 954-791-1435
Email: info@raiderdemo.com
Website: www.raiderdemo.com

Southland Demolition
8619 Western Way
Jacksonville, FL 32256
Phone: 904-731-1232
Email: tuengef@southland-enviro.com
Website: www.suthland-enviro.com

Svinga Brothers Corp.
206 NE 9th Street
Ocala, FL 34470
Phone: 352-351-2841
Fax: 352-351-3560

WR Townsend Contracting
1465 CR 210 W
Jacksonville, FL 32259
Phone: 904-354-9202

Georgia

Re Use the Past, Inc.
98 Moreland Street
Grantville, GA 30220
Phone: 770-583-3111
Email: bocastle@mindspring.com

Reaves Wrecking Co. Inc.
701 10th Street
Columbus, GA 31901
Phone: 706-322-8923
Fax: 706-322-1182
Email: billreaves@reaveswrecking.com
Website: www.reaveswrecking.com

Southern Pine Company of Georgia
P.O. Box 2152
Savannah, GA 31402
Phone: 912-236-4112
Email: info@southernpinecompany.com
Website: www.southernpinecompany.com
Species: Heart pine, cypress,

Idaho

Building Material Thrift Store
3990 Woodside Boulevard
Hailey, ID 83333
Phone: 208-788-0014
Fax: 208-788-0816
Email: bmtbruce@earthlink net
Website:
www.woodriverlandtrust.org/store/store.html

Engineered Demolition Inc.
3901 N Schreiber Way
Coeur D'Alene, ID 83815
Phone: 208-676-9900
Fax: 208-676-9800
Email: bwelch@bigblast.com
Website: www.bigblast.com

Salavatori's Cut and Run
1006 Elk Grove Road
Sandpoint, ID 83864
Phone: 208-265-7843
Email: tonto@coldreams.com

Trestlewood
933 South Frontage Road
Blackfoot, ID 83221
Phone: 208-785-1151
Fax: 208-785-0458
Email: info@trestlewood.com
Website: www.Trestlewood.com
Species: Fir, Pine, Oak

Illinois

A & T Wrecking & Lumber Co.
16461 Wood Street
Markham, IL 60426-5824
Phone: 708-333-4700

Brandenburg Industrial Service Company
2625 S. Loomis Street
Chicago, IL 60608
Phone: 312-326-5800
Fax: 312-326-5065
Email: moowila@brandenburg.info
Website: www.brandenburg.info

Darrah-Barns
104 N Prairie Street
Rockton, IL 61072
Phone: 815-624-4434
Fax: 815-624-4547
Email: darrahbarns@hotmail.com

Environmental Cleansing Corporation
16602 S. Crawford Avenue
Markham, IL 60426
Phone: 708-532-7000
Fax: 708-636-3996
Email: envirocleansing@aol.com
Website: www.environmentalcleansing.com

Heneghan Wrecking Co. Inc.
1321 W Concord Place
Chicago, IL 60622
Phone: 773-342-9009
Fax: 773-342-6123
Website: www.heneghanwrecking.com

River City Demolition
P.O. Box 726
Peoria, IL 61602
Phone: 309-655-0447
Fax: 309-767-1415
Email: rivercitydemo@aol.com
Website: www.rivercitydemolition.com

Indiana

Bringing It Back
5726 University Avenue
Indianapolis, IN 46219
Phone: 317-322-8388
Email: housesalvager@aol.com

Capellier Salvage and Wrecking
11640 N. East Drive
Camby, IN 46113
Phone: 317-831-4533
Fax: 317-834-3057
Email: sjack1306@aol.com

First Saturday Construction Salvage
Route 3 Box 405
Spencer, IN 47460
Phone: 812-876-6347
Fax: 812-876-6347
Email: construcsalvage@smithville net
Website: www.constructionsalvage.com
Species: Pine, Oak, Walnut

Hannells Wrecking Co.
3118 W U.S. Highway 40
Clayton, IN 46118
Phone: 317-539-6464
Fax: 317-539-2246
Species: Pine

Searcy Antique Woods
Cedar Grove, IN 47016
Phone: 812-926-9775
Fax: 765-647-6454
Email: sales@searcyantiquewoods.com
Website: www.searcyantiquewoods.com

White River Architectural Salvage
1325 W 30th Street
Indianapolis, IN 46208
Phone: 317-924-4000
Email:
whiteriversalvage@whiteriversalvage.com
Website: www.whiteriversalvage.com

Iowa

Jim's Small Demolition
P.O. Box 1235
Dubuque, IA 52004
Phone: 563-583-8673

Deconstruction/Soft-Stripping (DC)—Con.

Rock Creek Tree and Building Salvage
1538 325th Street
Osage, IA 50461
Phone: 641-732-4025

The Salvage Barn
1147 S Riverside Dr
Iowa City, IA 52246
Phone: 800-541-8656
Email: salvagebarn@ic-fhp.org
Website: www.ic-fhp.org/salvagebarn html

Kansas

Bahm Demolition
3840 NW Hodges Road
Silver Lake, KS 66539
Phone: 785-582-5190
Fax: 582-412-8785
Email: djb977@aol.com
Website: www.bahmdemolition.com
Species: Pine, Oak

Louisiana

Crescent City Architectural
3101 Tchoupitoulas Street
New Orleans, LA 70115
Phone: 504-891-0500
Fax: 504-891-1895
Email: cca@architectural-salvage.com
Website: www.architectural-salvage.com

Maine

Interstate Building Salvage
307 Stanley Road
New Vineyard, ME 04956
Phone: 207-778-9340

Maryland

Power Component Systems Inc.
7526-R Connelley Drive
Hanover, MD 21076
Phone: 410-760-0022
Fax: 410-760-0028
Email: toby@powercomponentsystems.com
Website:
www.powercomponentsystems.com

Second Chance
1645 Warner Street
Baltimore, MD 21230
Phone: 410-385-1101
Email: info@secondchanceinc.org
Website: www.secondchanceinc.org

The Loading Dock
2523 Gwynns Falls Parkway
Baltimore, MD 21216
Phone: 410-728-3625
Fax: 410-728-3633
Email: stafford@loadingdock.org
Website: www.loadingdock.org

Massachusetts

Architectural Timber and Millwork
49 Mount Warner Road
Hadley, MA 01035
Phone: 413-586-3045
Fax: 413-586-3046
Email: tmh@atimber.com
Website: www.atimber.com

Boston's ReStore Inc.
P.O. Box 240881
Dorchester, MA 02124
Phone: 617-288-8400
Email: bperkins@bostonrestore.org
Website: www.bostonrestore.org

Colonial Barn Restoration
269 Old Bay Road
Bolton, MA 01740
Phone: 978-779-9865
Email: Tim@ColonialBarn.com
Website: www.colonialbarn.com

Costello Dismantling
2 Rocky Gutter Street
Middleborough, MA 02346
Phone: 508-946-0880
Fax: 508-947-3093
Email: costello99@attby.com
Website: www.costellodismantling.com
Species: Pine

Environmental Futures Inc.
530 Atlantic Avenue
Boston, MA 02210
Phone: 617-443-1300

Longleaf Lumber
70 Webster Avenue
Sommerville, MA 02143
Phone: 617-625-3659
Fax: 617-625-3615
Email: info@longleaflumber.com
Website: www.longleaflumber.com

New England Demolition & Salvage
3065 Cranberry Highway
East Wareham, MA 02538
Phone: 508-291-7258
Fax: 508-273-0274
Email: homeneds@aol.com
Website: www nedsalvage.com

Pioneer Valley Deconstruction
235 Eastern Avenue
Springfield, MA 01109
Phone: 413-827-0781
Fax: 413-827-0780
Email: johndunne.pvp@verizon net

RJ O'Brien Building Wrecking & Salvage
460 Forest Street
Rockland, MA 02370
Phone: 781-878-1961
Email: OBrienRJO@gateway.com

Michigan

Dore & Associates Contracting, Inc.
900 Harry S Truman Pkwy
Bay City, MI 48707
Phone: 800-344-7876
Fax: 989-684-6663
Email: dore@concentric.net
Website: www.doreandassociates.com

Dore & Associates Contracting, Inc.
1221 E McNichols
Detroit, MI 48203
Phone: 800-344-7876
Email: dore@concentric.net
Website: www.doreandassociates.com

Odom Re-Use and Consulting
5555 Brentwood Avenue N
Grawn, MI 49637
Phone: 231-276-6330
Email: reusebruce@coslink net
Website: www.odomreuse.com

Pitsch Wrecking
675 Richmond Street NW
Grand Rapids, MI 49504
Phone: 616-363-4895

21st Century Salvage
10750 Martz Road
Ypsilanti, MI 48197
Phone: 734-485-4855

Minnesota

Bauer Brothers Salvage
2432 2nd Street N
Minneapolis, MN 55411
Phone: 612-331-9492
Fax: 612-521-0494

Carl Bolander & Sons Co.
251 Streetarkey Street
Saint Paul, MN 55107
Phone: 800-676-6504; 651-224-6299
Fax: 651-223-8197
Email: info@bolander.com
Website: www.bolander.com

Deconstruction/Soft-Stripping (DC)—Con.

Century Construction Co., Inc.
820 N Concord Street, Suite 101
South St. Paul, MN 55075
Phone: 651-451-1020
Fax: 651-451-2745
Email: info@centuryconstruct.com
Website: www.centuryconstruct.com

City Salvage Antiques
505 1st Avenue NE
Minneapolis, MN 55413
Phone: 612-627-9107
Email: mail@citysalvage.com
Website: www.citysalvage.com

Deconstruction Services
2316 E Lake Street
Minneapolis, MN 55407
Phone: 612-728-9388
Fax: 612-724-2288
Website: www.greeninstitute.org

F.M. Frattalone Excavating
3066 Spruce Street
St. Paul, MN 55117
Phone: 651-484-0448
Fax: 651-484-7839
Email: jimw@fmfrattalone.com
Website: www fmfrattalone.com
Species: Pine, Fir, Oak

Minnesota Timber Salvage
13737 100th Street
Foreston, MN 56330
Phone: 320-369-4507

North Shore Architectural Antiques
521 7th Street
Two Harbors, MN 55616
Phone: 218-834-0018
Email: jmccarthy@frontiernet net
Website:
www.north-shore-architectural-antiques com

Old Growth Woods
6456 160th Street
Rosemount, MN 55068
Phone: 651-690-3188
Fax: 651-698-6641
Email: sales@oldgrowthwoods.com
Website: www.oldgrowthwoods.com

SKB Environmental
251 Starkey Street
St Paul, MN 55107
Phone: 651-224-6329
Fax: 651-223-5053
Email: info@skbinc.com
Website: www.skbinc.com

The Reuse Center
2216 E Lake Street
Minneapolis, MN 55407
Phone: 612-724-2608
Fax: 612-724-2288
Email: JanetMester@Greeninstitude.org
Website:
www.greeninstitute.org/reusecenter.htm

Mississippi

Back Road Architectural Salvage Services
836 C Ridgewood Road Ext
Ridgeland, MS 39157
Phone: 601-957-3777
Email: cjej@a2ldial.net

Old Mississippi Lumber
P.O. Box 562
Holly Springs, MS 38634
Phone: 662-252-3395
Email: broev@bellsouth net
Website: www heartpinefloors.com

Missouri

Anderson Fine Carpentry and Salvage
228 W. 4th Street
Kansas City, MO 64111
Phone: 816-531-5976
Email: TheThaine@aol.com

Deco Companies
2101 Manchester Traffic Way
Kansas City, MO 64126
Phone: 816-483-5656
Fax: 816-483-51586
Email: judir@deco.com
Website: www.deco-kc.com

Habitat for Humanity ReStore
4535 W Chestnut Expressway
Springfield, MO 65802
Phone: 417-829-4001
Fax: 417-829-4003
Email: restore@drury.edu
Website: www habitatrestore.com

Habitat ReStore
4701 Deramus
Kansas City, MO 64120
Phone: 816-231-6889

Heartwood Associates Int'l.
5068 Tholozan Avenue
St. Louis, MO 63109
Phone: 314-352-9242
Fax: 314-752-2152
Email: longleaf1@prodigy net
Website: www heartwoodassociates.com

Pitchpine Lumber
19864 Gore Drive
Sainte Genevieve, MO 63670
Phone: 573-747-1733
Fax: 573-747-1680
Email: lloyd@pitchpine.com
Website: www.pitchpine.com
Species: Heartpine, Oak, Cypress

Montana

Big Timberworks Inc.
P.O. Box 368
Gallatin Gateway, MT 59730
Phone: 406-763-4639
Fax: 406-763-4818
Email: bigtimberworks.com

Nevada

Arcadia Demolition Services
2620 S Maryland Parkway
Las Vegas, NV 89109
Phone: 702-388-4498
Fax: 702-388-4473
Email: info@arcadiademo.com
Website: www.arcadiademo.com

Roldan Construction, Inc.
3280 W Hacienda Avenue
Las Vegas, NV 89118
Phone: 702-739-DEMO
Fax: 702-739-6909
Email: Jerry@roldaninc.com
Website: www roldaninc.com

New Hampshire

Admac Salvage
111 Saranac Street
Littleton, NH 03561
Phone: 603-444-1200
www musar.com/trader/admac html

Great Northern Barns
182 Grafton Tpk
Canaan, NH 03741
Phone: 603-523-7134
Fax: 603-523-8248
Email: info@greatnorthernbarns.com
Website: greatnorthernbarns.com

T-REX Corporation
532 Mammoth Road
Londonderry, NH 03053
Phone: 603-425-6660
Website: www.trexcorporation.com

Deconstruction/Soft-Stripping (DC)—Con.

New Jersey

R. Baker & Son All Industrial Services, Inc.
1 Globe Court
Red Bank, NJ 07701
Phone: 732-222-3553
Email: info@RBaker.com
Website: www.rbaker.com

Relics Reconstruction:
Architectural Salvage
201 Church Street
Millburn, NJ 07041
Phone: 201-376-4745

Restoration Materials Company
1260 New Market Avenue
South Plainfield, NJ 07080
Phone: 800-336-6548

New York

A-1 Salvage
Route 26
South Otselic, NY 13155
Phone: 315-653-4409
Email: norton@ascent net

American Architectural Salvage
and Demolition
245 S Greenfield Road
Greenfield Center, NY 12833
Phone: 518-580-1849

Barnstormers Flooring
166 Malden Turnpike
Saugerties, NY 12477
Phone: 845-246-3622
Fax: 845-246-3623
Email: safesol@frontier net
Website: www.safesolutionsllc.com
Species: Chestnut, Maple, Oak

Big Wood
P.O. Box 24
East Bethany, NY 14054
Phone: 315-986-8119
Fax: 315-986-2622
Email: larry@big-wood net
Website: www.big-wood net
Species: Longleaf pine, Fir

BRB Contracting, Inc.
20 Denker Drive
Ballston Lake, NY 12019
Phone: 518-693-6348
Email: brbci@hotmail.com

Demolition Depot
216 E 125th Street
New York, NY 10035
Phone: 212-860-1138
Fax: 212-860-1560
Email: info@demolitiondepot.com
Website: www.demolitiondepot.com

Gateway Demolition
134-22 32nd Avenue
Flushing, NY 11354
Phone: 718-359-1400
Fax: 718-461-6558
Email: info@gatewaydemolition.com
Website: www.gatewaydemolition.com

International Chimney Corp.
55 S Long Street
Williamsville, NY 14221
Phone: 716-634-3967
Fax: 716-634-3983
Website: www.internationalchimney.com

Legacy Antique Woods
114 Sibley Road
Honeoye Falls, NY 14472
Phone: 585-624-1011
Fax: 716-624-1094
Email: legacywood99@aol.com
Website: www.legacyantiquewoods.com
Species: Chestnut, Heartpine, Oak

New York Wastewatch
253 Broadway, Rm 302
New York, NY 10004
Phone: 212-942-5219
Email: jrosenfield@itac.org

Ontario Specialty Contracting Inc.
333 Ganson Street
Buffalo, NY 14203
Phone: 716-856-3333
Fax: 716-842-1785
Email: bwegrzyn@ontariospecialty.com
Website: www.ontariospecialty.com

Pioneer Millworks
1180 Commercial Drive
Farmington, NY 14425
Phone: 585-924-9970
Fax: 585-924-9962
Email: jonathen@pioneermillworks.com
Website: www.pioneermillworks.com

Sabre Demolition Corporation
73 Generese Street
Baldwinsville, NY 13027
Phone: 315-635-3759
Fax: 315-635-3790
Email: sabredemo@aol.com
Website: www.sabre-demolition.com

North Carolina

Airedale Woodworks LLC
P.O. Box 307
Murfreesboro, NC 27855
Phone: 800-489-0639
Fax: 252-398-8429
Email: sales@airedalewoodworks.com
Website: www.airedalewoodworks.com

Architectural Salvage of Greensboro
300 W Bellemeade Street
Greensboro, NC 27402
Phone: 336-389-9118
Email: asg@blandwood.org

D.H. Griffin Wrecking Co.
1600 North Graham Street
Charlotte, NC 28206-3024
Phone: 704-331-9400
Fax: 704-336-6860

D. H. Griffin Wrecking Co., Inc.
4700 Hilltop Road
Greensboro, NC 27407
Phone: 888-336-DEMO
Email: elwalker@dhgriffin.com
Website: www.dhgriffin.com

Fayetteville ReStore
443 Franklin Street
Fayetteville, NC 28301
Phone: 910-322-9822

Pete Hendricks
1414 Jenkins Road
Wake Forest, NC 27587
Phone: 919-556-2284

Rike Wrecking Co. Inc.
1005 Rundell Street
Winston Salem, NC 27105
Phone: 336-725-8789
Fax: 336-725-8789
Species: Oak, Pine

Salvage King
204 Cooper Road
Staley, NC 27355
Phone: 336-622-1595
Fax: 336-622-3883
Email: salvageking@msn.com
Website: www.salvageking.com

Scotland Neck Heartpine
105 Creek Street
Tarboro, NC 27886
Phone: 252-826-2755
Email: wburgwyn@yahoo.com

Deconstruction/Soft-Stripping (DC)—Con.

Ohio

Allied Erecting and Dismantling
2100 Poland Av
Youngstown, OH 44502
Phone: 330-744-0808
Fax: 330-744-3218
Email: info@aed.cc
Website: www.aed.cc

B and B Wrecking and Excavating Inc.
5801 Train Avenue
Cleveland, OH 44102
Phone: 216-651-9090
Fax: 216-651-9095
Email: bandbwrecking@ameritech.net
Website: www.bbwrecking.com

Barnwares
1888 Jacoby Road
Copley, OH 44321
Phone: 330-335-9907
Fax: 330-334-2097
Email: info@barnwares.com
Website: www.barnwares.com

Broadway Contracting Inc.
3950 E 89th Street
Cleveland, OH 44105
Phone: 800-709-4129
Fax: 216-271-3944
Email: ger1056@aol.com
Website: www.broad3939.com

Build It Again Center
3529 Cleveland Avenue
Columbus, OH 43224
Phone: 614-267-7778
Fax: 614-267-6655
Email: biac@habitat-columbus.org
Website: www habitat-columbus.org

Cleveland Deconstructors Inc.
6270 Greenwood Pkwy #305
Sagamore Hills, OH 44067
Phone: 330-467-7595
Email: nickkack@bright net

Eagle Creek Designs, Inc.
6025 Schustrich P.O. Box 163
Mantua, OH 44255
Phone: 330-274-2041
Fax: 330-274-3370
Email: hfs1917@aol.com

The Rose Group Ltd
778 Winding River Boulevard
New Lebanon, OH 45065
Phone: 513-494-9444
Fax: 810-963-2625
Email: webmaster@rose-grp.com
Website: www.rose-grp.com

Oregon

BRING Recycling
86641 Franklin Boulevard
Eugene, OR 97403
Phone: 541-746-3023
Fax: 541-746-3023
Email: davidw@bringrecycling.org
Website: www.bringrecycling.org

Capital Products
P.O. Box 719
Philomath, OR 97370
Phone: 541-929-5308
Deconstruction Management Group
12345 NW Harborton Drive
Portland, OR 97231
Phone: 503-341-3050
Email: jprimdahl@ilsr.org

Heartwood ReSources
355 Atlanta Street
Roseburg, OR 97470
Phone: 541-673-4070
Fax: 541-673-4223
Email:
heartwoodresources@umpquacdc.org
Website: www heartwoodresources.com

Norhwest Demolition
8200 Hunziker SW
Tigard, OR 97223
Phone: 503-638-6900

Storie Steel and Wood Products Co.
P.O. Box 12490
Portland, OR 97212
Phone: 503-287-1775
Fax: 503-282-9884
Email: clearcut@earthlink.net

The ReBuilding Center
3625 N. Mississippi Avenue
Portland, OR 97227
Phone: 503-331-1877
Fax: 503-331-1873
Website: www rebuildingcenter.org

Pennsylvania

Barnguys Recycled Materials, Inc., PA
Phone: 610-847-2616
Email: thebarnguy@aol.com
Website: www.barnguys.com

Barnwood Connection (The)
91 Bull Road
Barto, PA 19504
Phone: 610-845-3101
Fax: 610-845-3167
Email: info@barnwoodconnection.com
Website: www.barnwoodconnection.com

Central Salvage
124 N Narbeth Avenue
Narbeth, PA 19072
Phone: 610-667-1186
Fax: 610-667-1920
Email: adam@centralsalvagepa.com

Centre Mills Antique Floors
P.O. Box 16
Aspers, PA 17304
Phone: 717-334-0249
Fax: 717-334-6223
Website: www.igateway.com/
mall/homeimp/wood/index.htm

Cronin Builders and Supply
11106 Terry HWY P.O. 436
Meadville, PA 16335
Phone: 814-336-4523

Empire Services
1420 Clarion Street
Reading, PA 19601
Phone: 610-372-6511
Fax: 610-372-3402
Website: www.empireservicesberks.com

McHugh Dismantlement Services
P.O. Box 109
Berwyn, PA 19312
Phone: 610-640-1444
Fax: 610-640-1457
Email: mchughdemo@aol.com

Patina Woods
3363 New Franklin Road
Chambersburg, PA 17201
Phone: 717-264-8009
Website:
www.penmar net/patinawoods/index html

Recycle Shack
814 2nd Avenue
Royersford, PA 19468
Phone: 484-686-7641
Email: recycall@hotmail.com

Sable Construction Inc.
1609 N. Delaware Avenue
Philadelphia, PA 19125
Phone: 215-427-1462
Fax: 215-427-1796
Email: rcw@sableinc.com
Website: www.sableinc.com

Deconstruction/Soft-Stripping (DC)—Con.

Selective Dismantlement, Inc.
998 Shavertown Road
Boothwyn, PA 19061
Phone: 610-361-8793
Fax: 610-361-8798

U.S. Recycling and Wrecking
390 Eckman Road
Lancaster, PA 17603
Phone: 717-393-2992
Fax: 717-464-1845

Wood Natural Restorations
3038 Woodlane Avenue
Orefield, PA 18069
Phone: 610-395-6451
Email: ken@woodnatural.com
Website: www.woodnatural.com

Rhode Island

National Wrecking Company
64 Grotto Street
Pawtucket, RI 02860
Phone: 401-723-1545
Fax: 401-723-1547

South Carolina

Big Wood
SC
Phone: 864-898-1655
Fax: 864-898-1675
Website: www.big-wood net

South Dakota

Keetagilly
528 Suni Avenue
Baltic, SD 57003
Phone: 605-529-6152
Email: salvage@keetagilly.com

Second Chance Lumber
Viborg, SD 57070
Phone: 605-766-5145
Email: mellamy001@yahoo.com

Tennessee

American Heritage Preservation
1869 Highway 52 E
Portland, TN 37148
Phone: 888-427-2276
Fax: 615-325-2701
Email: nbced@mindspring.com
Website:
www.americanheritagepreservation.com
Species: Oak, Chestnut

Havron Contracting
1513 Williams Street
Chattanooga, TN 37408
Phone: 423-265-8883
Fax: 423-265-3627
Email: havron@mindspring.com
Website: www.demolitionsalvage.com
Species: Heartpine

Wilmot Inc.
3654 Knollwood Road
Nashville, TN 37215
Phone: 615-533-0696
Fax: 615-385-5744
Email: Tiffany_Wilmot@Yahoo.com
Website: www.Wilmotandassoc.com

Texas

American Demolition Inc.
2318 Chavaneaux
San Antonio, TX 78214
Phone: 210-627-2377
Email: gus@americandemolition.com
Website: www.americandemolition.com

Austin Habitat for Humanity Re-Store
310 Comal, #101
Austin, TX 78733
Phone: 512-478-2165
Fax: 512-478-9477
Email: dbmackie@aol.com
Website: www re-store.com

Cherry Demolition
6131 Selinsky
Houston, TX 77048
Phone: 713-987-0000
Fax: 713-991-6236
Email: mike@cherrydemolition.com
Website: www.cherrydomolition.com

Heritage Restorations
Brazos de Dios
Elm Mott, TX 76640
Phone: 254-717-5531
Email: info@heritagebarns.com
Website: www heritagebarns.com

Ken Richter Dismantling
2203 Lillie Lane
Taylor, TX 76574
Phone: 512-924-3108

McKinney Wrecking
18 Ruhlen Court
El Paso, TX 79925
Phone: 915-533-2006
Fax: 915-542-0032
Species: Pine, Oak

Steven L. Remley
2737 Bryan Avenue
Fort Worth, TX 76104
Phone: 817-924-9300
Fax: 817-924-9380
Email: elrinc@flash net
Website: www.lightrecyclers.com

Utah

Trestlewood
292 North 2000 W
Lindon, UT 84042
Phone: 801-443-4002
Email: info@trestlewood.com
Website: www.Trestlewood.com
Species: Fir, Pine, Oak

Vermont

David D. Parker Structural Restoration
P.O. Box 6458
Brattleboro, VT 05302
Phone: 802-251-0000
Fax: 802-251-0001
Website: www.parkerrestoration.com

Mason Brothers Architectural Salvage
11 Maple Street
Essex Junction, VT 05452
Phone: 802-879-4221
Species: Pine, Fir

ReCycle North
266 Pine Street
Burlington, VT 05401
Phone: 802-658-4143
Email: info@recyclenorth.org
Website: www recyclenorth.org

Second Harvest Antique Lumbers
Box 240 Willson Road
Jeffersonville, VT 05464
Phone: 802-644-8169
Fax: 802-644-8005
Species: Pine, Spruce, Hemlock

Shiningwater Enterprises
484 Mill Road
Lincoln, VT 05443
Phone: 802-453-2825
Email: jaxfam@sover.net
Website: www.traditional-building.com/
brochure/members/1architecturalsalvage.shtml

The Barn People
2218 U.S. Route 5
Windsor, VT 05089
Phone: 802-674-5898
Fax: 802-674-6310
Email: barnman@sover net
Website: www.thebarnpeople.com

Deconstruction/Soft-Stripping (DC)—Con.

Vermont Salvage Exchange
2-4 Gates Street
White River Junction, VT 05001
Phone: 802-295-7616
Fax: 802-295-5744
Email: help@vermontsalvage.com
Website: www.vermontsalvage.com

Virginia

Appalachian Woods
1240 Cold Springs Road
Stuarts Draft, VA 24477
Phone: 540-337-1801
Fax: 540-337-1030
Email: jonas@appalachianwoods.com
Website: www.appalachianwoods.com
Species: Heartpine, Oak, Fir

Big Wood
Afton, VA 22920
Phone: 434-361-9300
Fax: 434-361-1873
Website: www.big-wood net

E.T. Moore Manufacturing
3100 N Hopkins Road, Suite 101
Richmond, VA 23224
Phone: 804-231-1823
Fax: 804-231-0759
Email: orders@etmoore.com
Website: www.etmoore.com
Species: Longleaf pine, Cypress

Kings Arrow Antiques Lumber
11175 Tattersall Trail
Oakton, VA 22124
Phone: 703-407-5912
Email: kingsarrow@prodigy net
Species: Chestnut, Longleaf pine

Mountain Lumber
P.O. Box 289
Ruckersville, VA 22968
Phone: 800-445-2671
Fax: 804-985-4105
Email: sales@mountainlumber.com
Website: www mountainlumber.com

Shenandoah Valley Reclaimed Lumber
3586 Horizons Way
Harrisonburg, VA 22801
Phone: 540-896-7600
Fax: 540-896-5455
Email: butlerj@horizonsva.com
Website: svreclaimedlumber.com
Species: Pine, Oak, Chestnut

The Housewright Shop
187 Pine Tree Lane
Fort Valley, VA 22652
Phone: 540-933-6458
Email: pwcj@yahoo.com

Virginia Antique Building Materials
600 Greenview Court
Pulaski, VA 24301
Phone: 540-980-4232
Fax: 540-980-4338
Email: tdalton@i-plus.net
Species: Heartpine, Oak, Chestnut

Washington

BCR Barn Dismantling
734 Harrison Avenue
Beloit, WA 53511
Phone: 608-363-0012

Resource Woodworks Inc.
627 E 60th
Tacoma, WA 98404
Phone: 253-474-3757
Fax: 253-474-1139
Website: www rw-timber.com

Re-Tech Wood Products
1324 Russell Road
Forks, WA 98331
Phone: 360-374-4141
Fax: 360-374-4141
Email: RETECH@OLYPEN.COM
Website:
WWW.RETECHWOODPRODUCTS.COM
Species: Fir, Cedar

The ReStore
600 W Holly Street
Bellingham, WA 98225
Phone: 360-647-5921
Email: restore@re-sources.org
Website: www re-sources.org
Species: Fir, Oak, Maple

The ReStore
1440 NW 52nd Street
Seattle, WA 98107
Phone: 206-297-9119
Email: patfinn@Seattle@re-sources.org
Website: www re-sources.org/contact.htm

West Virginia

Antique Cabins and Barns
106 E Washington Street
Lewisburg, WV 24901
Phone: 304-645-7612
Fax: 304-925-3303

Vintage Log and Lumber
P.O. Box 130 Route 219 N
Renick, WV 24966
Phone: 304-497-2700
Fax: 304-497-3651
Email: sales@vintagelog.com
Website: www.vintagelog.com

Wisconsin

DeConstruction Inc.
1010 Walsh Road
Madison, WI 53714
Phone: 608-244-8759
Fax: 908-244-8981
Email: deconstruct@mailbag.com
Website: www.deconstructinc.com

Eckert Wrecking Inc.
4743 U.S. Highway 8
Rhinelander, WI 54501
Phone: 715-362-6550
Fax: 715-362-1837

Old House Salvage
4404 Stewart Avenue
Wausau, WI 54401
Phone: 715-849-5077
Email: delirevanceman@aol.com

Reclaimed Lumber Co.
633 Ellis Avenue
Baraboo, WI 53913
Phone: 608-356-8849
Email: David@reclaimed-lumber.com
Website: www reclaimed-lumber.com

Reclaimed Lumber Company
585 Kossow Road
Waukesha, WI 53186
Phone: 262-798-8986
Fax: 262-798-9401
Email: david@old-barn-wood.com
Website: www.old-barn-wood.com

Urban Evolutions
867 Valley Road
Menasha, WI 54952
Phone: 920-380-4149
Fax: 920-380-4184
Website: www.urbanevolutions.com
Species: Pine, Oak, Ash

Demolition/Selective Dismantling (DM)

Alabama

Old South Wrecking Co.
400 Paul Road
Montgomery, AL 36108
Phone: 334-264-6744

Arizona

A-Cal Wrecking Company
13443 N 20th Street
Phoenix, AZ 85022
Phone: 602-247-2650

Atwell Salvage & Demolition
3001 W Pima Street
Phoenix, AZ 85009
Phone: 602-484-7301
Fax: 602-484-0132

Avitia Demolition
1321 N Camino De Juan
Tucson, AZ 85745
Phone: 520-622-3366
Email: avitiainc@aol.com

B&C Contractors Inc.
1324 W El Caminito Place
Tucson, AZ 85705
Phone: 520-888-2681
Fax: 520-292-3173
Email: alyweber@worldnet.att net

B.C.S. Enterprises, Inc.
1275 W Houston Avenue
Gilbert, AZ 85233
Phone: 480-633-8300
Fax: 480-633-8309
Website: www.bcsdemo.com

Breinholt Contracting
2915 W Pima Street
Phoenix, AZ 85009
Phone: 602-322-1100

Catclaw Contractors
10519 E Tanque Verde Road
Tucson, AZ 85749
Phone: 520-760-0185

Kuhles Services LLC
219 E Navajo Drive
Prescott, AZ 86301
Phone: 928-445-8446

Taylor Demolition and Recycling
2140 S Freeway
Tucson, AZ 85713
Phone: 520-623-0410
Fax: 520-623-0399

Arkansas

Dore & Associates Contracting, Inc.
1400 Brookwood
Little Rock, AR 72202
Phone: 800-344-7876
Email: dore@concentric.net
Website: www.doreandassociates.com

California

A.E. Schmidt Co.
14212 Lang Station Road
Canyon Country, CA 91387
Phone: 800-479-2901; 661-251-2901
Fax: 661-251-3130
Website: www.aeschmidt.com

AWS Construction Services, Inc.
6621 E Pacific Coast Highway #130
Long Beach, CA 90803
Phone: 562-799-4436
Email: aws@awsconstruction.com
Website: www. awsconstruction.com

Cal-Demo Inc.
9515 Soquel Drive # 212
Aptos, CA 95003
Phone: 877-460-DEMO
Website: www.cal-demo.com

Casper Company
3825 Bancroft Drive
Spring Valley, CA 91977
Phone: 619-589-6001
Fax: 619-589-7158
Website: www.caspercompany.com

Clauss Construction
8956 Winter Garden Boulevard
Lakeside, CA 92040
Phone: 888-463-2291; 619-390-4944
Fax: 619-390-4944
Email: bernard@claussconstruction.com
Website: www.claussconstruction.com

Cleveland Wrecking Company
628 E Edna Place
Covina, CA 91723
Phone: 626-967-9799
Fax: 626-967-1479
Website: ww.clevelandwrecking.com

Cleveland Wrecking Company
2833 Leonis Boulevard # 210
Vernon, CA 90058
Phone: 213-269-0633

CST Environmental Inc.
404 N Berry Street
Brea, CA 92821
Phone: 714-672-3500
Fax: 714-672-3501
Email: demolition@cstenv.com
Website: cstenvironmental.com

Evans Brothers, Inc.
7589 National Drive
Livermore, CA 94550
Phone: 925-443-0225
Fax: 925-443-0229
Email: info@evansbrothers.com
Website: www.evansbrothers.com

Heim Bros. Inc.
375 Arthur Road
Martinez, CA 94553
Phone: 925-229-1610
Fax: 925-229-0447
Website: www heimbros.com

House Demolition & Land Clearing
2817 Ostrom Road
Marysville, CA 95901
Phone: 916-743-9305

Iconco Inc.
303 Derby Avenue
Oakland, CA 94601
Phone: 510-261-1900
Fax: 510-261-2459
Email: iconco@pacbell net
Website: www.iconco-inc.com

Interior Demolition Inc.
6841 Foothill Boulevard
Tujunga, CA 91042
Phone: 818-353-4804

Kroeker Demolition & Recycling
Contractors Inc.
4627 S Chestnut Avenue
Fresno, CA 93725
Phone: 559-237-3764
Fax: 559-268-3366
Email: rodneya@kroekerinc.com
Website: www kroekerinc.com

Presco Building Materials
291 S Waterman Avenue
San Bernardino, CA 92408
Phone: 909-889-0084
Fax: 909-889-0085

Demolition/Selective Dismantling (DM)—Con.

Randazzo Enterprises Inc.
13550 Blackie Road
Castroville, CA 95012
Phone: 831-384-7644
Email: jrandazzo@sol.com

RWH Construction
12722 Carmenita Road
Santa Fe Springs, CA 90670
Phone: 562-407-0694
Fax: 562-407-0696

SIM J. Harris Company
9229 Harris Plant Road
San Diego, CA 92145
Phone: 619-277-5481
Fax: 619-277-4517
Email: simjharris@aol.com

Stockton Recycling
1533 Waterloo Road
Stockton, CA 95205
Phone: 209-942-2267
Fax: 209-942-2289

West Coast Land Clearing
P.O. Box 90126
Long Beach, CA 90803
Phone: 562-599-2882
Fax: 562-599-2787
Email: rthomas@westcoastlc.com
Website: www.westcoastlc.com

Colorado

Allied Demolition, Inc.
7901 Highway 85
Commerce City, CO 80037
Phone: 303-289-3366
Fax: 303-289-3543
Website:
www.barnettlumber.com/demo htm

Mendoza Used Brick
701 W. 64th Avenue # B
Denver, CO 80221
Phone: 303-427-5675

Connecticut

Earth Technology, Inc.
250 Sackett Point Road
North Haven, CT 06473
Phone: 203-230-2040
Fax: 203-230-0302
Website: www.earthtechnology.com

Manafort Brothers, Inc.
414 New Britain Avenue
Plainville, CT 06062
Phone: 860-229-4853
Fax: 860-747-4861
Website: www manafortbrothers.com

Stamford House Wrecking
1 Barry Place
Stamford, CT 06902
Phone: 203-324-9537

District of Columbia

All Aboard Contracting Inc.
4214 Hunt Place NE
Washington, DC 20019
Phone: 202-388-4252
Fax: 202-388-3840

Florida

A Action Recycling Corporation
1405 CR 210 W
Jacksonville, FL 32259
Phone: 904-356-8869

Absolute Concrete Cutting
17265 SW 83rd CT.
Miami, FL 33157
Phone: 305-969-3644
Fax: 305-969-1320
Email: absodemo@bellsouth net
Website: www.absolute-demolition.cc

Arwood Wrecking
13255 Lanier Road
Jacksonville, FL 32226
Phone: 904-751-1628

Beasley & Son Inc.
4922 N 56th Street
Tampa, FL 33610
Phone: 813-626-0978

Burkhalter Wrecking, Inc.
P.O. Box 2407
Jacksonville, FL 32203
Phone: 904-354-7813
Fax: 904-354-7815
Email: pjb@burkhalters.com
Website: www.burkhalters.com

D.H. Griffin Wrecking Co., Inc.
1312 West Nine Mile Road
Pensacola, FL 32534
Phone: 850-478-1262

Dore & Associates Contracting, Inc.
1715 E Fowler, Suite 217
Tampa, FL 33612
Phone: 800-344-7876
Email: dore@concentric.net
Website: www.doreandassociates.com

Florida Dismantling
7520 NW 7th Avenue
Miami, FL 33150
Phone: 305-696-8855

Florida Wrecking and Salvage
8814 Honeywell Road
Gibsonton, FL 33534
Phone: 813-741-0405

Insul-Coat
2049 W Central Boulevard
Orlando, FL 32805
Phone: 407-447-1684
Fax: 407-447-1679
Email: kklein@cleanbuilding.com
Website: www.cleanbuilding.com

Raider Demolition
4970 SW 52nd Street
Davie, FL 33063
Phone: 954-791-9913
Fax: 954-791-1435
Email: info@raiderdemo.com
Website: www raiderdemo.com

Standard Demolition Corporation
1607 43rd Street
Tampa, FL 33605
Phone: 813-626-6552
Fax: 813-626-0840
Email: info@standarddemo.com
Website: www.standarddemo.com

WR Townsend Contracting
1465 CR 210 W
Jacksonville, FL 32259
Phone: 904-354-9202

Georgia

AMC Demolition Specialists, Inc.
1525 Northridge Road
Atlanta, GA 30338
Phone: 770-395-1400
Fax: 770-395-0222
Email: amcdemo@mindspring.com
Website: www.amcdemolition.com

America Demolition Contractors
1906 Ford Avenue
Savannah, GA 31405
Phone: 912-232-0053

Demolition/Selective Dismantling (DM)—Con.

Cooper Equipment Contracting
301 Miller Street
Valdosta, GA 31601
Phone: 229-244-7696

Raze Demolition and Contractors, Inc.
1605 Whitaker Street
Savannah, GA 31401
Phone: 912-201-9440
Fax: 912-447-6888
Species: Heartpine

Hawaii

Island Demo, Inc.
2769 Kilihau Street
Honolulu, HI 96819
Phone: 808-839-5522
Fax: 808-839-5515
Email: islanddemo@yahoo.com
Website:
www.gtesupersite.com/islanddemo

Illinois

A & T Wrecking and Lumber
1550 W 88th Street
Chicago, IL 60636
Phone: 773-445-3100

American Demolition Corp.
305 Ramona Avenue
Elgin, IL 60120
Phone: 847-608-0010
Fax: 847-608-0060
Website:
www.americandemolitioncorp.com

Delta Demolition, Inc.
1230 N. Kostner
Chicago, IL 60651
Phone: 773-252-6370
Fax: 773-252-8263

Heneghan Wrecking Co. Inc.
1321 W Concord Place
Chicago, IL 60622
Phone: 773-342-9009
Fax: 773-342-6123
Website: www.heneghanwrecking.com

N.F. Demolition
4333 S Knox Avenue
Chicago, IL 60632
Phone: 773-284-8300
Fax: 773-284-9316
Email: nfdemo@NFDemolition.com
Website: www.nfdemolition.com

Omega Demolition Corporation
1536 Brandy Parkway
Stearmwood, IL 60107
Phone: 630-837-3000
Fax: 630-837-2300
Email: chuckg@omega-demolition.com
Website: www.omega-demolition.com

Robinette Demolition, Inc.
0 S. 560 Highway 83
Oakbrook Terrace, IL 60181
Phone: 630-833-7997
Fax: 630-833-8047
Email: info@rdidemolition.com
Website: www rdidemolition.com

United Demolition Incorporated
2123 Oxford Road
Des Plaines, IL 60018
Phone: 847-296-2600
Fax: 847-816-4718

Indiana

Crowe Wrecking Co.
2400 Grove Street
Evansville, IN 47710
Phone: 812-425-6511

Northlake Excavation & Demolition
1332 Grant Street
Gary, IN 46404
Phone: 219-886-9368
Fax: 219-886-9603
Website: www northlakegary.com

Richey Salvage and Demolition
5782 N CR 420 W
Greensburg, IN 47240
Phone: 812-663-6512

Iowa

Cedar Valley Recovery and Demolition
553 Reed Street
Waterloo, IA 50703
Phone: 319-234-3075

Fuller Salvage and Wrecking
2113 E Mitchell Avenue
Waterloo, IA 50702
Phone: 391-233-2546

Iowa Demolition and Recycling Services
6400 Seminole Court NE
Cedar Rapids, IA 52411
Phone: 319-393-9013

J. Myron Olson & Son Inc.
1718 18th Street
Sioux City, IA 51105
Phone: 712-258-5615

Kansas

Bill Porter Wrecking
4949 E 63rd Street S
Derby, KS 67037
Phone: 316-788-7300

Bob Smith Salvage
4999 E Old Highway 40
New Cambria, KS 67470
Phone: 785-823-8877

McPherson Wrecking Inc.
2333 Barton Road
Grantville, KS 66429
Phone: 785-246-3012
Fax: 785-246-3014

Kentucky

Hedges Demolition
3201 W. Highway 146
LaGrange, KY 40031
Phone: 502-222-0779
Fax: 502-222-7258

Louisiana

Gulf Coast Dismantling and Salvage
P.O. Box 628
Oakdale, LA 71463
Phone: 318-335-9944

Louisiana/Chemical Dismantling Co., Inc.
24 27th Street
Kenner, LA 70062
Phone: 504-464-0770
Fax: 504-464-4419
Email: LaChem@aol.com
Website: www.lcdc-invirex.com

Maryland

Custom Demolition
3208 Kimberly Drive
Mount Airy, MD 21771
Phone: 410-635-3144

Massachusetts

Associated Building Wreckers Inc.
352 Albany Street
Springfield, MA 01105
Phone: 413-732-3179
Fax: 413-734-6224

Atlantic Building Salvage
178 E Union Street
Ashland, MA 01721
Phone: 508-231-1473

Demolition/Selective Dismantling (DM)—Con.

Hercules Building Wrecking
138 Wilder Street
Brockton, MA 02401
Phone: 508-588-3390
Fax: 508-580-0334

Neptune Demolition Corporation
70 Tenney Street
Georgetown, MA 01883
Phone: 978-352-6210

Michigan

Adamo Demolition
300 E Seven Mile Road
Detroit, MI 48203
Phone: 313-892-7330
Fax: 313-892-4656
Email: support@citrisonic.com
Website: www.adamodemolition.com

Best Wrecking Co.
601 Beaufait Avenue
Detroit, MI 48201
Phone: 800-820-2378
Fax: 313-259-7250
Email: best@bestwrecking.com

Bierlein Companies, Inc.
2000 Bay City Road
Midland, MI 48642
Phone: 800-336-6626; 989-496-0066
Email: info@bierlein.com
Website: www.bierlein.com

D&M Wrecking Co., Inc./Axxiom, Inc.
250 S 4th Street
Kalamazoo, MI 49009
Phone: 616-375-1313
Fax: 616-375-2767

Dore & Associates Contracting, Inc.
900 Harry S Truman Pkwy
Bay City, MI 48707
Phone: 800-344-7876
Fax: 989-684-6663
Email: dore@concentric.net
Website: www.doreandassociates.com

Dore & Associates Contracting, Inc.
1221 E McNichols
Detroit, MI 48203
Phone: 800-344-7876
Email: dore@concentric.net
Website: www.doreandassociates.com

North American Dismantling Corp.
P.O. Box 307
Lapeer, MI 48446
Phone: 810-664-2888
Fax: 810-664-6053
Email: cshuler@nadc1.com
Website: www.nadc1.com

Upright Wrecking
P.O. Box 241580
Detroit, MI 48224
Phone: 313-331-7000

Minnesota

Kellington Construction Inc.
20110 Auger Aev
Corcoran, MN 55340
Phone: 612-416-3200
Fax: 612-416-3201
Email: rlewis@kellington.com
Website: www.kellington.com

Mississippi

Gibsons Demolition Inc.
52 Minor Street
Natchez, MS 39120
Phone: 601-445-2214

Missouri

Madget & Griffin Inc.
2425 S. 6th Street
St. Joseph, MO 64501
Phone: 816-232-6210
Fax: 816-232-8573

Spirtas Wrecking Company
951 Skinker Parkway
St. Louis, MO 63112
Phone: 314-862-9800
Fax: 314-862-9802
Email: info@spirtas.com
www.spirtas.com
Website: www.spiritas.com

Montana

Envirocon, Inc.
101 International Way
Missoula, MT 59808
Phone: 406-523-1150
Fax: 406-543-7987
Email: Market@envirocon.com
Website: www.envirocon.com

Industrial Salvage and Demolition
P.O. Box 17767
Missoula, MT 59808
Phone: 406-543-8893

New Hampshire

Lead Source
23 Horne Street
Dover, NH 03820
Phone: 603-749-9274
Fax: 603-742-5044
Email: curtk@lead-source net
Website: www.lead-source net

New Jersey

American Demolition Corp.
2 English Lane
Egg Harbor Township, NJ 08234
Phone: 609-926-7373

American Wrecking Corporation of NJ
P.O. Box 29
Perth Amboy, NJ 08862
Phone: 732-442-6990
Fax: 732-442-0036
Email: info@awcnj.com
Website: www.awcnj.com

Bace Demolition, Inc.
135 Columbia Turnpike
Florham Park, NJ 07932
Phone: 973-822-3322

Mazzocchi Wrecking
32 Williams Parkway
East Hanover, NJ 07940
Phone: 973-884-8682
Fax: 973-337-7464
Email: grace@mazzocchiwrecking.com
Website: www.mazzocchiwrecking.com

R. Baker & Son All Industrial Services, Inc.
1 Globe Court
Red Bank, NJ 07701
Phone: 732-222-3553
Email: info@RBaker.com
Website: www.rbaker.com

Recmediation Inc.
396 Whitehead Avenue
South River, NJ 08882
Phone: 732-698-9699
Fax: 732-698-0991
Email: info@recmediation.com
Website: www.recmediation.com

Yannuzzi Demolition and Recycling
563 White Street
Orange, NJ 07050
Phone: 973-672-8333
Fax: 973-672-5523
Website: www.yannuzi net

Demolition/Selective Dismantling (DM)—Con.

New Mexico

Coronado Wrecking & Salvage Co.
4200 Broadway Boulevard Swest
Albuquerque, NM 87105
Phone: 505-877-2821

New York

Bianchi-Trison Corp.
300 Long Branch Road
Syracuse, NY 13209
Phone: 800-DEMO-201
Website: www.bianchitrison.com

BRB Contracting, Inc.
20 Denker Drive
Ballston Lake, NY 12019
Phone: 518-693-6348
Email: brbci@hotmail.com

Frasier Wrecking Contractors
212 E State Extension
Gloversville, NY 12078
Phone: 518-725-1915

Gateway Demolition
134-22 32nd Avenue
Flushing, NY 11354
Phone: 718-359-1400
Fax: 718-461-6558
Email: info@gatewaydemolition.com
Website: www.gatewaydemolition.com

Gramercy Group, Inc.
100 Grand Street
Westbury, NY 11590
Phone: 516-876-0020
Fax: 516-876-0021
Website: www.gramercygroupinc.com

International Chimney Corp.
55 S Long Street
Williamsville, NY 14221
Phone: 716-634-3967
Fax: 716-634-3983
Website: www.internationalchimney.com

Jackson Demolition Service
2754 Aqueduct Road
Schenectady, NY 12309
Phone: 800-440-2113
Fax: 518-372-1116
Email: jackdemo@capital net
Website: www.jacksondemolition.com

Lebis Enterprises, Inc.
P.O. Box 606 262 Woodward Avenue
Kenmore, NY 14217
Phone: 877-600-DEMO
Fax: 716-875-6252
Email: angela@lebis.com
Website: www.lebis.com

LVI Demolition Services Inc.
80 Broad Street
New York, NY 10004
Phone: 212-951-3661
Fax: 212-481-9895
Email: corporate@lviservices.com
Website: www.lviservices.com

Ontario Specialty Contracting Inc.
333 Ganson Street
Buffalo, NY 14203
Phone: 716-856-3333
Fax: 716-842-1785
Email: bwegrzyn@ontariospecialty.com
Website: www.ontariospecialty.com

Original Doors of Rochester
203 Milburn Street
Rochester, NY 14607
Phone: 716-271-6290

Sabre Demolition Corporation
73 Generese Street
Baldwinsville, NY 13027
Phone: 315-635-3759
Fax: 315-635-3790
Email: sabredemo@aol.com
Website: www.sabre-demolition.com

Van's Demolition, Inc.
422 Magazine Street
Albany, NY 12204
Phone: 518-438-1936

North Carolina

D.H. Griffin Wrecking Co.
1600 North Graham Street
Charlotte, NC 28206-3024
Phone: 704-331-9400
Fax: 704-336-6860

D. H. Griffin Wrecking Co., Inc.
4700 Hilltop Road
Greensboro, NC 27407
Phone: 888-336-DEMO
Email: elwalker@dhgriffin.com
Website: www.dhgriffin.com

D.H. Griffin Wrecking Company
304 N 3rd Street
Smithfield, NC 27577
Phone: 919-989-7564
Email: dhgwc@constructionnet net
Website: www.dhgriffin.com

Piedmont Grading & Wrecking Co., Inc.
3652 Beatties Ford Road
Charlotte, NC 28216
Phone: 800-968-2374
Email: Piedmontgrading@aol.com

Ohio

American Services Group, Inc.
5695 State Route 128
Cleves, OH 45002
Phone: 800-498-2450
Website: www.amersvs.com

Angelo Building Wreckers
375 W Park Avenue
Columbus, OH 43223
Phone: 614-279-9700

Buckeye Wrecking
1800 19th Street NE
Canton, OH 44714
Phone: 330-445-0088

Dayton Demolition & Contracting Inc.
222 Washington Street
Dayton, OH 45402
Phone: 937-228-3525
Fax: 937-228-1516

King Wrecking Co., Inc.
5038 Beech Street
Cincinnati, OH 45212
Phone: 513-241-1116
Email: kingwrecking@fuse net
Website: www kingwrecking.com

L & L Demolition Excavating Inc.
715 Dayton Road
Springfield, OH 45506
Phone: 937-324-0122

O'Rourke Wrecking Company
660 Lunken Park Drive
Cincinnati, OH 45226
Phone: 800-354-9850
Fax: 513-871-1313
Email: info@orourkewrecking.com
Website: www.orourkewrecking.com

Precision Environmental
5722 Schaaf Road
Independence, OH 44131
Phone: 216-642-6040
Email: inquiries@precision-env.com
Website: www.precision-env.com

Raisch John P Contractor
1312 Fairway Court
Miamisburg, OH 45342
Phone: 937-866-3094

Demolition/Selective Dismantling (DM)—Con.

Stark Wrecking Company
7081 Germantown Pike
Miamisburg, OH 45342
Phone: 937-866-5032

The Stone Salvage Company
Cleveland, OH 44077
Phone: 440-352-7686
Fax: 440-357-7076
Email: stonemaon@stonemason.com
Website: www.stonesalvage.com

Oklahoma

Ark Wrecking Co. of OKLA Inc.
1800 S 49th W Avenue
Tulsa, OK 74103
Phone: 918-583-0488

Midwest Wrecking Company
P.O. Box 3757
Edmond, OK 73083
Phone: 405-478-8833

Oregon

Elder Demolition
5635 SE 111th Avenue
Portland, OR 97266
Phone: 503-760-6330
Fax: 503-497-3115
Email: kdriver@viser.net

Norhwest Demolition
8200 Hunziker SW
Tigard, OR 97223
Phone: 503-638-6900

Northwest Demolition & Dismantle
P.O. Box 930
Wilsonville, OR 97070
Phone: 503-638-6900
Fax: 503-638-1019
Email: m.smith6273@aol.com

Pennsylvania

Empire Services
1420 Clarion Street
Reading, PA 19601
Phone: 610-372-6511
Fax: 610-372-3402
Website: www.empireservicesberks.com

Noralco Corporation
1920 Lincoln Road
Pittsburgh, PA 15235
Phone: 412-361-6678
Fax: 412-361-6535
Email: noralco@aol.com
Website: www.noralco.com

PDG Environmental
1386 Beulah Road
Pittsburgh, PA 15235
Phone: 800-972-7341
Website: www.pdge.com

Russo Demolition & Salvage
800 31st Street
Altoona, PA 16602
Phone: 814-946-3215
Fax: 814-946-3176

Zuk Lumber & Demolition
530 W Broad Street
Bethlehem, PA 18018
Phone: 610-868-7440

Rhode Island

AA Wrecking & Asbestos Abatement
1307 Hartford Avenue
Johnston, RI 02919
Phone: 401-351-1188

Atlantic Industrial Services
7 Echo Drive
Barrington, RI 02806
Phone: 401-247-2426

Gladu Wrecking & Recycling
Beacon Avenue
Woonsocket, RI 02895
Phone: 401-769-9125

Ocean State Wrecking &
Asbestos Removal
32 Shun Pike
Johnston, RI 02919
Phone: 401-946-6131

South Carolina

Browns Housewrecking & Salvage
609 Meeting Street
Charleston, SC 29403
Phone: 843-722-1643

Charleston Wrecking Co.
Charleston, SC 29401
Phone: 843-723-1322

Tennessee

Boyzie Turner Coal Co.
1924 Leslie Avenue
Knoxville, TN 37921
Phone: 865-522-7902

Burnett Demolition and Salvage
1220 Prosser Road
Knoxville, TN 37914
Phone: 865-637-3996

Chandler Demolition Company
1223 N Watkins Street
Memphis, TN 38108
Phone: 901-276-5459
Fax: 901-276-5450
Website: www.chandlerdemolition.com
Memphis Wrecking Company Inc.
2301 S 3rd Street
Memphis, TN 38109
Phone: 901-774-4011
Website:
http://yp.bellsouth.com/sites/memwreck/

Texas

A&R Demolition Inc.
13201 FM812
Del Valle, TX 78617
Phone: 512-243-0512

AAA Demolishing Co. Inc.
220 S Lockwood
Houston, TX 77011
Phone: 713-926-3018

AAA Salvage & Demolition
200 Corinth Street
Dallas, TX 75207
Phone: 214-428-1888
Fax: 214-428-1889

All Universal Service Co.
4021 Oak Lane
Bacliff, TX 77518
Phone: 281-339-1333

American Demolition Inc.
2318 Chavaneaux
San Antonio, TX 78214
Phone: 210-627-2377
Email: gus@americandemolition.com
Website: www.americandemolition.com

ATCO Company
2001 Moneda Street
Haltorn City, TX 76117
Phone: 817-834-2055

Demolition/Selective Dismantling (DM)—Con.

DYN-O-Mite Demolition
6916 CF Hawn Freeway
Dallas, TX 75217
Phone: 214-398-6496
Fax: 214-398-6497

Midwest Steel Company, Inc.
9825 Moers Road
Houston, TX 77075
Phone: 713-991-7843
Fax: 713-992-4745
Email: chrisgiven@midwest-steel.com
Website: www.midwest-steel.com

Miller Enterprises
136 W McLeroy
Saginaw, TX 76179
Phone: 817-626-1941

Utah

Demolition Salvage Supply Company
430 Slade Place
Salt Lake City, UT 84102
Phone: 801-539-1140

George's Demolition & Salvage
430 E 900 S
Salt Lake City, UT 84111
Phone: 801-521-8717

Pappas Brick & Stone
1860 Lincoln Avenue
Ogden, UT 84401
Phone: 801-621-1613

Virginia

Cmc
4509 Pouncey Tract Road
Glen Allen, VA 23059
Phone: 804-369-2120

Dwight Snead Construction
11255 Washington Highway
Glen Allen, VA 23059
Phone: 804-798-1611
Fax: 804-798-8224
Email: dwight@sneadconstruction.com
Website: www.sneadconstruction.com

Pryor's Hauling Company
4509 Pouncey Tract Road
Glen Allen, VA 23059
Phone: 804-360-2120

Washington

Northwest Demolition and Dismantling
Seattle, WA 98101
Phone: 206-243-2270
Website: www.nwdemolition.com

Nuprecon
35131 SE Center Street
Snoqualmie, WA 98065
Phone: 425-881-0623
Fax: 425-881-2072
Email: sales@Nuprecon.com
Website: www.nuprecon.com

R.W. Rhine Inc.
1124 112th Street E
Tacoma, WA 98554
Phone: 253-531-7223
Fax: 253-531-9548

Wisconsin

American Resource Recovery
9168 N 124th Street
Milwaukee, WI 53224
Phone: 414-355-8500

Azarian, Sam Wrecking
726 Water Street
Racine, WI 53403
Phone: 262-637-4153
Fax: 262-637-7520

Beaver Wrecking and Salvage
W8025 State Road 33
Beaver Dam, WI 53916
Phone: 920-887-7030
Fax: 920-887-7030

Gerovac Wrecking Company
11836 W Saint Martins Road
Franklin, WI 53132
Phone: 414-425-1500

Pagenkopf Scott
Green Bay, WI 54301
Phone: 920-498-1755

Scarboro River Barn and Lumber
Green Bay, WI 54301
Phone: 920-498-1755

Scs of Wisconsin Inc.
4001 W Loomis Road
Milwaukee, WI 53221
Phone: 414-281-8733

Equipment Related to Deconstruction (EQ)

Colorado

ReConnX, Inc.
P.O. Box 3009
Boulder, CO 80307
Phone: 303-554-8554
Fax: 303-554-8556
Email: jxg@reconnx.com
Website: www.reconnx.com/

Maine

Auburn Enterprises
P.O. Box 3065
Auburn, ME 04212-3065
Phone: 207-784-4244
Email: tlabrie@auburnmachinery.com

Massachusetts

Professional Engineering Co.
110 Ferry Street
Lawrence, MA 01841
Phone: 888-205-2555
Website: www.ceilingdemo.com

Ohio

Kent Demolition Tool
711 Lake Street
Kent, OH 44240
Phone: 800-527-2282
Email: sales@kenttool.com
Website: www.kentdemolition.com

Environmental Services (EV)

Arizona

A-Cal Wrecking Company
13443 N 20th Street
Phoenix, AZ 85022
Phone: 602-247-2650

Catclaw Contractors
10519 E Tanque Verde Road
Tucson, AZ 85749
Phone: 520-760-0185

California

Plant Reclamation
912 Harbour Way S.
Richmond, CA 94804
Phone: 510-233-6552
Fax: 510-237-6739
Website: www.plantreclamation.com

Environmental Services (EV)—Con.

New Hampshire

Lead Source
23 Horne Street
Dover, NH 03820
Phone: 603-749-9274
Fax: 603-742-5044
Email: curtk@lead-source net
Website: www.lead-source net

New York

LVI Demolition Services Inc.
80 Broad Street
New York, NY 10004
Phone: 212-951-3661
Fax: 212-481-9895
Email: corporate@lviservices.com
Website: www.lviservices.com

Ohio

Precision Environmental
5722 Schaaf Road
Independence, OH 44131
Phone: 216-642-6040
Email: inquiries@precision-env.com
Website: www.precision-env.com

Rhode Island

Ocean State Wrecking &
Asbestos Removal
32 Shun Pike
Johnston, RI 02919
Phone: 401-946-6131

Materials Recycler (RC)

Arizona

Kuhles Services LLC
219 E Navajo Drive
Prescott, AZ 86301
Phone: 928-445-8446

California

Ace Recycling & Scrap Metal
21252 Nordhoff Street
Chatsworth, CA 91311
Phone: 818-772-4891

Adams Steel
3200 E Frontera
Anaheim, CA 92806
Phone: 714-630-6523
Website: www.adamssteel.com

California Wood Recycling Inc.
2950 Johnson Drive
Ventura, CA 93003
Phone: 805-650-1616

Circosta Iron and Metal
1801 Evan Avenue
San Francisco, CA 94124
Phone: 415-282-8568
Fax: 415-641-7804

Dan Copp Crushing Corp
1300B North Hancock Street
Anaheim, CA 92807-1921
Phone: 714-777-6400
Fax: 714-777-6410

Delta Scrap and Salvage
1371 Main Street
Oakley, CA 94561
Phone: 925-754-1474
Website: www.deltademo.com

Gator Crushing and Recycling
2363 Willow Road
Arroyo Grande, CA 93420
Phone: 805-343-6277
Fax: 805-995-3281

Rossel Lumber Recycling
1960 Laredo Lane
Fontana, CA 92337
Phone: 909-371-3255
Fax: 909-361-3255
Email: rosselp@yahoo.com

San Francisco Community Recyclers
701 Amador Street
San Francisco, CA 94124
Phone: 415-731-6720
Fax: 415-566-0102

Colorado

Oxford Recycling
2400 W Oxford Avenue
Englewood, CO 80110
Phone: 303-762-1160
Fax: 303-762-1746
Email: info@oxfordrecycling.com
Website: www.oxfordrecycling.com

Recycle Materials
6385 W 53nd Avenue
Arvada, CO 80002
Phone: 303-431-3701
Email: rmc@rmci-usa.com
Website: www rmci-usa.com

Waste Not Recycling
1205 Hope Avenue
Pierce, CO
Phone: 800-584-9912
Email: recycle@waste-not.com
Website: www.waste-not.com

Delaware

D&D Dismantling
P.O. Box 600
Milford, DE 19963
Phone: 302-422-0922
Fax: 302-422-8051

Service Disposal of Delaware
P.O. Box 661
New Castle, DE 19720
Phone: 302-326-9155
Fax: 302-376-9882

District of Columbia

Institute for Local Self-Reliance
927 15th Street, NW 4th Floor
Washington, DC 20005
Phone: 202-898-1610
Email: nseldman@ilsr.oreg
Website: www.ilsr.org

Florida

Arwood Wrecking
13255 Lanier Road
Jacksonville, FL 32226
Phone: 904-751-1628

Georgia

H.F. Bloodworth, Inc.
Route 1 / P.O. Box 1975
McIntyre, GA 31054
Phone: 912-628-5218

Industrial Metals & Surplus
1635 Marietta Road NW
Atlanta, GA 30318
Phone: 404-355-0486
Website: www.steel-cheap.com

Owltown Recycling
4012 Sudderth Road
Buford, GA 30518
Phone: 770-271-3366

Iowa

Central C&D Recycling
1300 Lincoln Street
Des Moines, IA 50265
Phone: 515-243-6402

Materials Recycler (RC)—Con.

Concrete Recyclers Ltd
110 Main Street
Ossian, IA 52161
Phone: 583-532-9215

Iowa Demolition and Recycling Services
6400 Seminole Court NE
Cedar Rapids, IA 52411
Phone: 319-393-9013

Kentucky

City Salvage and Recycling
2495 Greenville Road
Hopkinsville, KY
Phone: 270-886-5606

Maine

The Green Store
71 Main Street
Belfast, ME 04915
Phone: 207-338-4045
Fax: 207-338-5988

Maryland

Tri-State Reuse Centre
225 W Main Street
Hancock, MD 21750
Phone: 301-678-6160
Fax: 301-678-7841

Michigan

Detroit Recycled Concrete Co.
14294 Myers Road
Detroit, MI 48227
Phone: 313-934-7677

Minnesota

SKB Environmental
251 Streetarkey Street
St Paul, MN 55107
Phone: 651-224-6329
Fax: 651-223-5053
Email: info@skbinc.com
Website: www.skbinc.com

Montana

ANS Metals
2100 Meadowlark Lane
Butte, MT 59701
Phone: 406-494-1661
Fax: 406-494-1607

New Hampshire

LL&S Wood Recycling
87 Lowell Road
Salem, NH 03079
Phone: 603-898-4098

New Jersey

ATS Wood Recycling
15 Polhemus Lane
Bridgewater, NJ 08807
Phone: 908-725-8484

Bace Demolition, Inc.
135 Columbia Turnpike
Florham Park, NJ 07932
Phone: 973-822-3322

New York

Full Circle, Inc.
509 Manida Street
Bronx, NY 10474
Phone: 800-775-1516
Fax: 718-328-4462

North Carolina

D.H. Griffin Wrecking Company
304 N 3rd Street
Smithfield, NC 27577
Phone: 919-989-7564
Email: dhgwc@constructionnet net
Website: www.dhgriffin.com

Miller C&D Recycling
131 Rowan Street
Salisbury, NC 28146
Phone: 704-279-2012
Fax: 704-279-2015

Salvage King
204 Cooper Road
Staley, NC 27355
Phone: 336-622-1595
Fax: 336-622-3883
Email: salvageking@msn.com
Website: www.salvageking.com

Ohio

Complete Resources Co.
3483 E Fulton Street
Columbus, OH 43219
Phone: 614-445-9485
Website: www.complete-resources.com

United Salvage Co.
921 Hazel Street
Akron, OH 44305
Phone: 330-253-2403

Oregon

BioReclaim
P.O. Box 246
Sheridan, OR 97378
Phone: 503-843-6262
Fax: 503-843-7717
Email: mgilham@onlinemac.com
Website: http://sites.onlinemac.com/
bioreclaim/contacts.htm

Texas

Environmental Light Recyclers, Inc.
2737 Bryan Avenue
Fort Worth, TX 76104
Phone: 800-755-4117
Fax: 817-924-3692

Washington

Earthwise, Inc.
2462 1st Avenue S
Seattle, WA 98134
Phone: 206-624-4510
Email: earthwise@qwest net
Website: www.earthwise-salvage.com

Rabanco Recycling
2733 3rd Avenue S
Seattle, WA 98134
Phone: 425-646-2576
Fax: 206-624-2991

West Virginia

Fultineers's Wood Recycling
P.O. Box 131
Lost Creek, WV 26385
Phone: 304-622-0535

Used Building Materials (UMS)

Alabama

Dixie Salvage
3630 Gault Avenue N
Fort Payne, AL 35967
Phone: 256-845-5475

Elrod's Building Material and Salvage
430 4th Avenue N
Bessemer, AL 35020
Phone: 205-426-8788

Fuller Surplus and Supply
3101 Jeff Davis Avenue
Selma, AL 36703
Phone: 334-872-7409

Used Building Materials (UMS)—Con.

James and Company Antique
Timbers and Flooring
482 County Road 209
Collinsville, AL 35961
Phone: 256-997-0703
Fax: 256-997-0773
Email: jamesandcompany@cs.com
Website: www.jamesandcompany.com
Species: White Oak, Longleaf pine,
Chestnut

Reaves Wrecking Co. Inc.
201 A Boulevard
Valley, AL 36854
Phone: 334-756-3237
Email: reaveswrecking@mindspring.com
Species: Pine

Southern Accents Architectural Antiques
308 2nd Avenue SE
Cullman, AL 35055
Phone: 205-737-0554

Surplus and Salvage Sales
910 40th Street N
Birmingham, AL 35222
Phone: 205-592-8306

Alaska

Alaska Materials Exchange
555 Cordova Street
Anchorage, AK 99501
Phone: 907-269-7586

Second Chance
3106 Spenard Road
Anchorage, AK 99503
Phone: 902-277-2748

Valley Materials Exchange
Big Lake Road
Big Lake, AK 99652
Phone: 907-892-7188

Arizona

Al's Building Materials and Supplies
9733 E Main Street
Mesa, AZ 85207
Phone: 480-986-4909

Atwell Salvage & Demolition
3001 W Pima Street
Phoenix, AZ 85009
Phone: 602-484-7301
Fax: 602-484-0132

Barnett & Shore Contractors
819 W Silverlake Road
Tucson, AZ 85713
Phone: 520-791-0286

Eric Building Supply
2112 N West Street
Flagstaff, AZ 86004
Phone: 928-774-3732

Gerson's Used Building Materials
1811 S Park Avenue
Tucson, AZ 85713
Phone: 520-624-8585
Email: dgerson@aol.com

Habitat Home Supply
215 W Leroux Street
Prescott, AZ 86303
Phone: 928-771-1777

Old Pueblo Adobe
9353 N Casa Grande Highway
Tucson, AZ 85713
Phone: 520-744-9268
Website: www.oldpuebloadobe.com

Old Pueblo Remodelers
1700 South 4th Avenue
Tucson, AZ 85713
Phone: 520-884-8685

ReStore/Community Closet
2958 E. 22nd Street
Tucson, AZ 85713
Phone: 520-326-1936
Website: www.tmmfs.org/

Salvage Depot Inc.
5701 W San Miguel
Glendale, AZ 85301
Phone: 623-680-4874
Fax: 623-972-1341
Email: daveschueller@worldnet.att net
Species: Fir

Stardust Building Supplies
1720 W Broadway Road
Phoenix, AZ 85202
Phone: 602-604-0605
Fax: 602-604-0207
Email: ala@stardustbuilding.org
Website: www.stardustbuilding.org

Valley of the Sun HFH ReStore
P.O. Box 20186
Phoenix, AZ 85036
Phone: 602-268-9022

Arkansas

Architectural Salvage by Ri-Jo
2309 Highway 71 S
Mena, AR 71953
Phone: 479-394-2438
Email: salvage@arkansas net

Bear's Building Salvage
510 Huntsville Road
Fayetteville, AR 72701
Phone: 501-443-2327
Fax: 501-442-4279
Email: bear1942@nwark.com

California

ABDO S. Allen Co
718 Douglas Avenue
Oakland, CA 94603
Phone: 510-569-2070

Albion Doors & Windows
P.O. Box 220
Albion, CA 95410
Phone: 707-937-0078
Email: bysawyer@knobsession.com
Website: www knobsession.com

Almquist Lumber
P.O. Box 875
Blue Lake, CA 95525
Phone: 707-668-5652
Fax: 707-668-5454
Email: almquist@tidepool.com
Website: www.almquistlumber.com

Antique Building Material Co.
3707 5th Avenue
San Diego, CA 92101
Phone: 619-233-1144

Antique Building Materials
6152 Wenrich Dr
San Diego, CA 92120
Phone: 619-583-3791
Fax: 619-583-9087
Email: ancientmaterials@cox net
Website: www.ancientarchitecture.com

Antique Building Materials
3175 17th Street
San Francisco, CA 94110
Phone: 415-565-0287

Architectural Antique and Salvage
Company of Santa Barbara
726 Anacapa Street
Santa Barbara, CA 93101
Phone: 805-965-2446

Used Building Materials (UMS)—Con.

Architectural Detail
299 N Altadena Dr
Pasadena, CA 91107
Phone: 626-844-6604
Fax: 626-844-6651
Website: www.pasadenasalvage.com

Architectural Salvage of San Diego
1971 India Street
San Diego, CA 92101
Phone: 619-696-1313

Armstrong Antique Plumbing & Lighting
2820 W Orange Avenue
Anaheim, CA 92804
Phone: 714-761-1320
Fax: 714-761-1320
Email: jarmst2534@aol.com

Battle Lumber & Hardware
2605 Imperial Avenue
San Diego, CA 92102
Phone: 619-234-5118

Bayshore Materials
512 Solano Avenue
Vallejo, CA 94590
Phone: 707-644-0859

Berkeley Architectural Salvage
1167 65th Street
Oakland, CA 94608
Phone: 510-655-2270

Best New and Used Building Materials
1129 E 6th Street
Corona, CA 92879
Phone: 909-279-5079

Beyond Waste
607 W Sierra
Cotati, CA 94952
Phone: 707-792-2555
Fax: 707-792-2565
Email: precycle@sonic.net
Website: www.beyondwaste.com
Species: Redwood, Fir

Big Ten Building Materials
757 W Woodbury Road
Altadena, CA 91001
Phone: 626-791-9747

Black's Farmwood
7 Mount Lassen Road, Suite C-125
San Rafael, CA 94912
Phone: 415-499-8300
Fax: 415-499-8309
Website: www.blacksfarmwood.com

Blue Diamond Materials
1245 Arrow Highway
Baldwin Park, CA 91706
Phone: 626-303-2623

Bourget Brothers Building Materials
1636 11th Street
Santa Monica, CA 90404
Phone: 310-450-6556

Bright Ideas
P.O. Box 586
Brookdale, CA 9507
Phone: 831-338-2522
Email: dondowell@yahoo.com
Website:
Species: Oak, Maple, Redwood

Building Materials Distributors
1708 Cactus Road
San Diego, CA 92173
Phone: 619-661-7181

Building Materials Recycling
6467 Datsun Street
San Diego, CA 92173
Phone: 619-661-8155
Building Resources
701 Amador Street
San Francisco, CA 94124
Phone: 415-285-7814
Fax: 415-285-4689
Email: brsfcr@yahoo.com
Website: www.bulidingresources.org

C & K Salvage
718 Douglas Avenue
Oakland, CA 94603
Phone: 510-569-2070
Fax: 510-569-2074
Email: cksalvage@aol.com
Species: Fir

C&M Diversified
330 N Montgomery
San Jose, CA 94124
Phone: 408-294-5185

Caldwell's Building Salvage
Resource/Wreckers
195 Bayshore Boulevard
San Francisco, CA 94124
Phone: 415-550-6777
Fax: 415-550-0349
Website: http://caldwell-bldg-salvage.com/

Castroville Used Building Materials
10900 Merritt Street
Castroville, CA 95012
Phone: 831-633-0369

Community Woodworks
2420 Ukraine Street Oakland Army Base
Building 823
Oakland, CA 94607
Phone: 510-835-7690
Fax: 510-835-7691
Website: www.communitywoodworks.org/

Cornerstone Salvage Company
40927 Airport Road
Littleriver, CA 95456
Phone: 707-937-5011
Species: Redwood

Daley Marketing Corporation
151 Kalmus Drive
Costa Mesa, CA 92626
Phone: 714-662-0755
Email: daleydmc@sprintmail.com

Earth Source Forest Products
1618 28th Street
Oakland, CA 94608
Phone: 510-208-7257
Fax: 510-547-7252
Email: selluwood@yahoo.com
Website: www.earthsourcewood.com

EcoTimber
1611 4th Street
San Rafael, CA 94901
Phone: 415-258-8454
Fax: 415-258-8455
Email: ecotimber@ecotimber.com
Website: www.ecotimber.com

El Dorado County Habitat for Humanity
5781 Pleasant Valley Road
El Dorado, CA 95623
Phone: 530-621-3972
Fax: 530-295-8972
Email: drisso@edchabitat.org
Website: www.edchabitat.org

El Toro Materials Co.
20851 El Toro Road
Lake Forest, CA 92630
Phone: 949-458-7993
Fax: 949-859-5138

European Reclamation
4520 Brazil Street
Los Angeles, CA 90039
Phone: 818-241-2152
Fax: 818-547-2734
Email: htc@wgn.net
Website: www.historictile.com

Ewles Materials
16081 Construction Circle W
Irvine, CA 92606
Phone: 949-552-6008
Fax: 949-552-7084

Used Building Materials (UMS)—Con.

Freeway Building Materials
1124 S Boyle Avenue
Los Angeles, CA 90023
Phone: 323-261-8904

Garbage Reincarnation, Inc.
500 Mecham Road
Santa Rosa, CA 95402
Phone: 707-584-8666
Fax: 707-584-8291
Email: brecycle@pacbell.net
Website: www.garbage.org

Gilman Street Salvage
808 Gilman Street
Berkeley, CA 94710
Phone: 510-524-5500
Fax: 510-524-5192
Email: info@gilmansalvage.com
Website:
www.gilmansalvage.com/welcome html

Habitat for Humanity
P.O. Box 770
Fort Bragg, CA 95437
Phone: 707-964-0942

Habitat for Humanity
2219 San Joaquin Street
Fresno, CA 93721
Phone: 559-237-4102

Habitat for Humanity Pomona Valley
2111 Bonita Avenue
La Verne, CA 91750
Phone: 909-596-7098
Fax: 909-596-2279
Email: pvhab@juno.com
Website: http://pomvalhabitat.org

Habitat for Humanity
6414 Brace Road
Loomis, CA 95650
Phone: 916-652-1045

Habitat for Humanity
1010 Doyle Street
Menlo Park, CA 94025
Phone: 650-324-2266

Habitat for Humanity
2301-B Woodland Avenue
Modesto, CA 95358
Phone: 209-575-4585

Habitat for Humanity–East Bay
2619 Broadway
Oakland, CA 94612
Phone: 510-251-6303

Habitat for Humanity of Ventura County
167 Lambert Street
Oxnard, CA 93030
Phone: 805-485-6065
Email: info@habitatventura.org
Website: www habitatventura.org

Habitat for Humanity
San Fernando/Santa Clarita Valleys
Pacoima, CA 91331
Phone: 818-897-0940

Habitat for Humanity
El Dorado County, Inc.
180 Industrial Drive #E
Placerville, CA 95667-6803
Phone: 530-621-3972

Habitat for Humanity
851 Commerce Street
Redding, CA 96002
Phone: 530-224-9684

Habitat for Humanity ReStore
426 N 7th Street
Sacramento, CA 95814
Phone: 916-440-1215
Email: info@shfh.org
Website: www.shfh.org

Habitat for Humanity
P.O. Box 1834
San Andreas, CA 95249
Phone: 209-754-5331

Habitat for Humanity
888 N First Street
San Jose, CA 94124
Phone: 408-294-6464

Habitat for Humanity Orange County
2165 S Grand Avenue
Santa Ana, CA 92705
Phone: 714-434-6202
Fax: 714-434-1222
Email: manager@restoreoc.org
Website: www restoreoc.org

Habitat for Humanity
1543 Sunnyvale Avenue # 101
Walnut Creek, CA 94596
Phone: 925-933-1296

Habitat for Humanity Orange County
13925 Edwards
Westminster, CA 92683
Phone: 714-891-6998

Hayward Lumber
10 Ragsdale Drive, Suite 100
Monterey, CA 93940
Phone: 831-643-1900
Website: www haywardlumber.com

Hexagram Antiques
426 3rd Street
Eureka, CA 95501
Phone: 707-443-4334

Iconco Inc.
303 Derby Avenue
Oakland, CA 94601
Phone: 510-261-1900
Fax: 510-261-2459
Email: iconco@pacbell net
Website: www.iconco-inc.com

Into the Woods
1205 N McDowell
Petaluma, CA 94954
Phone: 707-763-0159

J P Dolan Lumber
1701 Rumrill Boulevard
Richmond, CA 94806
Phone: 510-232-1273

Jackel Enterpise Inc.
347 Locust Street
Watsonville, CA 95076
Phone: 831-768-3880
Fax: 831-768-3883
Email: jackel@cruzil.com
Website: www.jackelenterprises.com
Species: Fir, Redwood

Jessie's Lumber
3609 Britton Avenue
Chula Vista, CA 91911
Phone: 619-426-3574

Liz's Antique Hardware
453 S La Brea
Los Angeles, CA 90036
Phone: 323-939-4403
Website: www.lahardware.com

M. Maselli & Sons, Inc.
519 Lakeville Street
Petaluma, CA 94952
Phone: 707-763-1562
Fax: 707-763-6964
Email: info@m-maselliandsons.com
Website: www m-maselliandsons.com

Maxwell Pacific
P.O. Box 4127
Malibu, CA 90264
Phone: 310-457-4533

Nunez and Sons Used Building Material
4024 E Chavez Avenue
Los Angeles, CA 90063
Phone: 323-266-0518

Used Building Materials (UMS)—Con.

Off the Wall
P.O. Box 4561
Carmel, CA 93923
Phone: 831-624-6165

Ohmega Salvage
2407 San Pablo Avenue
Berkeley, CA 94702
Phone: 510-843-7368
Fax: 510-843-7123
Email: ohmegasalvage@earhtlink net
Website: www.ohmegasalvage.com

Olympic Used Building Material
2860 E Olympic Boulevard
Los Angeles, CA 90023
Phone: 323-780-9163

Omega Too
2204 San Pablo Avenue
Berkeley, CA 94702
Phone: 510-843-3636
Fax: 510-843-0666

Pacific Heritage Wood Supply Co.
P.O. Box 1329
El Granada, CA 94018
Phone: 877-728-9231
Fax: 650-728-9231
Email: sales@phwood.com
Website: www.phwood.com

Pacific Post and Beam
P.O. Box 13708
San Luis Obispo, CA 93406
Phone: 805-543-7565
Fax: 805-543-1287

Pinocchio's
18651 Hare Creek Ter.
Fort Bragg, CA 95437
Phone: 707-964-6272
Fax: 707-964-0458
Website: www mcn.org/b/rmoore

Premier Architectural Materials
P.O. Box 22667
Carmel, CA 93923
Phone: 831-662-3450

Presco Building Materials
291 S Waterman Avenue
San Bernardino, CA 92408
Phone: 909-889-0084
Fax: 909-889-0085

Ralph's Used Building Material
1444 Island Avenue
San Diego, CA 92101
Phone: 619-232-2633

Recycletown-Reuse-Recycling
403 Meacham Road
Petaluma, CA 94952
Phone: 707-795-3660

Resale Lumber Products
4056 N Highway 101
Eureka, CA 95501
Phone: 707-822-5705
Fax: 707-822-3074
Email: konicke@urchin.net

Re-Sets
12215 Montague Avenue
Pacoima, CA 91331
Phone: 818-890-6499

Reusable Lumber Company
895 La Honda Road
Woodside, CA 94062
Phone: 650-529-9122
Fax: 650-529-3082
Email: info@reusablelumber.com
Website: www reusablelumber.com

Reuse People
15165 Golden Gate Drive
San Leandro, CA 94579
Phone: 510-351-5628

Ruiz Antique Lighting
2333 Clement Avenue
Alameda, CA 94501
Phone: 510-769-6082
Fax: 510-769-1374

RWH Construction
12722 Carmenita Road
Santa Fe Springs, CA 90670
Phone: 562-407-0694
Fax: 562-407-0696

San Diego Habitat ReStore
3653 Costa Bella Street
Lemon Grove, CA 92101
Phone: 619-463-0464
Fax: 619-668-2149
Email: johnl@habiatatsdiego.org
Website: www habitatsdiego.org

Santa Fe Wrecking Company
1600 S Santa Fe Avenue
Los Angeles, CA 90021
Phone: 213-623-3119
Fax: 213-623-3119
Website: www.santafewrecking.com

Savvy Salvage
4385 Piedmont Avenue
Oakland, CA 94611
Phone: 510-655-8877

Sepulveda Building Materials
359 E Gardena Boulevard
Gardena, CA 90248
Phone: 310-217-0134

Sink Factory
2140 San Pablo Avenue
Berkeley, CA 94702
Phone: 510-540-8193
Fax: 510-540-8212
Website: www.sinkfactory.com

Surplus City of Oroville
4514 Pacific Heights Road
Oroville, CA 95965
Phone: 530-534-9956

Terra Mai
P.O. Box 696
McCloud, CA 96057
Phone: 800-220-9062
Email: info@terramai.com
Website: www.terramai.com

The Reuse People
2100 Ferry Point #150
Alameda, CA 94501
Phone: 510-522-2722
Email: info@TheReusePeople.org
Website: www.thereusepeople.com

The Reuse People
23010 Lake Forest Dr, Suite D-302
Laguna Hills, CA 92653
Phone: 888-588-9490
Email: info@TheReusePeople.org
Website: www.thereusepeople.com

This & That
1701 Rumrill Boulevard
Richmond, CA 94805
Phone: 510-232-1273

This & That
1701 Rumrill Boulevard
San Pablo, CA 94806
Phone: 510-232-1273

Tony's Architectural Salvage
123 N Olive
Orange, CA 92866
Phone: 714-538-1900
Fax: 714-538-1966
Email:
webmaster@tonysarchitecturalsalvage.com
Website:
www.tonysarchitecturalsalvage.com

Used Building Materials (UMS)—Con.

Urban Ore
900 Murray Street
Berkeley, CA 94710
Phone: 510-841-7283

Urban Ore Inc.
6082 Ralston Avenue
Richmond, CA 94805-1202
Phone: 510-232-7724
Fax: 510-235-0198
Email: marylouvan@aol.com

Valley Base Materials
9050 Norris Avenue
Sun Valley, CA 91352
Phone: 818-767-3088

Vintage Architectural
1861-B Main Street
San Diego, CA 92113
Phone: 619-239-7636
Email: vintage@vintagearchitectural.com
Website: www.vintagearchitectural.com

Vintage Timberworks
47100 Rainbow Canyon Road
Temecula, CA 92592
Phone: 909-695-1003

Wesco Used Lumber
910 Ohio Avenue
Richmond, CA 94804
Phone: 510-235-9995
Fax: 510-236-2863

Westco Used Lumber
P.O. Box 1136
El Centro, CA 94530
Phone: 510-235-9995
Fax: 510-236-2863

Whole House Building Supplies
1955 Pulgas Avenue
East Palo Alto, CA 94303
Phone: 650-328-8731
Fax: 650-327-1933
Email: gardner@.net.com
Website: www.driftwoodsalvage.com
Species: Redwood, Oak, Pine

Whole House Building Supply
731-D Loma Verde Avenue
Palo Alto, CA 94303
Phone: 650-856-0634
Fax: 650-856-0634
Email: pgard0634@aol.com
Website: www.driftwoodsalvage.com

Youth Employment Partnership
2300 International Bvld
Oakland, CA 94601
Phone: 510-533-3447
Website: www.yep.org

Colorado

A Garrett Lumber and Wrecking Company
7360 Grape Street
Commerce City, CO 80022
Phone: 303-288-4946
Fax: 303-843-9682

Allied Demolition, Inc.
7901 Highway 85
Commerce City, CO 80037
Phone: 303-289-3366
Fax: 303-289-3543
Website: www.barnettlumber.com/demo.htm

Alpine Bargain Center
3915 N Garfield Avenue
Loveland, CO 80538
Phone: 970-622-8307
Fax: 970-669-9667
Website: www.alpinebargaincenter.com

Architectural Antiques
2669 Larimer Street
Denver, CO 80205
Phone: 303-297-9722
Fax: 303-297-9290
Website: www.archantiques.com

Architectural Salvage
504 E Pikes Peak Avenue
Colorado Springs, CO 80903
Phone: 719-633-9294

Architectural Salvage, Inc.
1215 Delaware Street
Denver, CO 80204
Phone: 303-615-5432

Building for Health Materials Center
P.O. Box 113
Carbondale, CO 81623
Phone: 970-963-0437
Fax: 970-963-3318
Email: contactus@buildingforhealth.com
Website: http://buildingforhealth.com

Carlisle Restoration Lumber
1445 Market Street
Denver, CO 80202
Phone: 303-893-3937

Construction Junction
695 Buggy Circle
Carbondale, CO 81623
Phone: 970-963-1016
Fax: 970-963-4913
Email: staff@constructionjunction1.com

Do-It-Ur-Self Plumbing
3120 Brighton Boulevard
Denver, CO 80216
Phone: 303-297-0455
Fax: 303-295-0147

Habitat for Humanity Home Supply Store
4001 S Taft Hill Road
Ft. Collins, CO
Phone: 970-223-9909
Email: www habitatstore.org

Habitat for Humanity Thrift Store
5250 N Highway 287
Loveland, CO 80537
Phone: 970-669-7343
Fax: 970-461-0303

Mendoza Used Brick
701 W. 64th Avenue # B
Denver, CO 80221
Phone: 303-427-5675

Old Grain Reclaimed Wood Specialists
P.O. Box 854
Carbondale, CO 81623
Phone: 970-704-9745
Fax: 970-704-9745
Email: info@oldgrain.com
Website: www.oldgrain.com

Queen City Architectural Salvage
4750 Brighton Boulevard
Denver, CO 80216
Phone: 303-296-0925

ReSource 2000
1702 Walnut Street
Boulder, CO 80302
Phone: 303-441-3278
Fax: 303-441-4367
Email: mmckinne@earthnet net
Website: www resource2k.org
Species: Oak, Fir, Pine

Uncle Benny's Building Supplies LLP
1815 S. County Road 13C
Loveland, CO 80537
Phone: 970-593-1667
Fax: 970-461-0900
Email: unclebennys@earthlink net
Website: unclebennysonline.com

Used Building Materials (UMS)—Con.

Used Again Building Materials
506 W Cucharras
Colorado Springs, CO 80905
Phone: 719-473-2150

Connecticut

A Reclaimed Lumber co.
9 Old Post Road
Madison, CT 06443
Phone: 203-214-9705
Email: info@whitecedar.com
Website: www.reclaimedlumberco.com
Species: Pine, Fir, Cypress

American Timbers LLC
P.O. Box 430
Canterbury, CT 06331
Phone: 800-461-8660
Fax: 860-546-9334
Email: sales@americantimbers.com
Website: www.americantimbers.com
email:amtimbers@compol net

Board and Beam
P.O. Box 1235
Washington, CT 06793
Phone: 860-868-6789
Fax: 860-868-0721
Email: bbeams@rcn.com
Website: www.boardandbeam.com
Species: Pine, Oak, Chestnut

Material Exchange
62 Cherry Street
Bridgeport, CT 06605
Phone: 203-335-3452

Old Wood Workshop, LLC
193 Hampton Road
Pomfret Center, CT 06259
Phone: 860-655-5259
Email: Info@Oldwoodworkshop.com
Website: www.oldwoodworkshop.com
Species: Chestnut, Oak, Pine

United House Wrecking
535 Hope Street
Stamford, CT 06906
Phone: 203-348-5371
Fax: 203-961-9472
Website: www.united-antiques.com

V and T Used Brick
254 N Hoadly
Naugatuck, CT 06770
Phone: 203-729-9436

Violette Used Brick
1400 New Britain Avenue
Farmington, CT 06032
Phone: 860-676-0411

Delaware

The Warehouse Project
500 Duncan Road
Wilmington, DE 19809
Phone: 302-477-1671

Townsend Building Supply
4324 N DuPont Highway
Townsend, DE 19734
Phone: 302-378-8846

District of Columbia

The Brass Knob
2329 Champlain Street NW
Washington, DC 20009
Phone: 202-265-0587
Email: bd@thebrassknob.com
Website: www.thebrassknob.com/

The Brass Knob
2311 18th Street NW
Washington, DC 20009
Phone: 202-265-0587
Fax: 202-332-5594

Florida

A Rainbow Lumber
450 Canaveral Groves Boulevard
Cocoa, FL 32926
Phone: 321-638-3800

A Thrift Store Habitat for Humanity
3962 Central Avenue
St. Petersburg, FL 33711
Phone: 727-322-9730

Adam and Eve Architectural Salvage
528 16th Street
West Pam Beach, FL 33407
Phone: 561-655-1022
Website:
adamandevearchitecturalsalvage.com

All Surplus Inc.
4350 NE 6th Avenue
Oakland Park, FL 33334
Phone: 954-567-0977
Fax: 954-491-8679
Email: johns567@bellsouth net

Allison's Architectural Antique
5716 Georgia Avenue
West Palm Beach, FL 33405
Phone: 561-582-2224

American Salvage
7001 NW 27th Avenue
Miami, FL 33147
Phone: 305-691-7001
Fax: 305-691-0001
Email: trw@americansalvage.com
Website: www.americansalvage.com

Architectural Artifacts
1900 N Miami Avenue
Miami, FL 33136
Phone: 305-573-4169

Architectural Design and Artifacts
515 N Andrews Avenue
Ft. Lauderdale, FL 33301
Phone: 954-525-1212

Atlantic Building Salvage
7526 NW 7th Avenue
Miami, FL 33150
Phone: 305-693-2910

Builders Bargain Surplus Inc.
3045 NE 12th Terrace
Ft. Lauderdale, FL 33334
Phone: 954-564-7375

Cash & Carry Surplus Building Supply
718 Farmer's Market Road
Fort Pierce, FL 34982
Phone: 561-461-3999

Central Environmental Services Inc.
3210 Friendly Avenue
Orlando, FL 32808
Phone: 407-295-7005
Fax: 407-295-7004
Website: www.centralenvironmental.com
Species: Heartpine, Oak, Maple

Charlotte County HFH ReStore
P.O. Box 6028
Port Charlotte, FL 33949
Phone: 941-639-1261

Discount Building Materials
735 Carswell Avenue
Daytona Beach, FL 32117
Phone: 386-255-0002

Florida Victorian Architectural Antiques
112 W. Georgia Avenue
DeLand, FL, FL 32720
Phone: 904-734-9300
Fax: 904-734-1150
Website: www floridavictorian.com

Used Building Materials (UMS)—Con.

Giant Mart
5485 Haines Road N
St. Petersburg, FL 33714
Phone: 727-526-1494
Fax: 727-526-1494

Government Sales Associates
4972 N Orange Avenue
Winter Park, FL 32792
Phone: 407-679-1759
Fax: 407-679-1567
Email: govsls@magicnet net

Habitat for Humanity Inc. (Tampa)
8100 N Florida Avenue
Tampa, FL 33604
Phone: 813-935-8805

Handyman's Dreamland Inc.
18522 U.S. Highway 19
Hudson, FL 34667
Phone: 813-869-2588
Email: jjexport@gte net

Layman's Used Merchandise
12190 U.S. Highway 19 N
Clearwater, FL 33764
Phone: 727-531-3801

Norwood Surplus Plywood
6200 Norwood Avenue
Jacksonville, FL 32208
Phone: 904-768-6818

Orange County Community
Distribution Center
2000 Lucerne Terrace
Orlando, FL 32806
Phone: 407-836-4680

Pensacola Salvage 7
1245 N Warrington Road
Pensacola, FL 32506
Phone: 850-455-7000

Pinellas Habitat for Humanity ReStore
3962 Central Avenue
St. Petersburg, FL 32608
Phone: 727-322-9730

Pinetree Builders
814 SE 23rd Street
Ft. Lauderdale, FL 33316
Phone: 954-760-5800
Fax: 954-760-5833
Email: info@pinetreebuilders.com
Website: www.pinetreebuilders.com
Species: Heartpine, Cypress

Reilly Bros Inc.
3026 E Riverside Drive
Fort Myers, FL 33916
Phone: 239-334-1567

Resources Limited
3100 Woodville Highway
Tallahassee, FL 32305
Phone: 850-878-5450
Email: lwelbon@comcast net

ReUser Building Products
622 SE 2nd Street
Gainesville, FL 32601
Phone: 352-379-4600
Fax: 352-377-0037
Email: pollyodel@gru net

Roz's Reusable Building Materials
18260 Paulson Drive
Port Charlotte, FL 33954
Phone: 941-766-0004

S&M Used Building Materials
5275 Haines Road N.
St. Petersburg, FL 33714
Phone: 727-526-8888
Fax: 727-522-8800
Email: custsvc@salvageitems.com
Website: www.salvageitems.com

Sarasota Architectural Salvage
1143 Central Avenue
Sarasota, FL 34236
Phone: 941-358-7730
Email: info@sarasotasalvage.com

Surplus Shop Inc.
10121 SE Highway 441
Belleview, FL 34420
Phone: 352-245-4640
Fax: 352-245-6172

Svinga Brothers Corp.
206 NE 9th Street
Ocala, FL 34470
Phone: 352-351-2841
Fax: 352-351-3560

Used Stuff Inc.
1404 Central Avenue
Sarasota, FL 34236
Phone: 941-953-5100
Email: usedstuff@comcast net

Georgia

Architectural Accents
2711 Piedmont Road
Atlanta, GA 30305
Phone: 404-266-8700
Fax: 404-266-0074
Email: archaccent@aol.com

Atlanta Salvage Outlet
1034 Howell Mill Road
Atlanta, GA 30318
Phone: 404-873-4416

Builder's Salvage
109 Addington Drive NW
Rome, GA 30165
Phone: 706-232-8869

Cooper Equipment Contracting
301 Miller Street
Valdosta, GA 31601
Phone: 229-244-7696

DBM Imports Exports
2905 Amwiler Road
Atlanta, GA 30360
Phone: 770-729-0159

Flint River HFH ReStore
P.O. Box 710
Albany, GA 31702
Phone: 912-430-7942

Great Gatsby's
5070 Peachtree Ind Boulevard
Atlanta, GA 30341
Phone: 770-457-1905

Habitat for Humanity
723 Spring Street
Americus, GA 31709
Phone: 229-931-9899
Fax: 229-931-6188
Email: restore@newhorizonshabitat.org
Website: www newhorizonshabitat.org

Home Resource Interchange
750 Glenwood Avenue SE
Atlanta, GA 30316
Phone: 404-624-4434
Fax: 404-624-5299

Hudgins & Company, Inc.
640 North Avenue NW
Atlanta, GA 30318
Phone: 404-523-2791

Used Building Materials (UMS)—Con.

Metropolitan Artifacts
4783 Peachtree Road
Atlanta, GA 30341
Phone: 707-986-0007

Pinch of the Past
109 W Broughton Street
Savannah, GA 31401
Phone: 912-232-5563
Email: pinchopast@aol.com
Website: www.pinchofthepast.com

Re Use the Past, Inc.
98 Moreland Street
Grantville, GA 30220
Phone: 770-583-3111
Email: bocastle@mindspring.com

Restorations & Antiques
Supplies of Savannah
600 W 51st Street
Savannah, GA 31405
Phone: 912-236-7724

Restorations and Antique Supplies
600 W 51st Street
Savannah, GA 31405
Phone: 912-236-7724

Sawmill Treasures
Highway 57
Irwinton, GA 31042
Phone: 478-946-2510
Email: guerryholder@hotmail.com
Website: www.sawmilltreasures.com

Second Chance
230 7th Street
Macon, GA 31201
Phone: 478-742-7874

Vintage Lumber Products
325 Swift Street
Toccoa, GA 30577
Phone: 706-282-0077

Vintage Lumber Sales
18757 Highway 85
Gay, GA 30218
Phone: 706-538-0180
Fax: 706-538-6558
Website: www.vintagelumbersales.com
Species: Heartpine, Cypress, Oak

Wrecking Barn
292 Mooreland Avenue
Atlanta, GA 30307
Phone: 404-525-0468

Idaho

Building Material Thrift Store
3990 Woodside Boulevard
Hailey, ID 83333
Phone: 208-788-0014
Fax: 208-788-0816
Email: bmtbruce@earthlink net
Website:
www.woodriverlandtrust.org/store/store.html

Ross Lumber
391 Highway. 75 Box 519
Shoshone, ID 83352
Phone: 208-886-7778
Fax: 208-886-7779
Email: rosslumber.com
        rickross@micron.com

Trestlewood
933 South Frontage Road
Blackfoot, ID 83221
Phone: 208-785-1151
Fax: 208-785-0458
Email: info@trestlewood.com
Website: www.Trestlewood.com
Species: Fir, Pine, Oak

Wasankari Construction
2730 Highway 95 S
Moscow, ID 83843
Phone: 208-883-4362

Illinois

A & T Wrecking & Lumber Co.
16461 Wood Street
Markham, IL 60426-5824
Phone: 708-333-4700

American Barn Company
3808 N Clark Street
Chicago, IL 60613
Phone: 773-327-1560

Archaic Architectural
4304 S Michigan Avenue
Chicago, IL 60653
Phone: 773-268-0100

Architectural Artifacts
4325 N Ravenswood Avenue
Chicago, IL 60613
Phone: 773-348-0622
Fax: 773-348-6118

Asset Recovery Contracting
5441 Fargo Avenue
Skokie, IL 60077
Phone: 847-674-3366
Fax: 847-674-8660
Email: jim@arcdem.com
Website: www.arcdemo.com

Builders Salvage
30347 U.S. 150 Highway
Farmer City, IL 61842
Phone: 309-928-2344

Carlson's Barnwood Company
8066 N 1200 Avenue
Cambridge, IL 61238
Phone: 309-522-5550
Fax: 309-522-5123
Email: info@carlsonsbarnwood.com
Website: www.carlsonsbarnwood.com

Colonial Brick Inc.
2222 S Halstead Street
Chicago, IL 60608
Phone: 312-733-2600
Website: www.colonialbrickchicago.com

Darrah-Barns
104 N Prairie Street
Rockton, IL 61072
Phone: 815-624-4434
Fax: 815-624-4547
Email: darrahbarns@hotmail.com

Dix Lumber and Recycling
202 E Washington Street
Dix, IL 62830
Phone: 618-266-7665

HFH of McLean County
P.O. Box 3432
Bloominton, IL 61702
Phone: 309-827-3931

J Stuart Corsa–Purveyors
of Salvage Material
6528 Charles Street
Rockford, IL 61108
Phone: 815-229-0377
Email: stuart51@aol.com

Jan's Antiques
225 N Racine Avenue
Chicago, Il 60607
Phone: 312-563-0275

Lockett's Lumber & Salvage
2104 Baker Avenue
East St Louis, IL 62207
Phone: 618-274-1884

Used Building Materials (UMS)—Con.

Lowder Construction Architectural Salvage
116 E State Street
Waverly, IL 62692
Phone: 217-435-9618

Mid-America Architectural Salvage
P.O. Box 926
Grayslake, IL 60030
Phone: 847-223-5772
Fax: 847-223-5775
Website: www.architectural-antqs.com

Old House Heaven
602 E State Street
Jacksonville, IL 62650
Phone: 217-479-8020
Fax: 217-479-8332
Email: oldhouse@csi.net
Website: www.oldhouseheaven.com

River City Demolition
P.O. Box 726
Peoria, IL 61602
Phone: 309-655-0447
Fax: 309-767-1415
Email: rivercitydemo@aol.com
Website: www.rivercitydemolition.com

Salvage One
1524 S Sangamon Street
Chicago, IL 60608
Phone: 312-733-0098
Email: salvoone@aol.com
Website: www.salvageone.com

Spiess Architectural Antiques
230 E Washington Street
Joliet, IL 60433
Phone: 815-722-5639
Fax: 815-722-0171
Email: SPIESSANTQ@AOL.COM

The Renovation Source Inc.
3512 N Southport Avenue
Chicago, IL 60657
Phone: 773-327-1250
Fax: 773-327-1250
Species: Oak, Pine, Poplar

The Restoration Place
305 20th Street
Rock Island, IL 61201
Phone: 309-786-0004
Fax: 309-786-5834

The Storehouse of Vision
5001 W. Harrison
Chicago, IL 60644
Phone: 773-921-3900 ext. 315
Fax: 773-921-3953
Email: sjpincham@thestorehouse.org
Website: www.thestorehouse.org

Indiana

Capellier Salvage and Wrecking
11640 N. East Drive
Camby, IN 46113
Phone: 317-831-4533
Fax: 317-834-3057
Email: sjack1306@aol.com

Crowe Wrecking Co.
2400 Grove Street
Evansville, IN 47710
Phone: 812-425-6511

Edgewood Building Supply
1580 E Epler Avenue
Indianapolis, IN 46227
Phone: 317-786-9208
Fax: 317-788-4023

First Saturday Construction Salvage
Route 3 Box 405
Spencer, IN 47460
Phone: 812-876-6347
Fax: 812-876-6347
Email: construcsalvage@smithville net
Website: www.constructionsalvage.com
Species: Pine, Oak, Walnut

Foursquare Antiques and Architectural
Salvage
727 W 5th Street
Bloomington, IN 47404
Phone: 812-337-8577

Hannells Wrecking Co.
3118 W U.S. Highway 40
Clayton, IN 46118
Phone: 317-539-6464
Fax: 317-539-2246
Species: Pine

Harris Building and Salvage
2027 W 500 S
Morocco, IN 47963
Phone: 219-285-6029

Rehab Resource, Inc.
3029 E Washington Street
Indianapolis, IN 46205
Phone: 800-685-4686
Email: rresource@iquest net
Website: www.rehabresource.org/

Tim & Billy's Salvage Store
970 Fort Wayne Avenue
Indianapolis, IN 46202
Phone: 317-632-7161
Fax: 317-632-0047
Website: www.architecturalantiques net

Tim and Avi's Salvage Store
2442 Central Avenue
Indianapolis, IN 46205
Phone: 317-925-6071

White River Architectural Salvage
1325 W 30th Street
Indianapolis, IN 46208
Phone: 317-924-4000
Email:
whiteriversalvage@whiteriversalvage.com
Website: www.whiteriversalvage.com

Iowa

Building Savers
3301 Main Street
Emmetsburg, IA 50536
Phone: 712-852-3057

Eco-Youth
3351 Square D Drive SW
Cedar Rapids, IA 52404
Phone: 319-365-3501
Fax: 319-365-0104
Website: www nahp net

Gavin Historical Bricks
2050 Glendale Road
Iowa City, IA 52245
Phone: 319-354-5251
Email: info@historicalbricks.com
Website: www historicalbricks.com

Home Recycling Exchange
805 SE 14th Court
Des Moines, IA 50317
Phone: 515-282-9296
Email: lballhre@aol.com

House and Garden Restoration Specialties
1410 19th Street
Des Moines, IA 50314
Phone: 515-243-3985
Fax: 515-282-3892

Ken Hunt Building Supply & Salvage
2050 E Army Post Road
Des Moines, IA 50320
Phone: 515-287-0007
Fax: 515-287-0007

Used Building Materials (UMS)—Con.

ReStore HfH Quad Cities
2235 Grant Street
Bettendorf, IA 52722
Phone: 563-359-9066
Email: dancin@mcleodusa net
Website: www.restoreqc.org

The Salvage Barn
1147 S Riverside Dr
Iowa City, IA 52246
Phone: 800-541-8656
Email: salvagebarn@ic-fhp.org
Website: www.ic-fhp.org/salvagebarn html

Kansas

Bahm Demolition
3840 NW Hodges Road
Silver Lake, KS 66539
Phone: 785-582-5190
Fax: 582-412-8785
Email: djb977@aol.com
Website: www.bahmdemolition.com
Species: Pine, Oak

Bill Porter Wrecking
4949 E 63rd Street S
Derby, KS 67037
Phone: 316-788-7300

Bob Smith Salvage
4999 E Old Highway 40
New Cambria, KS 67470
Phone: 785-823-8877

BOGE Iron and Metal Company Inc.
800 S Saint Francis Street
Wichita, KS 67211
Phone: 316-263-8241

McPherson Wrecking Inc.
2333 Barton Road
Grantville, KS 66429
Phone: 785-246-3012
Fax: 785-246-3014

Novick Iron & Metal
1997 E 21st Street N
Wichita, KS 67214
Phone: 316-265-6661
Fax: 316-265-6677

Reeves Lumber & Surplus
2800 E Macarthur Road
Wichita, KS 67216
Phone: 316-524-0730

Wise Buys
RR 2 Box 33A
Beloit, KS 67420
Phone: 785-738-4333

Kentucky

City Salvage and Recycling
2495 Greenville Road
Hopkinsville, KY
Phone: 270-886-5606

Hedges Demolition
3201 W. Highway 146
LaGrange, KY 40031
Phone: 502-222-0779
Fax: 502-222-7258

Joe Ley Antiques, Inc.
615 Market Street
Louisville, KY 40202
Phone: 502-583-4041

Salvage Building Materials of Lexington
573 Angliana Avenue
Lexington, KY 40508
Phone: 859-255-4700

WD Architectural Salvage
618 E Broadway Street
Louisville, KY 40202
Phone: 502-589-0670

Louisiana

Antique Woods and Architecturals
113 Heymann Boulevard
Lafayette, LA 70503
Phone: 337-291-1139

Architectural Antiques Materials Company
871 Polk Street
New Orleans, LA 70124
Phone: 504-942-7000

Armadillo South Architectural
4801 Washington Avenue
New Orleans, LA 70125
Phone: 504-486-1150

Builders Antique Menagerie Co.
7925 Tom Drive
Baton Rouge, LA 70806
Phone: 225-925-9582
Fax: 225-925-9506

Carrollton Brick Co.
535 Iris Avenue
New Orleans, LA 70121
Phone: 504-835-0074

Carrollton Lumber and Wrecking Company
2938 Leonidas Street
New Orleans, LA 70118
Phone: 504-861-3681
Fax: 504-861-2681
Email: ContactUs@CarrolltonLumber.com
Website: www.carrolltonlumber.com

Discount Building Materials and Salvage
905 N Lee Road
Covington, LA 70433
Phone: 985-898-2164

Green Project
520 S Alexander Street
New Orleans, LA 70119
Phone: 504-488-6853

Habitat ReStore New Orleans
2830 Royal Street
New Orleans, LA 70117
Phone: 504-943-2240
Fax: 504-943-2214
Email: restore@habitat-nola.org
Website: www habitat-nola.org/restore

HFH St. Tammany West
P.O. Box 3082
Covington, LA 70434
Phone: 504-893-3172

Louisiana Antique Woods
101 Templeton Drive
Lafayette, LA 70508
Phone: 337-269-1933

Ole Fashion Things
402 SW Evangeline Trailway
Lafayette, LA 70501
Phone: 337-234-4800

Ricca & Puderer Demolishing
& Building Materials
2645 Toulouse Street
New Orleans, LA 70119
Phone: 504-822-8200

Second Chance Construction Salvage
403 Richard Street
Gretna, LA 70053
Phone: 504-367-7717

Southern Specialty Contractors
210 Baronne Street
New Orleans, LA 70118
Phone: 504-525-4911

The Architectural Antiques Bank
1824 Felicity Street
New Orleans, LA 70113
Phone: 504-523-2702
Fax: 504-523-6055

Used Building Materials (UMS)—Con.

The Wreckers Warehouse
401 Short Street
New Orleans, LA 70118
Phone: 504-525-4911

Tiger Antique Woods
12539 S Choctaw Drive
Baton Rouge, LA 70815
Phone: 225-275-9132

Vintage Woods
301 Pecan Drive
Denham Springs, LA 70726
Phone: 225-665-0017

White Lumber and Architectural
Demolition
950 S Genois Street
New Orleans, LA 70112
Phone: 504-486-7576
Email: whitelumber@hotmail.com
Species: Longleaf pine, Oak, Cypress

Maine

Aroostock Building Materials Bank
4 Lombard Road P.O. Box 748
Caribou, ME 04736
Phone: 207-498-2575
Website: www.ccmaine.org/building-
materials html

Building Materials Exchange
169 Lewiston Road
Gray, ME 04039
Phone: 207-657-2957
Fax: 209-657-5910

Decorum
231 Commercial Street
Portland, ME 04101
Phone: 207-775-3346
Website: www.decorumonesource.com

Frederick Non-Profit Building Supply, Inc.
5813 Buckeystown Pike
Frederick, ME 21701
Phone: 301-662-2988

Interstate Building Salvage
307 Stanley Road
New Vineyard, ME 04956
Phone: 207-778-9340

Maine Antique Structures
Salvage Company
280 Rockland Street
Rockport, ME 04856
Phone: 207-594-0607

Maine Housing & Building
Materials Exchange
169 Lewiston Road
Gray, ME 04039
Phone: 207-657-2957
Fax: 207-657-5910
Email: MHBME169@yahoo.com
Website: www mainebme.org

Mid Coast HFH ReStore
93 Chestnut Street
Camden, ME 04843
Phone: 207-236-4974

Old House Parts Co.
24 Blue Wave Mall
Kennebunk, ME 04043
Phone: 207-985-1999
Fax: 207-985-1911
Email: restoration@oldhouseparts.com
Website: www.oldhouseparts.com

Penney Pincher Discount
24 Hartland Avenue
Pittsfield, ME 04967
Phone: 207-487-3696

Portland Architectural Salvage
919 Congress Street
Portland, ME 04101
Phone: 207-780-0634
Website: www.portlandsalvage.com

Seacoast Architectural Salvage
5 Lime
Rockport, ME 04856
Phone: 207-594-4836

Maryland

Newel Post
7600 Jefferson Avenue
Landover, MD 20785
Phone: 301-627-4499
Website: www.pghct.org/newelpost html

Second Chance
1645 Warner Street
Baltimore, MD 21230
Phone: 410-385-1101
Email: info@secondchanceinc.org
Website: www.secondchanceinc.org

The Loading Dock
2523 Gwynns Falls Parkway
Baltimore, MD 21216
Phone: 410-728-3625
Fax: 410-728-3633
Email: stafford@loadingdock.org
Website: www.loadingdock.org

Massachusetts

A Shapiro & Sons Inc.
341 Ashland Street
North Adams, MA 01247
Phone: 413-663-6525

Architechtural Timber and Millwork
49 Mount Warner Road
Hadley, MA 01035
Phone: 413-586-3045
Fax: 413-586-3046
Email: tmh@atimber.com
Website: www.atimber.com

Associated Building Wreckers Inc.
352 Albany Street
Springfield, MA 01105
Phone: 413-732-3179
Fax: 413-734-6224

Boston's ReStore inc.
P.O. Box 240881
Dorchester, MA 02124
Phone: 617-288-8400
Email: bperkins@bostonrestore.org
Website: www.bostonrestore.org

Building Materials Resource Center
100 Terrace Street
Boston, MA 02120
Phone: 617-442-8917
Fax: 617-427-2491
Email: info@bbmc.com
Website: www.bostonbmrc.org

Central Building Salvage Corp.
141 Boston Street
Everett, MA 02149
Phone: 617-387-3700

Colonial Barn Restoration
269 Old Bay Road
Bolton, MA 01740
Phone: 978-779-9865
Email: Tim@ColonialBarn.com
Website: www.colonialbarn.com

Hercules Building Wrecking
138 Wilder Street
Brockton, MA 02401
Phone: 508-588-3390
Fax: 508-580-0334

JC Antique Boards and Beams
P.O. Box 2079
Nantucket, MA 02554
Phone: 508-325-8808

Used Building Materials (UMS)—Con.

Neptune Demolition Corporation
70 Tenney Street
Georgetown, MA 01883
Phone: 978-352-6210

Nor'East Architectural Antiques
5 Market Square
Amesbury, MA 01913
Phone: 978-834-9088
Fax: 978-499-7136
Email: mail@noreast1.com
Website: www noreast1.com

Old Mansions
1305 Blue Hill Avenue
Mattapan, MA 02126
Phone: 617-296-0445

Old Woods Limited
202 N Spencer Road
Spencer, MA 01562
Phone: 508-885-6000

Restoration Resources
31 Thayer Street
Boston, MA 02118
Phone: 617-542-3033
Fax: 617-542-3034
Website:
http://members.aol.com/wcrres/index htm

ReStore Home Improvement Center
250 Albany Rear
Springfield, MA 01105
Phone: 413-788-6900
Fax: 413-788-6909
Email: hollym@cetonline.org
Website: www restoreonline.org

South Mountain Company
P.O. Box 1260
West Tisbury, MA 02575
Phone: 508-693-4850

South Shore HFH ReStore
28 River Street
Braintree, MA 02184
Phone: 781-843-9080

The Olde Bostonian Architectural Antiques
66 Von Hillern Street
Dorchester, MA 02125
Phone: 617-282-9300
Fax: 617-282-3565
Email: anthgr01@aol.com
Website: www.oldbostonian.com

Michigan

Architectural Salvage Wing-Grand Illusion
201 E Michigan Avenue
Grass Lake, MI 49240
Phone: 517-522-8715
Email: leede1@aol.com

D&M Wrecking Company, Inc./Axxiom, Inc.
250 S 4th Street
Kalamazoo, MI 49009
Phone: 616-375-1313
Fax: 616-375-2767

Detroit Building Materials
1551 Rosa Parks Boulevard
Detroit, MI 48216
Phone: 313-965-6520

Habitat ReStore Detroit
2718 Rosa Parks Boulevard
Detroit, MI 48216-1213
Phone: 313-891-7867
Email: jacob@ic.org

Heritage Architectural Salvage and Supply
150 N Edwards Street
Kalamazoo, MI 49009
Phone: 269-385-1004

Heritage Building and Materials Co.
13136 Puritan Street
Detroit, MI 48227
Phone: 313-345-3711

Home Repair Services
1100 S Division Avenue
Grand Rapids, MI 49507
Phone: 616-241-2601
Fax: 616-241-5151
Email: info@homerepairservices.org
Website: www homerepairservices.org

K D Used Brick & Building Material
10244 Harper Avenue
Detroit, MI 48213
Phone: 313-923-4129

Larry's Building Materials
13855 Grand River
Detroit, MI 48227
Phone: 313-273-4699
Fax: 313-272-8090

Materials Unlimited
2 W. Michigan Avenue
Ypsilanti, MI 48197
Phone: 734-483-6980; 800-299-9462
Fax: 734-482-3636
Email: materials@materialsunlimted.com
Website: www materialsunlimted.com

Motorcity Building Materials Center
4485 W Jefferson Avenue
Detroit, MI 48209
Phone: 313-843-7540

Odom Re-Use and Consulting
5555 Brentwood Avenue N
Grawn, MI 49637
Phone: 231-276-6330
Email: reusebruce@coslink net
Website: www.odomreuse.com

Recycle Ann Arbor
2420 S Industrial
Ann Arbor, MI 48104
Phone: 734-662-6288
Fax: 734-662-6649
Email: richard@recycleannarbor.org
Website: www recycleannarbor.org

Minnesota

All State Salvage Inc.
1354 Jackson Street
St. Paul, MN 55101
Phone: 651-488-6675

Architectural Antiques
1330 Quincy Street NE
Minneapolis, MN 55413
Phone: 612-332-8344
Fax: 612-332-8967
Email: sales@archantiques.com
Website: www.archantiques.com

Bauer Brothers Salvage
2432 2nd Street N
Minneapolis, MN 55411
Phone: 612-331-9492
Fax: 612-521-0494

City Salvage Antiques
505 1st Avenue NE
Minneapolis, MN 55413
Phone: 612-627-9107
Email: mail@citysalvage.com
Website: www.citysalvage.com

F.M. Frattalone Excavating
3066 Spruce Street
St. Paul, MN 55117
Phone: 651-484-0448
Fax: 651-484-7839
Email: jimw@fmfrattalone.com
Website: www fmfrattalone.com
Species: Pine, Fir, Oak

Guilded Salvage Antiques
1315 Tyler Street NE
Minneapolis, MN 55413
Phone: 612-789-1680
Fax: 612-789-1688

Used Building Materials (UMS)—Con.

North Shore Architectural Antiques
521 7th Street
Two Harbors, MN 55616
Phone: 218-834-0018
Email: jmccarthy@frontiernet net
Website: www.north-shore-architectural-antiques.com

PPL Shop
850 15th Avenue NE
Minneapolis, MN 55413
Phone: 612-789-3322
Fax: 612-789-2319

The Reuse Center
2216 E Lake Street
Minneapolis, MN 55407
Phone: 612-724-2608
Fax: 612-724-2288
Email: JanetMester@Greeninstitude.org
Website:
www.greeninstitude.org/reusecenter.htm

Mississippi

Back Road Architectural Salvage Services
836 C Ridgewood Road Ext
Ridgeland, MS 39157
Phone: 601-957-3777
Email: cjej@a2ldial.net

Gibsons Demolition Inc.
52 Minor Street
Natchez, MS 39120
Phone: 601-445-2214

H & K Salvage
14391 Highway 49
Gulfport, MS 39503
Phone: 228-832-9499

Metro Jackson HFH ReStore
P.O. Box 55634
Jackson, MS 39296-5634
Phone: 601-353-6000

T & E Salvage-Buy & Sell
13015 Highway 67
Biloxi, MS 39532
Phone: 228-392-9814

Missouri

Anderson Fine Carpentry and Salvage
228 W. 4th Street
Kansas City, MO 64111
Phone: 816-531-5976
Email: TheThaine@aol.com

Anderson Fine Carpentry and Salvage
228 W. 4th Street
Kansas City, MO 64111
Phone: 816-531-5976
Email: TheThaine@aol.com

Ben Tarbe Used Brick Inc.
1202 Genessee Street
Kansas City, MO 66102
Phone: 913-432-9726

Century Used Brick
12982 Maurer Industrial Drive
Sappington, MO 63127
Phone: 314-843-1213
Fax: 314-843-9203

Chuck's Stone and Brick Co.
2955 S Brentwood
St Louis, MO 63144
Phone: 314-968-2230
Fax: 314-968-7591
Email: cbrickston@aol.com

Fellenz Antiques and Architectural
Artifacts
439 N. Euclid Avenue
St. Louis, MO 63108
Phone: 314-367-0214

Habitat for Humanity ReStore
4535 W Chestnut Expressway
Springfield, MO 65802
Phone: 417-829-4001
Fax: 417-829-4003
Email: restore@drury.edu
Website: www.habitatrestore.com

Habitat ReStore
4701 Deramus
Kansas City, MO 64120
Phone: 816-231-6889

Hardico
Suite 130, 112 W Jefferson
Kirkwood, MO 63122
Phone: 314-965-3535
Fax: 314-965-7333
Email: hardico@swbell net

Mack Circle Used Brick and Wrecking
1414 Marcus Avenue
St. Louis, MO 63113
Phone: 314-531-2997

Perhat Lumber Co.
6023 S Broadway
St Louis, MO 63111
Phone: 314-481-9302

Peterson Wrecking Used Lumber
2008 Aull Lane
Lexington, MO 64067
Phone: 660-259-6500

St. Louis HFH ReStore
3763 Forest Park Avenue
St. Louis, MO 63108
Phone: 314-531-4155

Montana

Industrial Salvage and Demolition
P.O. Box 17767
Missoula, MT 59808
Phone: 406-543-8893

Nebraska

MT Salvage
3717 S 66th Street
Omaha, NE 68106
Phone: 402-391-5315

RPM Salvage
1109 Bellevue Boulevard
Omaha, NE 68005
Phone: 402-346-4470

Nevada

Phil's Salvage Emporium
1131 S Main Street
Las Vegas, NV 89104
Phone: 702-382-7528

Roldan Construction, Inc.
3280 W Hacienda Avenue
Las Vegas, NV 89118
Phone: 702-739-DEMO
Fax: 702-739-6909
Email: Jerry@roldaninc.com
Website: www roldaninc.com

New Hampshire

Admac Salvage
111 Saranac Street
Littleton, NH 03561
Phone: 603-444-1200
Website: www.musar.com/trader/admac.html

Architectural Salvage
3 Mill Street
Exeter, NH 03833
Phone: 603-773-5635
Email: arch@ttlc net
Website: www.oldhousesalvage.com

Used Building Materials (UMS)—Con.

Renovators Supply
P.O. Box 2515
Conway, NH 03818
Phone: 413-423-3737

Vermont Salvage
2 Lumber Lane
Manchester, NH 03102
Phone: 603-624-0868

New Jersey

Contractors Surplus
931 Asbury Avenue
Asbury Park, NJ 07712
Phone: 732-974-2871

Joseph Fazzio Inc.
2760 Glassboro Cross Keys Road
Glassboro, NJ 08028
Phone: 856-881-3185

Recycling the Past
381 N Main Street
Barnegat, NJ 08005
Phone: 609-660-9790
Fax: 800-878-3251
Email: whitey99@cybercomm net
Website: www recyclingthepast.com

Relics Reconstruction: Architectural Salvage
201 Church Street
Millburn, NJ 07041
Phone: 201-376-4745

Restoration Materials Company
1260 New Market Avenue
South Plainfield, NJ 07080
Phone: 800-336-6548

Trenton Materials Exchange
800 New York Avenue
Trenton, NJ 08638
Phone: 609-278-0033

New Mexico

Coronado Wrecking & Salvage Co.
4200 Broadway Boulevard Swest
Albuquerque, NM 87105
Phone: 505-877-2821

Frontier Wood
4523 State Highway 14
Sante Fe, NM 87508
Phone: 505-474-9663

Habitat for Humanity
5 Roberts Circle
Los Lunas, NM 87031
Phone: 505-747-7200

Habitat for Humanity ReStore
P.O. Box 238
Espanola, NM 87532
Phone: 505-747-2690

Habitat for Humanity ReStore
1143 Siler Park Lane
Sante Fe, NM 87507
Phone: 505-473-1114

La Puerta
1302 Cerrillos Road
Santa Fe, NM 87505
Phone: 505-984-8164
Fax: 505-986-5838

Salvation Army Thrift Store
1202 Camino Carlos Rey
Santa Fe, NM 87507
Phone: 505-473-7735

New York

Antiques and Vintage Woods of America
Route 199
Pine Plains, NY 12567
Phone: 518-398-1797

Architectural Antiques
105 Anderson Avenue
Rochester, NY 14607
Phone: 585-271-6290

Architectural Salvage Warehouse
337 Berry Street
Brooklyn, NY 11211
Phone: 718-388-4527

Arlyn Lumber and Home Center
715 E 98th Street
Brooklyn, NY 11236
Phone: 718-498-0600

ARROW Reuse Center
51-02 21st Street
Long Island, NY 11101
Phone: 718-472-1180
Email: nctai@att.net
Website: www.arrowonline.org

Big Wood
P.O. Box 24
East Bethany, NY 14054
Phone: 315-986-8119
Fax: 315-986-2622
Email: larry@big-wood net
Website: www.big-wood net
Species: Longleaf pine, Fir

BJ Corelli Inc.
1941 Jerome Avenue #A
Bronx, NY 10453
Phone: 718-731-2400

Breezy Point Lumber Co.
28 Market Street
Breezy Point, NY 11697
Phone: 718-634-2600

Cat House Antiques
136 Bruceville Road
High Falls, NY 12440
Phone: 845-687-0790

Chief's Used Brick
3221 Edson Avenue
Bronx, NY 10469
Phone: 718-379-1232

Creative Look
29 W 30th Street
New York, NY 10001
Phone: 212-330-9971

Demolition Depot
216 E 125th Street
New York, NY 10035
Phone: 212-860-1138
Fax: 212-860-1560
Email: info@demolitiondepot.com
Website: www.demolitiondepot.com

Dorp Salvage Co.
566 Broadway
Schenectady, NY 12305
Phone: 518-393-1744

Environmental Construction Outfitters
901 E 134th Street
Bronx, NY 10454
Phone: 800-238-5008
Website: www.environproducts.com

Gothic City Architectural Antiques
1940 Niagra Street
Buffalo, NY 14207
Phone: 716-874-4479
Fax: 716-875-1209
Email: charley@gothiccity.com
Website: www.gothiccity.com
Species: Heartpine, Oak, Walnut

Used Building Materials (UMS)—Con.

Grossman Lumber Co.
P.O. Box 772
Manhasset, NY 11030
Phone: 718-251-1020

Historic Albany Foundation
Architectural Parts
89 Lexington Avenue
Albany, NY 12206
Phone: 518-465-2987

Historic Home Supply
215 River Street
Troy, NY 12180
Phone: 518-266-0675
Fax: 518-266-0810
Email: homedupply@earthlink net
Website: www homesupply.com

Horsefeathers Architectural Antiques
346 Connecticut Street
Buffalo, NY 14213
Phone: 716-882-1581
Fax: 716-882-0215
Email: horsehoe@buffnet net
Website: www horsefeathers-antiques.com

House Parts
540 South Avenue
Rochester, NY 14620
Phone: 716-325-2329
Fax: 716-325-3613
Email: houseparts@msn.com

Hudson Valley Materials Exchange
1101 First Street
New Windsor, NY 12553
Phone: 845-567-1445
Fax: 845-567-1536
Website: www hvmaterialsexchange.com

Irreplaceable Artifacts
14 Second Avenue
New York, NY 10003
Phone: 212-777-2900

Legacy Antique Woods
114 Sibley Road
Honeoye Falls, NY 14472
Phone: 585-624-1011
Fax: 716-624-1094
Email: legacywood99@aol.com
Website: www.legacyantiquewoods.com
Species: Chestnut, Heartpine, Oak

Olde Good Things
124 W 24th Street
New York, NY 10011
Phone: 212-989-8401
Fax: 212-463-8005
Email: mail@oldegoodthings.com
Website: www.oldegoodthings.com

Pioneer Millworks
1180 Commercial Drive
Farmington, NY 14425
Phone: 585-924-9970
Fax: 585-924-9962
Email: jonathen@pioneermillworks.com
Website: www.pioneermillworks.com

Pittsford Lumber and Woodshop
50 State Street
Pittsford, NY 14534
Phone: 585-586-1877
Fax: 585-586-1934

ReHouse Inc.
1840 Kennedy Road
Webster, NY 14580
Phone: 585-872-1450
Email: scamprath@rehouseny.com
Website: www rehouseny.com

Shaver Brothers
32 Perrine Street
Auburn, NY 13021
Phone: 800-564-7206
Email: pjguerrette@a-znet.com

Significant Elements / Historic Ithaca, Inc.
212 Center Street
Ithaca, NY 14850
Phone: 607-277-3450
Fax: 607-273-4816
Email: elements@lightlink.com
Website: www.significantelements.org

Siwek Contractors
4340 Park Avenue
Bronx, NY 10457
Phone: 718-364-1400

Urban Archaeology
143 Franklin Street
New York, NY 10013
Phone: 212-431-4646
Fax: 212-343-9312

Vintage Barns, Woods & Restoration
333 Mossy Brook Road
High Falls, NY 12440
Phone: 845-340-9870
Fax: 845-339-4573
Email: info@vintagewoods.com
Website: www.vintagewoods.com
Species: Pine–white, Cypress, Oak

Zaborski Emporium
27 Hoffman Street
Kingston, NY 12401
Phone: 845-338-6465
Fax: 845-338-6465
Email: ZaborskiEmporium@aol.com
Website: www.stanthejunkman.com

North Carolina

Airedale Woodworks LLC
P.O. Box 307
Murfreesboro, NC 27855
Phone: 800-489-0639
Fax: 252-398-8429
Email: sales@airedalewoodworks.com
Website: www.airedalewoodworks.com

Architectural Salvage
P.O. Box 220193
Charlotte, NC 28222
Phone: 704-552-7560

Architectural Salvage of Greensboro
300 W Bellemeade Street
Greensboro, NC 27402
Phone: 336-389-9118
Email: asg@blandwood.org

Asheville Architectural Salvage
23 Rankin Avenue
Asheville, NC 28801
Phone: 828-281-2600

Asheville Recyclers
19 Biltmore Avenue
Asheville, NC 28801
Phone: 828-254-5700

Building Supply Recycling Center
302 E Pettigrew Street
Durham, NC 27701
Phone: 919-490-0414
Email: renovatenc@aol.com

Building Supply Salvage, Inc.
2207 English Road
High Point, NC 27262
Phone: 336-889-2207

Classic Antique Wood
12431 Walkers Meadow Lane
Charlotte, NC 28273
Phone: 704-506-1955
Website: www.classicantiquewood.com
Species: Pine

Fayetteville ReStore
443 Franklin Street
Fayetteville, NC 28301
Phone: 910-322-9822

Used Building Materials (UMS)—Con.

Gideons Home Building
Materials and Salvage
1700 W Lee Street
Greensboro, NC 27403
Phone: 336-294-0789

Habitat for Humanity of Greater
New Bern Inc.
1249 Pollack Street
New Bern, NC 28560
Phone: 252-633-9599
Fax: 252-633-4632

Habitat for Humanity ReStore
P.O. Box 34397
Charlotte, NC 28234
Phone: 704-376-2054

Habitat for Humanity Reuse Center
2400 Alwin Court
Raleigh, NC 27604
Phone: 919-833-6768
Fax: 919-833-8256
Website: www.habitatwake.org

Material Salvage and Recycling
1521 Huffman Mill Road
Burlington, NC 27215
Phone: 336-584-1193

Piedmont Salvage and Equipment
4620 Hilltop Road
Greensboro, NC 27407
Phone: 336-510-6905
Email: jdsmith510@triad rr.com

Preservation Hall
55 N. Main Street
Weaverville, NC 28787
Phone: 828-645-1047
Website: www.preservation-hall.com

Renovator Supply of NC
302 E Pettigrew Street
Durham, NC 27701
Phone: 919-490-0414
Email: rensup@aol.com
Website: www renovator-nc.com

ReStore
443 Franklin Street
Fayetteville, NC 28301
Phone: 910-321-0780

Rike Wrecking Co. Inc.
1005 Rundell Street
Winston Salem, NC 27105
Phone: 336-725-8789
Fax: 336-725-8789
Species: Oak, Pine

Rocky's Material and Salvage
409 Dover Road
Kinston, NC 28501
Phone: 252-522-2424

Salvage Building Materials
951 N Liberty Street
Winston Salem, NC 27101
Phone: 336-724-1739

The Salvage House
22-24 Bonlee-Bennett Road
Bonlee, NC 27213
Phone: 919-837-2376
Email: jeff@thesalvagehouse.com
Website: www.thesalvagehouse.com

Scotland Neck Heartpine
105 Creek Street
Tarboro, NC 27886
Phone: 252-826-2755
Email: wburgwyn@yahoo.com

Third Creek Salvage Company
2067 Shelton Avenue
Statesville, NC 28677
Phone: 704-872-7502
Fax: 704-872-9247
Email: wes@thirdcreeksalvage.com
Website: www.thirdcreeksalvage.com

Vintage Beams and Timbers
Architectural Salvage
P.O. Box 548
Sylva, NC 28779
Phone: 828-586-0755
Fax: 828-586-4647
Email: info@vintagebeamsandtimbers.com
Website: www.vintagebeamsandtimbers.com

Waughton Millwork and Salvage
Building Material
215 Cassell Street
Winston Salem, NC 27127
Phone: 336-788-0990

Wilmington Architectural Salvage
20 Brunswick Street
Wilmington, NC
Phone: 910-762-2511

Yesterday's Windows
327 Haywood Road
Asheville, NC 28806
Phone: 828-259-9936
Fax: 828-259-9936

Ohio

Acme Construction Services
3104 Syracuse Street
Cincinnati, OH 45206
Phone: 513-281-5151

Allied Erecting and Dismantling
2100 Poland Av
Youngstown, OH 44502
Phone: 330-744-0808
Fax: 330-744-3218
Email: info@aed.cc
Website: www.aed.cc

Angelo Building Wreckers
375 W Park Avenue
Columbus, OH 43223
Phone: 614-279-9700

Architectural Artifacts
20 S Ontario Street
Toledo, OH 43602
Phone: 419-243-6916
Fax: 419-243-0094
Email: architectural@speedvox net

B and B Wrecking and Excavating Inc.
5801 Train Avenue
Cleveland, OH 44102
Phone: 216-651-9090
Fax: 216-651-9095
Email: bandbwrecking@ameritech.net
Website: www.bbwrecking.com

Broadway Contracting Inc.
3950 E 89th Street
Cleveland, OH 44105
Phone: 800-709-4129
Fax: 216-271-3944
Email: ger1056@aol.com
Website: www.broad3939.com

Buckeye Wrecking
1800 19th Street NE
Canton, OH 44714
Phone: 330-445-0088

Build It Again Center
3529 Cleveland Avenue
Columbus, OH 43224
Phone: 614-267-7778
Fax: 614-267-6655
Email: biac@habitat-columbus.org
Website: www.habitat-columbus.org

Used Building Materials (UMS)—Con.

Habitat for Humanity ReStore
3529 Cleveland Avenue
Columbus, OH 43224
Phone: 614-267-7778

Habitat for Humanity ReStore
1041 S Patterson Boulevard
Dayton, OH 45402
Phone: 937-586-0860

L & L Demolition Excavating Inc.
715 Dayton Road
Springfield, OH 45506
Phone: 937-324-0122

Lincoln Street Salvage
14657 Lincoln Street SE
Minerva, OH 44657
Phone: 330-868-1375

Loewendick's
4248 Linnville Road
Health, OH 43056
Phone: 740-323-3127

Murphy's Plumbing Supplies
1927 Dryden Road
Dayton, OH 45439
Phone: 937-293-1142

National Salvage Supply, Inc.
1668 Copley Road
Akron, OH 44320
Phone: 330-922-9844

North Hill Salvage Store
813 Elma Street
Akron, OH 44310
Phone: 330-762-4509

Rex Salvage Store
1201 S Arlington Street
Akron, OH 44306
Phone: 330-773-8605

Salvage II
22045 Bates Road
Minerva, OH 44567
Phone: 330-868-3137

Salvage Masters
445 Fairport Nursery Road
Painesville, OH 44077
Phone: 440-942-8769
Email: salvagemasters@roundOhio
Website: http://webpost net/te/teammaker/
Salvage/quicktakes htm

Stark Wrecking Company
7081 Germantown Pike
Miamisburg, OH 45342
Phone: 937-866-5032

Stock Pile The
1387 Claredon Avenue SW
Canton, OH 44710
Phone: 330-455-4585

The Stone Salvage Company
Cleveland, OH 44077
Phone: 440-352-7686
Fax: 440-357-7076
Email: stonemaon@stonemason.com
Website: www.stonesalvage.com

United Salvage Co.
921 Hazel Street
Akron, OH 44305
Phone: 330-253-2403

Valley Building Materials The
2000 State Avenue
Cincinnati, OH 45214
Phone: 513-921-2822

Oklahoma

Apache Lumber Co.
2703 E Apache Street
Tulsa, OK 74110
Phone: 918-425-0295

Architectural Antiques
1900 Linwood Boulevard
Oklahoma City, OK 73106
Phone: 405-232-0759

Bibler Brothers Lumber Co.
5500 NW Texas
Idabel, OK 74745
Phone: 580-286-9470

Central Oklahoma HFH ReStore
1025 N. Broadway Avenue
Oklahoma City, OK 73102
Phone: 405-524-7151

Cherry Trucking and Wrecking
13336 NW Expressway Street
Piedmont, OK 73078
Phone: 405-373-2555

Cleveland County HfH
1835 Industrial Boulevard
Norman, OK 73069
Phone: 405-360-7868

Dawson Building Supply
5519 E Tecumseh Street
Tulsa, OK 74115
Phone: 918-832-0071
Fax: 918-835-4788
Species: Pine, Fir

Friendly Plumbing
15 SE 23rd Street
Oklahoma City, OK 73129
Phone: 405-236-1151

Habitat Renovation Station
1800 Broadway Avenue
Oklahoma City, OK 73103
Phone: 405-232-5592

Midwest Wrecking Company
P.O. Box 3757
Edmond, OK 73083
Phone: 405-478-8833

Shanbour Lindy
530 S Broadway Avenue
Oklahoma City, OK 73109
Phone: 405-239-7749

Tulsa Metro Area HFH ReStore
P.O. Box 1357
Tulsa, OK 74101
Phone: 918-592-4224

Oregon

1874 House Antiques
8070 SE 13th Avenue
Portland, OR 97202
Phone: 503-233-1874
Email: 1874store@aol.com

Asher Traditional Homes
15795 SW Serena Court
Portland, OR 97224
Phone: 503-620-6163

Aurora Mills Architectural Salvage
14971 1st Street NE
Aurora, OR 97002
Phone: 503-678-6083

Bend Area Habitat ReStore
540 NE 1st Street
Bend, OR 97702
Phone: 541-312-6709
Fax: 541-749-2553
Website: www.bendhabitat.org

Used Building Materials (UMS)—Con.

Brady Peeks Enterprises
P.O. Box 101
Curtin, OR 97428
Phone: 541-942-2079

BRING Recycling
86641 Franklin Boulevard
Eugene, OR 97403
Phone: 541-746-3023
Fax: 541-746-3023
Email: davidw@bringrecycling.org
Website: www.bringrecycling.org

Builders City
8905 N Vancouver Avenue
Portland, OR 97217
Phone: 503-285-0546
Fax: 503-240-1691

Capital Products
P.O. Box 719
Philomath, OR 97370
Phone: 541-929-5308

Craftmark Reclaimed Wood
P.O. Box 237
McMinnville, OR 97128
Phone: 503-472-6929
Fax: 503-472-5150
Website: www.craftmarkinc.com

Crosscut Hardwoods
3065 NW Front Avenue
Portland, OR 97210
Phone: 503-224-9663
Fax: 503-227-4670

Dillon & Associates inc
2545 SW Spring Garden Street
Portland, OR 97219
Phone: 503-244-2822

Environmental Building Supplies
819 SE Taylor Street
Portland, OR 97214
Phone: 503-222-3881
Fax: 503-222-3756
Email: ebs@ecohaus.com
Website: www.ecohaus.com

Gilmer Wood Company
2211 NW St. Helens Road
Portland, OR 97210
Phone: 503-274-1271
Fax: 503-274-9839
Email: gilmerwood@aol.com
Website: www.gilmerwood.com

Grand & Benedicts Annex
111 SE Belmont Street
Portland, OR 97214
Phone: 503-234-3792

Heartwood ReSources
355 Atlanta Street
Roseburg, OR 97470
Phone: 541-673-4070
Fax: 541-673-4223
Email: heartwoodre-
sources@umpquacdc.org
Website: www heartwoodresources.com

HfH ReStore
141 S Wasson Street
Coos Bay, OR 97420
Phone: 541-888-1103

HfH ReStore
740 NE 1st Street
Bend, OR 97701
Phone: 541-312-6709

HfH Restore
Box 11527
Portland, OR 97211
Phone: 503-283-6247

Hippo Hardware and Trading Company
1040 E Burnside Street
Portland, OR 97214
Phone: 503-231-1444
Fax: 503-201-5078
Website: www.hipponet.com

J & J Property Investments Corp.
Portland, OR 97223
Phone: 503-639-9584

Knez Building Materials
12301 SE Highway 212
Clacmus, OR 97223
Phone: 503-655-1991

Leslie Larry Lewisburg Auction
& Gen Store
5830 Northwest Highway 99
Corvallis, OR 97330
Phone: 541-745-5373

Morrow's Used Building Materials
2784 Jacksonville Highway # B
Medford, OR 97401
Phone: 541-770-6867

Oregon Breakers Inc. Wholesale
1926 SE 10th Avenue
Portland, OR 97214
Phone: 503-736-0921

Pakit Liquidators
903 Seast Armour Drive
Bend, OR 97702
Phone: 541-389-7047

Peddle'n Pete Secondhand Store
& Used Lumber
212 W Front
Merrill, OR 97633
Phone: 541-798-1037

Rejuvenation House Parts
1100 Seast Grand Avenue
Portland, OR 97214
Phone: 503-238-1900
Email: www rejuvenation.com

Storie Steel and Wood Products Co.
P.O. Box 12490
Portland, OR 97212
Phone: 503-287-1775
Fax: 503-282-9884
Email: clearcut@earthlink.net

The ReBuilding Center
3625 N. Mississippi Avenue
Portland, OR 97227
Phone: 503-331-1877
Fax: 503-331-1873
Website: www rebuildingcenter.org

Pennsylvania

A-1 New & Used Plumbing & Heating
30 Prospect Street
Somerville, PA 02143
Phone: 617-625-6140
Fax: 617-718-0827
Email: a-1plumbimg@rcn.com
Website:
www.antiqueplumbingandradiators.com

Aged Woods
2331 E Market Street, Suite 6
York, PA 17402
Phone: 800-233-9307
Fax: 717-840-1468
Email: info@agedwoods.com
Website: www.agedwoods.com

Antique Wood and Colonial Restoration
1273 Redding Avenue
Boyer Town, PA 19512
Phone: 610-367-8193
Fax: 610-367-6911
Email: antiquewds@aol.com
Website: vintagewoods.com
Species: Cypress, Hemlock, Pine

Used Building Materials (UMS)—Con.

Antique Woods
1600 Chestnut Tree Road
Elverson, PA 19520
Phone: 610-942-0973

Architectural Antiques Exchange
715 N 2nd Street
Philadelphia, PA 19123
Phone: 215-922-3669
Fax: 215-922-3680
Email: aaexchange@aol.com
Website: www.architectualantiques.com

Architectural Emporium
207 Adams Avenue
Canonsburg, PA 15317
Phone: 724-746-4301

Authentic Wood Floors
2301 N Cameron Street
Harrisburg, PA 17110
Phone: 717-234-0812

Bambi Used Brick
520 E Fornance Street
Norristown, PA 19401
Phone: 610-275-5777

Barnguys Recycled Materials, Inc.
PA
Phone: 610-847-2616
Email: thebarnguy@aol.com
Website: www.barnguys.com

Barnwood Connection (The)
91 Bull Road
Barto, PA 19504
Phone: 610-845-3101
Fax: 610-845-3167
Email: info@barnwoodconnection.com
Website: www.barnwoodconnection.com

Conklin's Authentic Antique Barnwood
RD 1 Box 70
Susquehanna, PA 18847
Phone: 717-465-3832
Fax: 717-465-3832
Website: www.conklinsbarnwood.com

Construction Junction
214 N Lexington Avenue
Pittsburgh, PA 15201
Phone: 412-243-5025
Fax: 412-243-5026
Website: www.constructionjunction.org
Species: Oak, Pine, Cherry

Cronin Builders and Supply
11106 Terry HWY P.O. 436
Meadville, PA 16335
Phone: 814-336-4523

Delaware Valley Recycling
3107 S. 61st Street
Philadelphia, PA 19153
Phone: 215-724-2244

Habitat ReStore of Lancaster County
1520 Lincoln Highway E
Lancaster, PA 17602
Phone: 717-293-0250

Lelinski John
729 Main Street
Bristol, PA 19007
Phone: 215-945-2475

LS Sadler Inc.
150 Sadler Drive
Indiana, PA 15701
Phone: 724-463-3044

Mayse Woodworking Company
319 Richardson Road
Lansdale, PA 19446
Phone: 215-822-8307
Fax: 215-822-8307
Species: Heartpine, Longleaf pine, Hemlock

Merritt's Antiques
1860 Weaverton Road
Douglassville, PA 19518
Phone: 610-689-9541
Fax: 610-689-4538

Olde Good Things
400 Gilligan Street
Scranton, PA 18508
Phone: 570-341-7668
Email: mail@oldegoodthings.com
Website: www.oldegoodthings.com

Recycle Shack
814 2nd Avenue
Royersford, PA 19468
Phone: 484-686-7641
Email: recycall@hotmail.com

ReStore
3016 E. Thompson Street
Philadelphia, PA 19134
Phone: 215-634-3474

Russo Demolition & Salvage
800 31st Street
Altoona, PA 16602
Phone: 814-946-3215
Fax: 814-946-3176

Sahd Frank Salvage
1045 Lancaster Avenue
Columbia, PA 17512
Phone: 717-684-8506
Email: fpuzz@aol.com
Website: www.demolition-salvage.com
Species: Pine

Stauffer & Sons Inc.
33 Glenola Drive
Leola, PA 17540
Phone: 717-656-2811

Sylvan Brandt LLC Resawn
& Antique Floors
651 E Main Street
Lititz, PA 17543
Phone: 717-626-4520
Fax: 717-626-5867
Email: dean@sylvanbrandt.com

Tullytown Metal & Iron Company
729 Main Street
Bristol, PA 19007
Phone: 215-945-2475

U.S. Recycling and Wrecking
390 Eckman Road
Lancaster, PA 17603
Phone: 717-393-2992
Fax: 717-464-1845

Victorian Memories
313 13th Street
Franklin, PA 16323
Phone: 814-437-9450
Email: Vmpostman@aol.com

W. W. Charles & Daughters Inc.
252 Hollow Road
New Providence, PA 17560
Phone: 717-786-3738

Rhode Island

AA Wrecking & Asbestos Abatement
1307 Hartford Avenue
Johnston, RI 02919
Phone: 401-351-1188

Columbus Door Co.
1884 Elmwood Avenue
Warwick, RI 02888
Phone: 401-781-7792
Fax: 408-467-3620

National Wrecking Company
64 Grotto Street
Pawtucket, RI 02860
Phone: 401-723-1545
Fax: 401-723-1547

Used Building Materials (UMS)—Con.

New England Architectural Center
334 Knight Street
Warwick, RI 02885
Phone: 401-732-1383
Email: ne_architectural@att net
Website: www nearchitecturalcenter.com

South Carolina

Antique Hardware and Home
19 Buckingham Plantation Drive
Buffington, SC 29910
Phone: 800-422-9982
Website: www.antiquehardware.com

Big Wood
SC
Phone: 864-898-1655
Fax: 864-898-1675
Website: www.big-wood net

Carolina Building Materials and Salvage
2440 Meeting Street Road
Charleston, SC 29405
Phone: 843-744-2575

Charleston Wrecking Co.
Charleston, SC 29401
Phone: 843-723-1322

Cogan's Antiques
110 N Palmer Street
Ridgeway, SC 29130
Phone: 803-337-3939

H&H Fencing and Salvage
739 Bruce Street
Columbia, SC 29223
Phone: 803-736-6631

HFH ReStore
122 Maxwell Avenue
Greenwood, SC 29646
Phone: 864-953-9880

HfH-Sumter ReStore
30 Bridge Court
Sumter, SC 29150
Phone: 803-934-9749

Old House Salvage
95 Big Survey Road
Piedmont, SC 29673
Phone: 864-243-5990

Sea Island HFH ReStore
3487 McGill Court
Johns Island, SC 29455-7232
Phone: 803-768-0998

Wild Clover Reclamation & Lumber Co., Inc.
P.O. Box 101
Murrells Inlet, SC 29576
Phone: 803-237-5490
Fax: 803-237-5091

Wolverine Brass Inc.
2951 Highway 501 E
Conway, SC 29526
Phone: 843-347-3122

South Dakota

Architectural Elements
818 E 8th Street
Sioux Falls, SD 57103
Phone: 605-339-9646
Email: architecturalelements@mail.com
Species: Fir, Oak

Materials Clearance and Salvage
1109 Creek Drive
Rapid City, SD 57701
Phone: 605-343-1993
Fax: 605-343-1993

Second Chance Lumber
Viborg, SD 57070
Phone: 605-766-5145
Email: mellamy001@yahoo.com

Tennessee

American Heritage Preservation
1869 Highway 52 E
Portland, TN 37148
Phone: 888-427-2276
Fax: 615-325-2701
Email: nbced@mindspring.com
Website:
www.americanheritagepreservation.com
Species: Oak, Chestnut

Architectural Exchange
1300 McCallie Avenue
Chattanooga, TN 37405
Phone: 423-697-1243
Email: ACR1300@aol.com
Website: http://mywebpages.comcast.net/
tnhotairpilot/archex/index html

Bob's Salvage
756 Old Hickory
Jackson, TN 38305
Phone: 731-668-9431

Boyzie Turner Coal Co.
1924 Leslie Avenue
Knoxville, TN 37921
Phone: 865-522-7902

Burnett Demolition and Salvage
1220 Prosser Road
Knoxville, TN 37914
Phone: 865-637-3996

Habitat for Humanity of Blount County
1620 W. Broadway, S215
Maryville, TN 37801
Phone: 423-458-8950

Hailey Salvage and Building Materials
1224 Dickerson Pike
Nashville, TN 37207
Phone: 615-226-0696

Hailey Salvage and Building Materials
725 Lebanon Road
Nashville, TN 37210
Phone: 615-224-9050

Havron Contracting
1513 Williams Street
Chattanooga, TN 37408
Phone: 423-265-8883
Fax: 423-265-3627
Email: havron@mindspring.com
Website: www.demolitionsalvage.com
Species: Heartpine,

HFH ReStore
169 Scott Street
Memphis, TN 38112
Phone: 901-323-9250

Holston HFH ReStore
P.O. Box 5265
Kingsport, TN 37663-0265
Phone: 423-239-7689

Knoxville HFH ReStore
2209 N Central Avenue
Knoxville, TN 37917
Phone: 423-521-4909

Loudon County HFH ReStore
204 Lakeside Plaza, Suite 115
Loudon, TN 37774
Phone: 423-458-8950

Loudon County Salvage and Building
410 Magnolia Avenue
Knoxville, TN 37917
Phone: 423-525-1926

Nashville Discount Building Materials
1400 51st Avenue N
Nashville, TN 37209
Phone: 615-292-7856

Used Building Materials (UMS)—Con.

North Hixson Salvage Door and Window
7505 Hixson Pike
Hixson, TN 37343
Phone: 423-847-6774

Regency Reclaimed Woods
5977 Old Dayton Pike
Chattanooga, TN 37415
Phone: 423-877-0879

Salvage and Building Materials
103 E Centre Stage Business
Clinton, TN 37716
Phone: 865-457-7897

Salvage Lumber Co.
2711 Western Avenue
Knoxville, TN 37921
Phone: 865-525-6645

Southeastern Salvage
6052 Lee Highway
Chattanooga, TN 37421
Phone: 423-892-5766
Fax: 423-899-4429

The Reuse Center
3010 Ambrose Avenue
Nashville, TN 37207
Phone: 615-254-6301

The Reuse Center
903 Dickerson Pike
Nashville, TN 37207
Phone: 615-650-5001

Wilmot Inc.
3654 Knollwood Road
Nashville, TN 37215
Phone: 615-533-0696
Fax: 615-385-5744
Email: Tiffany_Wilmot@Yahoo.com
Website: www.Wilmotandassoc.com

Texas

A & R Demolition
13201 Fm 812
Del Valle, TX 78617
Phone: 512-243-0512

A Full Service Co.
212 E Amarillo Boulevard
Amarillo, TX 79107
Phone: 806-379-6225

A Pallet Co.
610 E French Avenue
Temple, TX 76501
Phone: 254-742-1231

A&R Demolition Inc.
13201 FM812
Del Valle, TX 78617
Phone: 512-243-0512

AAA Salvage & Demolition
200 Corinth Street
Dallas, TX 75207
Phone: 214-428-1888
Fax: 214-428-1889

Abe's Salvage
2108 E Rosedale St
Fort Worth, TX 76104
Phone: 817-536-2381

Acme Brick Company
11261 Harry Hines Boulevard
Dallas, TX 75229
Phone: 972-241-1400

Adkins Architectural Antiques
3515 Fannin Street
Houston, TX 77004
Phone: 713-522-6547

All Universal Service Co.
4021 Oak Lane
Bacliff, TX 77518
Phone: 281-339-1333

Anderson New and Used Bricks
11126 Mesa Drive
Houston, TX 77078
Phone: 281-458-4752

Antique Lumber Co.
1811 Rock Island
Dallas, TX 75207
Phone: 214-428-7774
Fax: 214-428-1889
Email: sales@antiquelumber.com
Website: www.antiquelumber.com

Antique Lumber Company
104 Corsicana Street
Hillsboro, TX 76645
Phone: 214-686-7400
Fax: 254-580-0944
Email: hardgrove@airmail net
Website: www.antiquelumber.com
Species: Heartpine, Pine, Oak

Architectural Antiques Salvage
403 Dawson Streetreet
San Antonio, TX 78202
Phone: 210-226-6863
Fax: 210-224-4712
Email: oldhouseparts@juno.com
Website:
www.urweb net/architectural.antiques

Austin Brick Company
5180 Highway 290 W
Austin, TX 78735
Phone: 512-899-1550

Austin Habitat for Humanity Re-Store
310 Comal, #101
Austin, TX 78733
Phone: 512-478-2165
Fax: 512-478-9477
Email: dbmackie@aol.com
Website: www re-store.com

Brazoria County HFH ReStore
P.O. Box 2216C
Freeport, TX 77542
Phone: 409-823-7200

Building Materials Outlet
10421 NIH35
Austin, TX 78701
Phone: 512-836-1663
Email: bm010421@smart net

Cherry Demolition
6131 Selinsky
Houston, TX 77048
Phone: 713-987-0000
Fax: 713-991-6236
Email: mike@cherrydemolition.com
Website: www.cherrydomolition.com

Cunningham Construction
100 Private Road 331
Hillsboro, TX 76645
Phone: 254-582-3089
Fax: 254-582-3684
Email: tc45@hotmail.com
Species: Longleaf pine, Cedar, Cypress

Cyborg Palace
5952 W Highway 84-67
Bangs, TX 76823
Phone: 325-752-6267

Del Valley Recycling
1713 Hwy 71
Austin, TX
Phone: 512-385-4617

Used Building Materials (UMS)—Con.

Discount Home Warehouse
1750 Empire Central
Dallas, TX 75235
Phone: 214-631-2755
Email: dhw_1@msn.com
Website: www.dhwsalvage.com

DYN-O-Mite Demolition
6916 CF Hawn Freeway
Dallas, TX 75217
Phone: 214-398-6496
Fax: 214-398-6497

Family Resale
8000 Jensen Drive
Houston, TX 77093
Phone: 713-691-0506

Frenchman Lumber
206 G Street
Kerrville, TX 78028
Phone: 830-792-3381
Fax: 830-792-3381

Habitat for Humanity ReStore
119 Lake Street
Bryan, TX 77801
Phone: 409-823-7200

Habitat for Humanity ReStore
3020 Bryan Street
Dallas, TX 75204
Phone: 214-827-4037

Habitat for Humanity ReStore
3345 S Jones Street
Fort Worth, TX 76110
Phone: 817-926-9219
Fax: 817-926-8575
Email: info@fwhabitat.org

Habitat for Humanity ReStore
2910 Avenue N-R
Lubbock, TX 79405
Phone: 806-763-4663

Habitat for Humanity ReStore
311 Probandt
San Antonio, TX 78204
Phone: 210-223-5203

Habitat for Humanity ReStore
P.O. Box 6362
Tyler, TX 75711
Phone: 903-595-6630

Habitat for Humanity ReStore
1507 N Main Street
Victoria, TX 77901
Phone: 361-570-4700
Fax: 361-570-6170
Email: restore@icsi net

Historic Houston
P.O. Box 130463
Houston, TX 77219
Phone: 713-522-0542
Fax: 713-522-0566
Email: info@historichouston.org
Website: www historichouston.org

Ken Richter Dismantling
2203 Lillie Lane
Taylor, TX 76574
Phone: 512-924-3108

Landmark Brick
129 N Murphy Road
Plano, TX 75094
Phone: 972-578-8585

McKinney Wrecking
18 Ruhlen Court
El Paso, TX 79925
Phone: 915-533-2006
Fax: 915-542-0032
Species: Pine, Oak

Miller Enterprises
136 W McLeroy
Saginaw, TX 76179
Phone: 817-626-1941

Moore for Less Salvage
Discount Building Materials
Highway 114
Rhome, TX 76078
Phone: 817-636-2552

Old Lumber Yard Antiques
116 W Bailey Street
Ponder, TX 76259
Phone: 940-479-0203

Pam Gaylor Dismantling
Route1, Box 750-H
Elgin, TX 78621
Phone: 512-332-0819

Pieces of the Past
411 W Monroe
Austin, TX 78704
Phone: 512-326-5141
Fax: 512-326-5181
Email: kathy@pieces-of-the-past.com
Website: www.pieces-of-the-past.com

Pieces of the Past
3607 Broadway Street
San Antonio, TX 78209
Phone: 210-828-0757

Precision Woodworks
507 E Jackson Street
Burnet, TX 78611
Phone: 512-756-6950
Fax: 512-756-2804
Website: www.precisionwoodworks.com

Precision Woodworks
417 North Briery Road
Irving, TX 75061
Phone: 972-790-8831
Fax: 512-756-6950

Quality Surplus
1004 N Simmons Freeway
Lake Dallas, TX 75065
Phone: 940-497-3749
Fax: 940-494-2769
Species: Pecan, Oak, Pine

Ramirez Properties
3131 Balstrop Hwy
Austin, TX
Phone: 512-335-5512

Reed-Orr Wrecking Company
1903 Rock Island Street
Dallas, TX 75207
Phone: 214-428-7429

Restore
3020 Bryan Street
Dallas, TX 75204
Phone: 214-827-9083

Salvage Lumber of Texas
100 S Roberts Drive
West, TX 76691
Phone: 254-826-4458
Fax: 254-757-3103
Email: bergman@hot1 net

Scott's Salvage
13494 Gholson Road
Waco, TX 76705
Phone: 254-829-1448

Second Chance Building Components
817 Spring Street
Columbus, TX 78934
Phone: 409-732-6646

Strickland Lumber
115 Lee Street
Wichita Falls, TX 76301
Phone: 940-322-2716

Used Building Materials (UMS)—Con.

The Emporium
1800 Westheimer
Houston, TX 77098
Phone: 713-528-3808
Fax: 713-528-5494
Email: info@the-emporium.com
Website: www.the-emporium.com

The Wrecking Barn, Inc.
3111 Ross Avenue
Dallas, TX 75204
Phone: 214-827-7173
Fax: 214-747-4211

Thomas Elisha
2108 E Rosedale Street
Fort Worth, TX 76104
Phone: 817-536-2381

Town & Country Brick & Supply Inc.
15711 Fm 2920 Road
Tomball, TX 77375
Phone: 281-351-6356

Tuck Used Lumber
1303 Hutchins Road
Dallas, TX 75203
Phone: 214-948-7285

Union Salvage
2505 South Street
Nacogdoches, TX 75964
Phone: 936-560-4534

Union Salvage
104 Simonds Road
Seagoville, TX 75159
Phone: 972-287-5190

W K Lumber Company
4721 Airport Freeway
Haltorn City, TX 76117
Phone: 817-831-8847

Welpman & Son Door & Salvage
2200 E. Maddox Avenue
Fort Worth, TX 76104
Phone: 817-535-0906
Fax: 817-535-0906

Utah

Bowen Enterprises
P.O. Box 12005
Ogden, UT 84412
Phone: 801-621-3626

Community Development of Utah
501 E 1700 S
Salt Lake City, UT 84105
Phone: 801-994-7222
Email: slcdc@slcdc.org

Costello Co.
1240 Princeton Avenue
Salt Lake City, UT 84101
Phone: 801-581-0084

Demolition Salvage Supply Company
430 Slade Place
Salt Lake City, UT 84102
Phone: 801-539-1140

George's Demolition & Salvage
430 E 900 S
Salt Lake City, UT 84111
Phone: 801-521-8717

Trestlewood
292 North 2000 W
Lindon, UT 84042
Phone: 801-443-4002
Email: info@trestlewood.com
Website: www.Trestlewood.com
Species: Fir, Pine, Oak

Urban Forest Woodworks
1065 West 600 N
Logan, UT 84321
Phone: 435-752-7268
Fax: 435-752-4471
Email: ufww@urbanforestww.com
Website: www.urbanforestww.com

Vermont

Architectural Salvage Warehouse
53 Main Street
Burlington, VT 05401
Phone: 802-658-5011
Email: salvage@together.net
Website: www.architecturalsalvagevt.com
Species: www.greatsalvage.com

Mason Brothers Architectural Salvage
11 Maple Street
Essex Junction, VT 05452
Phone: 802-879-4221
Species: Pine, Fir

ReCycle North
266 Pine Street
Burlington, VT 05401
Phone: 802-658-4143
Email: info@recyclenorth.org
Website: www.recyclenorth.org

Second Harvest Antique Lumbers
Box 240 Willson Road
Jeffersonville, VT 05464
Phone: 802-644-8169
Fax: 802-644-8005
Species: Pine, Spruce, Hemlock

Virginia

Ahoora, Inc.
P.O. Box 826
Merrifield, VA 22116
Phone: 703-438-0957
Fax: 703-438-1726
Email: ahoora@aol.com

Antique Building Products
P.O. Box 206
Amherst, VA 24521
Phone: 804-946-0634
Fax: 804-946-0835
Website: www.antiquebuildingproducts.com

Appalachian Woods
1240 Cold Springs Road
Stuarts Draft, VA 24477
Phone: 540-337-1801
Fax: 540-337-1030
Email: jonas@appalachianwoods.com
Website: www.appalachianwoods.com
Species: Heartpine, Oak, Fir

Bargain Village
12197 Jefferson Davis Highway
Woodford, VA 22580
Phone: 804-448-0059

Big Wood
Afton, VA 22920
Phone: 434-361-9300
Fax: 434-361-1873
Website: www.big-wood net

Black Dog Salvage
902 13th Street SW
Roanoke, VA 24016
Phone: 540-343-6200
Fax: 540-343-6295
Email: info@blackdogsalvage.com
Website: www.blackdogsalvage.com

Caravati's Architectural Antiques
104 E 2nd Street
Richmond, VA 23224
Phone: 804-232-4175
Fax: 804-233-7109
Email: webmaster@recentruins.com
Website: www recentruins.com

Used Building Materials (UMS)—Con.

Cmc
4509 Pouncey Tract Road
Glen Allen, VA 23059
Phone: 804-369-2120

E.T. Moore Manufacturing
3100 N Hopkins Road, Suite 101
Richmond, VA 23224
Phone: 804-231-1823
Fax: 804-231-0759
Email: orders@etmoore.com
Website: www.etmoore.com
Species: Longleaf pine, Cypress

Empire Salvage & Recycling, Inc.
200 Thistle Street
Bluefield, VA 24605
Phone: 276-322-3554

Governors Antiques and Architectural
Supply
8000 Antique Lane
Mechanicsville, VA 23116
Phone: 804-746-1030
Fax: 804-730-8308
Email: governorsantiques@earthlink.net
Website: governorsantiques.net

Hamilton Salvage Building Materials
3201 Dwina Road
Coeburn, VA 24230
Phone: 276-762-5140

Imperial Building Supply
856 W 45th Street
Norfolk, VA 23508
Phone: 757-489-4254

Kings Arrow Antiques Lumber
11175 Tattersall Trail
Oakton, VA 22124
Phone: 703-407-5912
Email: kingsarrow@prodigy net
Species: Chestnut, Longleaf pine

Lantz Building Supply
138 Linville Avenue
Broadway, VA 22815
Phone: 540-896-7048

Mountain Lumber
P.O. Box 289
Ruckersville, VA 22968
Phone: 800-445-2671
Fax: 804-985-4105
Email: sales@mountainlumber.com
Website: www mountainlumber.com

Pryor's Hauling Company
4509 Pouncey Tract Road
Glen Allen, VA 23059
Phone: 804-360-2120

Shenandoah Valley Reclaimed Lumber
3586 Horizons Way
Harrisonburg, VA 22801
Phone: 540-896-7600
Fax: 540-896-5455
Email: butlerj@horizonsva.com
Website: svreclaimedlumber.com
Species: Pine, Oak, Chestnut

Showcase
1657 W Broad Street
Richmond, VA 23220
Phone: 804-340-1900

The Housewright Shop
187 Pine Tree Lane
Fort Valley, VA 22652
Phone: 540-933-6458
Email: pwcj@yahoo.com

Virginia Antique Building Materials
600 Greenview Court
Pulaski, VA 24301
Phone: 540-980-4232
Fax: 540-980-4338
Email: tdalton@i-plus.net
Species: Heartpine, Oak, Chestnut

Washington

Bear Creek Lumber
P.O. Box 669
Winthrop, WA 98862
Phone: 509-997-3110
Fax: 509-997-2040
Email: customerser-
vice@bearcreeklumber.com
Website: www.bearcreeklumber.com

Brown's Lumber Yard
112 N Erie Street
Spokane, WA 99202
Phone: 509-535-0112

Centralia Perks
113 N Tower Avenue
Centralia, WA 98531
Phone: 360-330-2882

Duluth Timber Co.
5715 Gilkey Avenue
Bow, WA 98232
Phone: 360-766-6253

Earthwise, Inc.
2462 1st Avenue S
Seattle, WA 98134
Phone: 206-624-4510
Email: earthwise@qwest net
Website: www.earthwise-salvage.com

Earthworks Recycling Inc.
1904 E Broadway Avenue
Spokane, WA 99202
Phone: 509-534-1638
Website: www.earthworksrecycling.com

Environmental Home Center
1724 4th Avenue S
Seattle, WA 98134
Phone: 206-682-7332
Fax: 682-206-8275
Email:
pattis@environmentalhomecenter.com
Website:
www.environmentalhomecenter.com

Grand and Benedicts
3825 1st Avenue S
Seattle, WA 98134
Phone: 206-223-1988

Habitat for Humanity–Builders
Surplus Store
E 850 Trent Avenue
Spokane, WA 99202
Phone: 509-535-9517

Montana Originals
33100 114th SE
Preston, WA 98050
Phone: 425-222-6497
Fax: 425-222-4567

Northwest Salvage & Second Hand
7402 NE St. Johns Road
Vancouver, WA 98665
Phone: 360-694-0662

Northwest Tub Co.
103 S Tower Avenue
Centralia, WA 98531
Phone: 360-888-8827

R.W. Rhine Inc.
1124 112th Street E
Tacoma, WA 98554
Phone: 253-531-7223
Fax: 253-531-9548

Ray's Demolition Warehouse
2101 E Broadway Avenue
Spokane, WA 99202
Phone: 509-533-1903

Used Building Materials (UMS)—Con.

Recovery 1
1630 18th Street E
Tacoma, WA 98421
Phone: 206-537-5852

Seattle Building Salvage
2114 Hewitt Avenue
Everett, WA 98201
Phone: 425-303-8500

Seattle Building Salvage
330 Westlake Avenue N
Seattle, WA 98103
Phone: 206-381-3453
Website: www.seattlebuildingsalvage.com

Second Use Building Materials
7953 2nd Avenue S
Seattle, WA 98108
Phone: 206-763-0436
Fax: 206-763-6021
Website: www.seconduse.com

Sound Builders Resource
210 Thurston Avenue NE
Olympia, WA 98501
Phone: 360-753-1575
Fax: 360-753-5402
Email: info@fbroly.org
Website: www.sbroly.org

The ReStore
600 W Holly Street
Bellingham, WA 98225
Phone: 360-647-5921
Email: restore@re-sources.org
Website: www re-sources.org
Species: Fir, Oak, Maple

The ReStore
1440 NW 52nd Street
Seattle, WA 98107
Phone: 206-297-9119
Email: patfinn@Seattle@re-sources.org
Website: www re-sources.org/contact.htm

TreeHouse Workshop Inc.
303 NW 43 Street
Seattle, WA 98107
Phone: 206-782-0208
Website: www.treehouseworkshop.com

Waste Not Want Not
724 E 1st Street
Port Angeles, WA 98362
Phone: 360-417-3016

Waste Not Want Not
304 10th ST
Port Townsend, WA 98368
Phone: 360-379-6838
Fax: 360-379-6838
Email: wnwn@cablespeed.com
Website: www.wastenot-recycle.com

Windfall Lumber Products
210 Thurston Avenue
Olympia, WA 98501
Phone: 360-352-2250
Fax: 603-894-5571
Website: www.windfalllumber.com

YV ReStore
2500 S 26th Avenue
Yakima, WA 98903
Phone: 509-576-8077
Email: Habitat@yvn net
Website: www.yakimahabitat.org

West Virginia

Almost Heaven HFH ReStore
P.O. Box 98
Circleville, WV 26804
Phone: 304-567-2300

Americo Inc.
One River Park 16th Street
McMechen, WV 26040
Phone: 304-232-1333
Fax: 304-233-1333
Website: www.americo.ohgolly.com

Fultineers's Wood Recycling
P.O. Box 131
Lost Creek, WV 26385
Phone: 304-622-0535

Southland Surplus Building Materials
216 Business Street
Beckley, WV 25801
Phone: 304-252-6515

Vintage Log and Lumber
P.O. Box 130 Route 219 N
Renick, WV 24966
Phone: 304-497-2700
Fax: 304-497-3651
Email: sales@vintagelog.com
Website: www.vintagelog.com

Wisconsin

Coughlin Contractors, Inc.
Welch Road
Watertown, WI 53098
Phone: 920-261-7637
Fax: 920-261-7658
Email: rjcmvc@execpc.com

DeConstruction Inc.
1010 Walsh Road
Madison, WI 53714
Phone: 608-244-8759
Fax: 908-244-8981
Email: deconstruct@mailbag.com
Website: www.deconstructinc.com

Gerovac Wrecking Company
11836 W Saint Martins Road
Franklin, WI 53132
Phone: 414-425-1500

HfH ReStore
208 Cottage Grove Road
Madison, WI 53716
Phone: 608-661-2813

Homesource Center
3701 W Lisbon Avenue
Milwaukee, WI 53208
Phone: 414-344-4142

I M Salvage Company
4025 W Loomis Road
Milwaukee, WI 53221
Phone: 414-281-8733

Old House Salvage
4404 Stewart Avenue
Wausau, WI 54401
Phone: 715-849-5077
Email: delirevanceman@aol.com

Pagenkopf S
Green Bay, WI 54301
Phone: 920-498-1755

Reclaimed Lumber Co.
633 Ellis Avenue
Baraboo, WI 53913
Phone: 608-356-8849
Email: David@reclaimed-lumber.com
Website: www reclaimed-lumber.com

Salvage Heaven Inc.
206 E Lincoln Avenue
Milwaukee, WI 53207
Phone: 414-329-7170

Scarboro River Barn and Lumber
Green Bay, WI 54301
Phone: 920-498-1755

Scs of Wisconsin Inc.
4001 W Loomis Road
Milwaukee, WI 53221
Phone: 414-281-8733

Used Building Materials (UMS)—Con.

Timeless Timber
2200 E Lake Shore Drive
Ashland, WI 54806
Phone: 888-653-5647
Fax: 715-685-9620
Email: sales@timelesstimber.com
Website: www.timelesstimber.com

Urban Evolutions
867 Valley Road
Menasha, WI 54952
Phone: 920-380-4149
Fax: 920-380-4184
Website: www.urbanevolutions.com
Species: Pine, Oak, Ash

Wyoming

Centennial Woods
7512 Ridge Road
Cheyenne, WY 82009
Phone: 307-778-8762
Fax: 307-778-8762

Antiquus Wood Products
Phone: 800-852-9224
Website: www.antiquuswood.com

HfH International ReStores
Website: www.habitat.org/env/restore.html

Reclaimed Forest
Email: info@reclaimedforest.com
Website: www.reclaimedforest.com

Savvy Salvage
Phone: 781-893-7211
Email: info@savvysalvage.com
Website: www.savvysalvage.com

Value-Added Products (VA)

Alabama

A.L. Roy Lumber Co. Inc.
1405 1st Avenue N
Bessemer, AL 35020
Phone: 800-476-8169
Fax: 205-425-2139
Email: david@roylumber.com
Website: www.roylumber.com

Southern Timberwrights
77 Baushore Place
Guntersville, AL 35976
Phone: 256-582-9299
Email: lrm@localaccess.net
Website: www.southerntimberwrights.com

Alaska

Hartvigson's Fine Furniture and Woodworking
7133 Arctic Boulevard, Suite 8
Anchorage, AK 99518
Phone: 907-344-6612
Website: www.hartvigsons.com

Arizona

Bowen Poles and Lumber
22402 N Black Canyon Highway
Phoenix, AZ 85080
Phone: 602-993-6350
Fax: 602-516-8172

California

Baka Production
1785 Egbert Avenue
San Francisco, CA 94124
Phone: 415-468-8090

Blue Log Lumber
P.O. Box 804
Mendocino, CA 95460
Phone: 707-937-1735
Website: www.goodwood.org
Species: redwood

California Hardwood Producers
1980 Grass Valley Highway
Auburn, CA 95603
Phone: 916-888-8191
Email: dave@californiahardwood.com
Website: www.californiahardwood.com

Community Woodworks
2420 Ukraine Street Oakland Army Base,
Building 823
Oakland, CA 94607
Phone: 510-835-7690
Fax: 510-835-7691
Website: www.communitywoodworks.org/

Crossroads Recycled Lumber
P.O. Box 928, 57839 Road 225
North Fork, CA 93643
Phone: 888-842-3201
Fax: 559-877-3646
Email: crlumber@netptc.net
Website: www.crossroadslumber.com

Holmes Wilson Furniture
30361 Seaview Road
Cazadero, CA 95421
Phone: 707-847-3747

Jim State Forest Products
Highway 3
Hayfork, CA 96041
Phone: 503-628-1101

Mad River Woodworks
P.O. Box 1067
Blue Lake, CA 95525
Phone: 707-668-5671
Fax: 707-668-5673
Email: info@madriverwoodworks.com
Website: www.madriverwoodworks.com

Maxwell Pacific
P.O. Box 4127
Malibu, CA 90264
Phone: 310-457-4533

Mendocino Specialty Lumber Company
P.O. Box 519
Hydesville, CA 95547
Phone: 707-726-0339
Fax: 707-726-0319
Email: wood@oldgrowth.com
Website: www2@oldgrowth.com

Michael Evenson Natural Resources
P.O. Box 157
Petrolia, CA 95558
Phone: 707-629-3679
Fax: 707-629-3679
Website: www.oldgrowthtimbers.com

Pacific Coast Lumber
225 Tank Farm Road #D4
San Luis Obispo, CA 93401
Phone: 805-543-5533
Fax: 805-543-1601

Value-Added Products (VA)—Con.

Pacific Heritage Wood Supply Co.
P.O. Box 1329
El Granada, CA 94018
Phone: 877-728-9231
Fax: 650-728-9231
Email: sales@phwood.com
Website: www.phwood.com

Pacific Post and Beam
P.O. Box 13708
San Luis Obispo, CA 93406
Phone: 805-543-7565
Fax: 805-543-1287

Pinocchio's
18651 Hare Creek Ter.
Fort Bragg, CA 95437
Phone: 707-964-6272
Fax: 707-964-0458
Website: www mcn.org/b/rmoore

Recycled Lumberworks
1825 Airport Park Boulevard
Ukiah, CA 95482
Phone: 707-462-2567
Fax: 707-462-6122
Website: www.oldwoodguy.com
Species: Fir

Sierra Timber Framers
P.O. Box 595
Nevada City, CA 95959
Phone: 530-292-9449
Fax: 530-292-9460
Website: www.sierratimberframers.com

Studio eg
442 Rich Street
Oakland, CA 94609
Phone: 510-596-8945
Email: info@studioeg.com
Website: www.studioeg.com

The Wooden Duck
2919 7th Street
Berkeley, CA 94710
Phone: 510-848-3575
Email: info@thewoodenduck.com
Website: www.thewoodenduck.com

USA Recovered Wood Resources
308 Fountain Avenue
Pacific Grove, CA 93950
Phone: 831-809-2627
Fax: 831-372-2766
Email: jbsfortord@aol.com

Vintage Timberworks
1155 Industrial Avenue
Escondido, CA 92029
Phone: 760-743-0744
Fax: 760-743-5714
Website: www.vintagetimber.com

Colorado

Mastercrafted Specialty Woods
P.O. Box 741
Edwards, CO 81632
Phone: 970-926-4552
Fax: 970-926-4574
Email: info@craftedwoods.com
Website: www.craftedwoods.com

Old Grain Reclaimed Wood Specialists
P.O. Box 854
Carbondale, CO 81623
Phone: 970-704-9745
Fax: 970-704-9745
Email: info@oldgrain.com
Website: www.oldgrain.com

Resource Wood Products, Inc.
7800 Hwy 82 Ste 102
Glenwood Springs, CO 81601
Phone: 970-945-5939
Email: rwtimber@aol.com
Website: www rw-timber.com

Singing Saw Woodworks, Inc.
67 Shady Hollow
Nederland, CO 80466
Phone: 303-258-0378
Fax: 303-258-0349
Website: www.singingsaw.com/singingsaw

Wind River Collections, Antique
Wood Flooring
7500 E Arapahoe Road #335
Englewood, CO 80112
Phone: 720-493-5572
Fax: 720-493-5626
Email: info@windrivercollections.com
Website: www.windrivercollections.com

Connecticut

A Reclaimed Lumber co.
9 Old Post Road
Madison, CT 06443
Phone: 203-214-9705
Email: info@whitecedar.com
Website: www reclaimedlumberco.com
Species: Pine, Fir, Cypress

Antique Specialty Flooring
100 W. Main Street
Plantsville, CT 06479
Phone: 860-621-6787
Fax: 860-276-0704

Chestnut Oak Company
3810 Old Mountain Road
West Suffield, CT 06093
Phone: 860-668-0382
Email: info@chestnutoakcompany.com
Website: www.chestnutoakcompany.com

Chestnut Specialists, Inc.
365 Harwinton Avenue
Plymouth, CT 06782
Phone: 860-283-4209
Fax: 860-283-4209
Website: www.chestnutspec.com

Chestnut Woodworking and
Antique Flooring
P.O. Box 204
West Cornwall, CT 06796
Phone: 860-672-4300
Fax: 860-672-2441
Email: info@chestnutwoodworking.com
Website: www.chestnutwoodworking.com

Horse Drawn Pine
273 Pendleton Hill Road
North Stonington, CT 06359
Phone: 860-599-4493
Fax: 860-599-4403

Sara E. Armster
9 Old Post Road
Madison, CT 06443
Phone: 203-245-1781
Fax: 203-245-0755
Website: www.whitecedar. com
Species: White Cedar, Cypress

Florida

Goodwin Heart Pine Company
106 SW 109th Place
Micanopy, FL 32667
Phone: 800-336-3118
Fax: 352-466-0339
Email: goodwin@heartpine.com
Website: www heartpine.com

Pinetree Builders
814 SE 23rd Street
Ft. Lauderdale, FL 33316
Phone: 954-760-5800
Fax: 954-760-5833
Email: info@pinetreebuilders.com
Website: www.pinetreebuilders.com
Species: Heartpine, Cypress

Value-Added Products (VA)—Con.

Georgia

Authentic Pine Floors
4042 Highway 42
Locust Grove, GA 30248
Phone: 770-957-6038
Fax: 770-914-2925
Email: info@authenticpinefloors.com
Website: www.authenticpinefloors.com

Georgia Heart Pine
1130 Sarracenia
Moultrie, GA 31768
Phone: 229-985-4100

Sawmill Treasures
Highway 57
Irwinton, GA 31042
Phone: 478-946-2510
Email: guerryholder@hotmail.com
Website: www.sawmilltreasures.com

Southern Pine Company of Georgia
P.O. Box 2152
Savannah, GA 31402
Phone: 912-236-4112
Email: info@southernpinecompany.com
Website: www.southernpinecompany.com
Species: Heart pine, cypress

Southern Wood Floors
472A-1 Flowing Wells Road
Augusta, GA 30907
Phone: 706-855-0779
Email: info@southernwoodfloors.com
Website: www.southernwoodfloors.com

Idaho

Alternative Timber Structures
1054 Rammel Mountain Road
Tectonia, ID 83452
Phone: 208-456-2711
Website:
www.alternativetimberstructures.com

Bell Hardwood Floor Inc.
325 N Holmes Avenue
Idaho Falls, ID 83401
Phone: 208-522-9694

Stein and Collett, Inc.
P.O. Box 4065
McCall, ID 83638
Phone: 208-634-8228
Fax: 208-634-8228

Trestlewood
933 South Frontage Road
Blackfoot, ID 83221
Phone: 208-785-1151
Fax: 208-785-0458
Email: info@trestlewood.com
Website: www.Trestlewood.com
Species: Fir, Pine, Oak

Illinois

Ecologic, Inc.
1140 Elizabeth Avenue
Waukegan, IL 60085
Phone: 800-899-8004
Fax: 847-244-5977

J. Hoffman Co.
1919 Cherry Hill Road
Joilet, IL 60433
Phone: 630-513-6680
Fax: 630-513-6687

Indiana

Searcy Antique Woods
Cedar Grove, IN 47016
Phone: 812-926-9775
Fax: 765-647-6454
Email: sales@searcyantiquewoods.com
Website: www.searcyantiquewoods.com

Kentucky

Longwood Antique Woods
330 Midland Place #3
Lexington, KY 40505
Phone: 869-233-2268
Email: longwood-inc@msn.com
Website: www.longwoodantiquewoods.com

Whiskey Wood
3658 State Road 1414
Hartford, KY 42347
Phone: 270-298-0084
Fax: 270-298-7755
Website: www.whiskeywood.com

Louisiana

Albany Woodworks, Inc.
P.O. Box 729
Albany, LA 70711
Phone: 225-567-1155
Fax: 225-567-5150
Website: www.albanywoodworks.com

Antique Lumber Millwork
1920 Ridge Road
Duson, LA 70529
Phone: 800-381-9585
Fax: 318-988-2703

Crescent City Architectural
3101 Tchoupitoulas Street
New Orleans, LA 70115
Phone: 504-891-0500
Fax: 504-891-1895
Email: cca@architectural-salvage.com
Website: www.architectural-salvage.com

New Orleans Cypressworks
3110 Magazine Street
New Orleans, LA 70115
Phone: 504-891-0001

What It's Worth
11550 N Harrells Ferry
Baton Rouge, LA 70816
Phone: 504-275-1867

Will Branch Antique Lumber
60407 Spring Valley Road
Bogalusa, LA 70427
Phone: 985-732-3798
Fax: 985-732-5555
Email: wse@willbranch net
Website: www.willbranch net

Maine

Auburn Enterprises
P.O.Box 3065
Auburn, ME 04212-3065
Phone: 207-784-4244
Email: tlabrie@auburnmachinery.com

The Green Store
71 Main Street
Belfast, ME 04915
Phone: 207-338-4045
Fax: 207-338-5988

Maryland

Colonial Lumber
207 W Ashby Ellis Road
Oakland, MD 21550
Phone: 301-334-3189
Email: coloniallmbr@gcnetmail net
Website: www.coloniallumber.com

Craftwright Timberframe Co.
100 Railroad Avenue 105
Westminster, MD 21157
Phone: 410-876-0999
Fax: 410-876-0999
Email: greyoak1@aol.com
Website:
www.craftwrighttimberframes.com
Species: Oak, Chestnut, Heartpine

Value-Added Products (VA)—Con.

International Wood Products
32203 Park Avenue
Queen Anne, MD 21657
Phone: 410-364-5031
Fax: 410-364-5905

Old Line Timberframes
400 Dilks Lane
Elkton, MD 21921
Phone: 410-287-1545
Fax: 410-287-1545
Email: joe@oldlinetimberframes.com
Website: www.oldlinetimberframes.com

Old Wood & Co.
1013 S Talbot Street
Saint Michaels, MD 21663
Phone: 410-745-0035

The Woods Co. Inc.
2357 Bottler Road
Brownsville, MD 21715
Phone: 301-432-8419

Vintage Lumber Company
1 Council Drive
Woodsboro, MD 21798
Phone: 301-845-2500
Fax: 301-845-6475
Email: woodfloors@vintagelumber.com
Website: www.vintagelumber.com
Species: Oak, Chestnut, Pine

Massachusetts

Cataumet Saw Mill
494 Thomas Landers Road
East Falmoth, MA 02536
Phone: 508-457-9239
Fax: 508-540-7974
Website: www.cataumet.com
Species: Heartpine, Fir, Oak

Craftsman Lumber Company
436 Main Street P.O. Box 222
Groton, MA 01450
Phone: 978-448-5621
Email: mark@craftsmanlumber.com
Website: www.craftsmanlumber.com

Jay Harding Construction
96 Brook Street
Clinton, MA 01754
Phone: 978-897-7411
Fax: 978-897-3609
Website: www.oldewood.com

Karp WoodWorks
136 Fountain Street
Ashland, MA 01721
Phone: 508-881-7000
Fax: 508-881-7084
Species: Oak, Maple, Heartpine

Longleaf Lumber
70 Webster Avenue
Sommerville, MA 02143
Phone: 617-625-3659
Fax: 617-625-3615
Email: info@longleaflumber.com
Website: www.longleaflumber.com

Nor'East Architectural Antiques
5 Market Square
Amesbury, MA 01913
Phone: 978-834-9088
Fax: 978-499-7136
Email: mail@noreast1.com
Website: www.noreast1.com

Minnesota

Duluth Timber Company
P.O. Box 16717
Duluth, MN 55816
Phone: 218-727-2145
Fax: 218-727-0393
Email: liz@duluthtimber.com
Website: www.duluthtimber.com
Species: Fir, Longleaf pine, Cypress

Minnesota Timber Salvage
13737 100th Street
Foreston, MN 56330
Phone: 320-369-4507

Old Growth Woods
6456 160th Street
Rosemount, MN 55068
Phone: 651-690-3188
Fax: 651-698-6641
Email: sales@oldgrowthwoods.com
Website: www.oldgrowthwoods.com

Mississippi

Old Mississippi Lumber
P.O. Box 562
Holly Springs, MS 38634
Phone: 662-252-3395
Email: broev@bellsouth net
Website: www heartpinefloors.com

Missouri

Heartwood Associates Int'l.
5068 Tholozan Avenue
St. Louis, MO 63109
Phone: 314-352-9242
Fax: 314-752-2152
Email: longleaf1@prodigy net
Website: www heartwoodassociates.com

Pitchpine Lumber
19864 Gore Drive
Sainte Genevieve, MO 63670
Phone: 573-747-1733
Fax: 573-747-1680
Email: lloyd@pitchpine.com
Website: www.pitchpine.com
Species: Heartpine, Oak, Cypress

Sanders Enterprise, Inc.
3019 Nash Road
Scott City, MO 63780
Phone: 314-334-9600
Fax: 314-334-2077

Stockton Heartwoods Limited
624 Holly Hills Avenue
St. Louis, MO 63101
Phone: 800-788-4828
Fax: 314-352-6110
Email: heartwoods@earthlink net
Website: www heartwoods.com
Species: Heartpine, Oak, Fir

Montana

Big Timberworks Inc.
P.O. Box 368
Gallatin Gateway, MT 59730
Phone: 406-763-4639
Fax: 406-763-4818
Email: bigtimberworks.com

Nellis Custom Woodworks
4470 Amsterdam Road
Manhattan, MT 59741
Phone: 406-282-9049
Fax: 406-282-9050
Email: eric@nelliscustomwoodworks.com
Website: http://www.nelliscustomwoodworks.
com/aboutus.html

Superior Hardwoods and Millwork
P.O. Box 4731 / 5120 Highway 93 S
(show room)
Missoula, MT 59801
Phone: 406-251-2272
Fax: 406-251-2520
Email: superhrdwds@blackfoot.net
Website: www.superior'hardwoods.com
Species: Fir, Oak

Value-Added Products (VA)—Con.

New Hampshire

Benson Woodworking Co. Inc.
6 Blackjack Crossing
Walpole, NH 03608
Phone: 603-756-3600
Email: info@bensonwood.com
Website: www.bensonwood.com

Carlisle Restoration Lumber
1676 Route 9
Stoddard, NH 03464
Phone: 800-595-9663
Fax: 603-446-3540
Email: info@wideplankflooring.com
Website: www.wideplankflooring.com
Species: Pine, Heartpine, Oak

Northfield Restoration
10 Kensington Road
Hampton Falls, NH 03844
Phone: 603-926-5383
Fax: 603-926-5383
Email: northfields@neaccess net
Website: www northfield.com
Species: Pine, Oak, Chestnut

New Jersey

American Antique and Specialty Woods
51 Mt. Bethel Road
Warren, NJ 07059
Phone: 908-822-0006
Fax: 908-822-7111
Website: www.americanwoodsnj.com
Species: All

MW Wood Enterprises
6 Bywood lane
Ewing, NJ 08628
Phone: 609-538-8680
Fax: 609-530-1922

Willard Brothers Saw Mill
300 Basin Road
Trenton, NJ 08619
Phone: 609-890-1990
Fax: 609-587-6750

New Mexico

Plaza Hardwood, Inc.
219 W Manhattan Street
Santa Fe, NM 87501
Phone: 505-992-3260
Fax: 505-992-8766
Email: paulfuge@certifiedwood.com
Website: www.plzfloor.com

New York

Accent Hardwood Flooring & Supply Corp.
390 Route 25, P.O. Box 180
Middle Island, NY 11953
Phone: 800-545-6435
Fax: 631-924-4584
Email: sales@accentflooring.com
Website: www.accentflooring.com

Barn Shadow Enterprises
32 Lee Place
Wellsville, NY 14895
Phone: 585-593-5075
Fax: 585-593-5075
Email: barnse@rctc.com
Website: www.barnshadow.com

Country Road Associates, Ltd
63 Front Street
Millbrook, NY 12545
Phone: 845-677-6041
Fax: 845-677-6532
Email: info@countryroadassociates.com
Website: www.countryroadassociates.com

Kaywood Flooring and Supply Co.
P.O. Box 314
Eastport, NY 11941
Phone: 631-325-0666
Fax: 631-325-8955
Email: oldfloor@optonline net
Website: www.antiquebarnwood.com

Kleine's Antique Barnwood
Flooring & Lumber
18 River Avenue
Eastport, NY 11941
Phone: 516-325-8955
Fax: 516-325-1465
Email: info@antiquebarnwood.com

M. Fine Lumber
1301 Metropolitan Avenue
Brooklyn, NY 11237
Phone: 718-381-5200
Fax: 718-366-8907
Email: rob@mfinelumber.com
Website: www mfinelumber.com
Species: Fir, Pine

New Energy Works Timber Framers, Inc.
1180 Commercial Drive
Farmington, NY 14425
Phone: 800-486-0661
Fax: 585-924-9962
Email: joinery@newenergyworks.com
Website: www.newenergyworks.com

Pioneer Millworks
1755 Pioneer Road
Shortsville, NY 14548
Phone: 716-289-3093
Fax: 716-289-3221
Website: www newenergworks.com

Pittsford Lumber and Woodshop
50 State Street
Pittsford, NY 14534
Phone: 585-586-1877
Fax: 585-586-1934

Shaver Brothers
32 Perrine Street
Auburn, NY 13021
Phone: 800-564-7206
Email: pjguerrette@a-znet.com

North Carolina

Artisan Woodworks
10837 Liberty Road
Liberty, NC 27298
Phone: 336-622-5441
Email: artisanwoodworks@intrex.net
Website: www.artisanwoodworks.com

Clark Woodworking
P.O. Box 53210
Fayetteville, NC 28305
Phone: 910-678-0899

Harmony Exchange
2700 Big Hill Road
Boone, NC 28607
Phone: 828-264-2314
Fax: 828-264-4770
Website: www harmonyexchange.com

Hawk Creek Hollow Timber Products
P.O. Box 147
Tryon, NC 28782
Phone: 828-859-5180
Fax: 828-859-5108
Email: ann@annielauries.com

Heartwood Pine Floors
P.O. Box 187 Highway 87 S
Pittsboro, NC 27312
Phone: 800-524-7463
Email: email@heartwoodpine.com
Website: www.heartwoodpine.com

J. L. Powell & Co., Inc.
723 Pine Log Road
Whiteville, NC 28472
Phone: 800-227-2007
Fax: 910-642-3164
Email: heather@palnkfloors.com
Website: www.plankfloors.com
Species: Longleaf pine, Pine

Value-Added Products (VA)—Con.

Natural Wood Flooring
119 Gail Drive
Roanoke Rapids, NC 27870
Phone: 800-726-PINE

The Joinery
P.O. Box 518
Tarboro, NC 27886
Phone: 919-823-3306
Fax: 919-823-0818

Vintage Beams and Timbers
Architectural Salvage
P.O. Box 548
Sylva, NC 28779
Phone: 828-586-0755
Fax: 828-586-4647
Email: info@vintagebeamsandtimbers.com
Website: www.vintagebeamsandtimbers.com

Woodhouse
P.O. Box 7336
Rocky Mount, NC 27801
Phone: 252-977-7336
Fax: 252-641-4477

North Dakota

Carlisle Restoration Lumber
NCR 32
Stoddard, ND 03464
Phone: 603-446-3937
Fax: 603-446-3540

Ohio

Barnwares
1888 Jacoby Road
Copley, OH 44321
Phone: 330-335-9907
Fax: 330-334-2097
Email: info@barnwares.com
Website: www.barnwares.com

Eagle Creek Designs, Inc.
6025 Schustrich P.O. Box 163
Mantua, OH 44255
Phone: 330-274-2041
Fax: 330-274-3370
Email: hfs1917@aol.com

J and J Barnwood
36019 Glasgow Road
Salineville, OH 43945
Phone: 330-424-4977

Oregon

Craftmark Reclaimed Wood
P.O. Box 237
McMinnville, OR 97128
Phone: 503-472-6929
Fax: 503-472-5150
Website: www.craftmarkinc.com

Endura Wood Products
1303 SE 6th Avenue
Portland, OR 97214
Phone: 503-233-7090
Fax: 503-233-7091
Email: EdM@EnduraWood.com
Website: www.endurawood.com

Environmental Building Supplies
819 SE Taylor Street
Portland, OR 97214
Phone: 503-222-3881
Fax: 503-222-3756
Email: ebs@ecohaus.com
Website: www.ecohaus.com

Green Mountain Woodworks
P.O. Box 1433
Phoenix, OR 97535
Phone: 541-535-5880
Fax: 514-535-5331
Email: mstella@mind net
Website:
www.greenmountainwoodworks.com

Jefferson Smurfit Recycling Company
1330 NW 14th Avenue
Portland, OR 97209
Phone: 503-294-1560
Fax: 503-742-9113

Oregon Lumber Company
543 3rd Street #81
Lake Oswego, OR 97034
Phone: 503-636-8191
Fax: 503-635-6140

The Timber Recycler
188 HWY99 N
Eugene, OR 97405
Phone: 541-687-0817
Fax: 541-485-0996
Email: ttrzirg@aol.com
Species: Fir

Pennsylvania

Authentic Wood Floors
2301 N Cameron Street
Harrisburg, PA 17110
Phone: 717-234-0812

Barnguys Recycled Materials, Inc., PA
Phone: 610-847-2616
Email: thebarnguy@aol.com
Website: www.barnguys.com

Centre Mills Antique Floors
P.O. Box 16
Aspers, PA 17304
Phone: 717-334-0249
Fax: 717-334-6223
Websiste: www.igateway.com/mall/
homeimp/wood/index htm

Conklin's Authentic Antique Barnwood
RD 1 Box 70
Susquehanna, PA 18847
Phone: 717-465-3832
Fax: 717-465-3832
Website: www.conklinsbarnwood.com

ERA, Inc.
68 Eisenhour Road
Myerstown, PA 17067
Phone: 231-768-5827

Hess Christopher D Inc.
3931 Cedar Drive
Walnut Port, PA 18088
Phone: 610-760-9533
Email: chbarndawg@entermail.net
Website: www.christopherdsinc.com
Species: Heartpine, Chestnut, Oak

Mayse Woodworking Company
319 Richardson Road
Lansdale, PA 19446
Phone: 215-822-8307
Fax: 215-822-8307
Species: Heartpine, Longleaf pine,
Hemlock

Patina Woods
3363 New Franklin Road
Chambersburg, PA 17201
Phone: 717-264-8009
Website:
www.penmar net/patinawoods/index html

Sylvan Brandt LLC Resawn & Antique
Floors
651 E Main Street
Lititz, PA 17543
Phone: 717-626-4520
Fax: 717-626-5867
Email: dean@sylvanbrandt.com

Value-Added Products (VA)—Con.

The Woods Co. Inc.
5045 Kansas Avenue
Chambersburg, PA 17201
Phone: 717-263-6524
Fax: 717-263-9346
woodfloors@thewoodscompany.com
Website: www.thewoodscompany.com
Species: Oak, Chestnut, Pine

Wood Natural Restorations
3038 Woodlane Avenue
Orefield, PA 18069
Phone: 610-395-6451
Email: ken@woodnatural.com
Website: www.woodnatural.com

Yesteryear Floorworks Company
2331 E Market Street, Suite 6
York, PA 17402
Phone: 800-233-9307
Fax: 717-840-1468
Website: www.agedwoods.com

Rhode Island

New England Timber Frames
188 Windstone Drive
Portsmouth, RI 02871
Phone: 401-683-2541
Fax: 401-682-2142
Email: netimbrfrm@aol.com
Website: http://members.aol.com/netimbrfrm

South Carolina

Heart Pine Lumber and Millworks
P.O. Box 1844
Orangeburg, SC 29116
Phone: 803-534-8478
Fax: 803-533-0051
Species: Heartpine

South Dakota

Keetagilly
528 Suni Avenue
Baltic, SD 57003
Phone: 605-529-6152
Email: salvage@keetagilly.com

Tennessee

America Heart Pine, Inc.
4626 Billy Maher Road
Memphis, TN 38135
Phone: 800-544-5765

Push Hard Lumber
4635 N Fairmount Road
Signal Mountain, TN 37377
Phone: 423-517-0089
Email: info@pushhardlumber.com
Website: www.pushhardlumber.com

Texas

Antique Lumber Co.
1811 Rock Island
Dallas, TX 75207
Phone: 214-428-7774
Fax: 214-428-1889
Email: sales@antiquelumber.com
Website: www.antiquelumber.com

Delta Lumber
4701 E. 5th Street
Austin, TX 78702
Phone: 512-385-8522
Species: Longleaf Yellow Pine

Gemini Forest Products
9104 Bellechase Road
Granbury, TX 76049
Phone: 817-573-7103
Fax: 817-713-5453
Email: greghalm@earthlink net
Species: Longleaf pine, Cypress

Heart of Texas Pine Company
4538 S IH 35
San Marcos, TX 78666
Phone: 512-392-1965
Email: texasheartpine@centurytel net

Heritage Restorations
Brazos de Dios
Elm Mott, TX 76640
Phone: 254-717-5531
Email: info@heritagebarns.com
Website: www heritagebarns.com

Hill Country Woodworks of Texas
E Jackson Street
Burnet, TX 78611
Phone: 512-756-6950
Fax: 512-756-2804
Email: byron@texaswoodwork.com
Website: www.texaswoodwork.com
Species: Longleaf pine, Mesquite,

Remanufactured Hardwoods
2630 Loop 35
Alvin, TX 77511
Phone: 281-331-7838
Fax: 281-331-6467
Email: recycle@poboxes.com
Website:
www.clever net/qms/hardwood htm

Texas Woods, Inc.
1192 Highway 304
Bastrop, TX 78602
Phone: 512-303-5667
Fax: 512-303-7700
Email: mesquite@bastrop.com
Website: www.texaswoods.com

The Phoenix Commotion
2913 Montgomery Road
Huntsville, TX 77340
Phone: 936-291-1333
Email: brnsqz@txucom net
Website: www.phoenixcommotion.com

The Woodshop of Texas
P.O. Box 202
Porter, TX 77365
Phone: 888-950-9663
Fax: 713-329-9969
Email: tlhurd@ev1.net
Website: www.antiquewoods net

What It's Worth
P.O. Box 162135
Austin, TX 78716
Phone: 512-328-8837
Fax: 512-328-8837

Utah

Alpine Barns
1060 Orchard Lane
Alpine, UT 84004
Phone: 801-310-5004
Email: info@alpinebarns.com
Website: www.alpinebarns.com

Trestlewood
292 North 2000 W
Lindon, UT 84042
Phone: 801-443-4002
Email: info@trestlewood.com
Website: www.Trestlewood.com
Species: Fir, Pine, Oak

Trestlewood Furniture
1035 South 800 W
Salt Lake City, UT 84104
Phone: 801-972-9970
Fax: 801-973-0999
Email: trestle@trestlewood.com

Urban Forest Woodworks
1065 West 600 N
Logan, UT 84321
Phone: 435-752-7268
Fax: 435-752-4471
Email: ufww@urbanforestww.com
Website: www.urbanforestww.com

Value-Added Products (VA)—Con.

Vermont

David D. Parker
P.O. Box 6458
Brattleboro, VT 05302
Phone: 802-251-0000
Fax: 802-251-0001
Website: www.parkerrestoration.com

David D. Parker Structural Restoration
P.O. Box 6458
Brattleboro, VT 05302
Phone: 802-251-0000
Fax: 802-251-0001
Website: www.parkerrestoration.com

J H Lumber & Wood Products
R D 2 Box 5320
Montpelier, VT 05602
Phone: 802-229-4148
Website: www.jhlumber.com

Shiningwater Enterprises
484 Mill Road
Lincoln, VT 05443
Phone: 802-453-2825
Email: jaxfam@sover.net
Website: www.traditional-building.com/
brochure/members/1architecturalsalvage.shtml

Virginia

Antique Building Products
P.O. Box 206
Amherst, VA 24521
Phone: 804-946-0634
Fax: 804-946-0835
www.antiquebuildingproducts.com

Cochran's Lumber and Millwork
33735 Snickersville Tnpk.
Bluemont, VA 20135
Phone: 540-554-8274
Website: www.lumberandmillwork.com

E.T. Moore Manufacturing
3100 N Hopkins Road, Suite 101
Richmond, VA 23224
Phone: 804-231-1823
Fax: 804-231-0759
Email: orders@etmoore.com
Website: www.etmoore.com
Species: Longleaf pine, Cypress

Heartwood International
141 Heartwood Circle
Afton, VA 22920
Phone: 804-361-1323
Fax: 804-361-1873
Email: contact@heartwoodinternational.com
Website: www.heartwoodinternational.com

Old Wood
4501 Liberty Hall Court
Quinton, VA 23141
Phone: 804-932-8013
Fax: 804-642-2532
Email: will@3bubbas.com
Species: Pine, Oak, Cypress

Vintage Pine Company
P.O. Box 85
Pamplin, VA 23958
Phone: 434-248-9000

Washington

Chuckanut Log Design
1421 N State Street
Bellingham, WA 98225
Phone: 360-647-2633
Fax: 360-647-3342

Eco-Woodworks
3016 Sapp Road
Tumwater, WA 98512
Phone: 360-943-3808
Fax: 360-943-4217

G.R. Plume Co.
1373 W Smith Road, Suite A1
Ferndale, WA 98248
Phone: 360-384-2800
Fax: 360-384-0035
Email: plumegr@plumes.com
Website: www.grplume.com

J Squared Timbers
5448 Shilshole Avenue NW
Seattle, WA 98107
Phone: 800-598-3074
Fax: 206-781-1600

Resource Woodworks Inc.
627 E 60th
Tacoma, WA 98404
Phone: 253-474-3757
Fax: 253-474-1139
Website: www.rw-timber.com

Re-Tech Wood Products
1324 Russell Road
Forks, WA 98331
Phone: 360-374-4141
Fax: 360-374-4141
Email: retech@olypen.com
Website: www.retechwoodproducts.com
Species: Fir, Cedar

Windfall Lumber Products
210 Thurston Avenue
Olympia, WA 98501
Phone: 360-352-2250
Fax: 603-894-5571
Website: www.windfalllumber.com

Wisconsin

Barnwood Products
Black River Falls, WI 54615
Phone: 715-284-2469
Email: ctrywdcrft@discover-net net
Website: www.barnwoodproducts.com

Glenville TimberWrights
S5390 St Road 13
Baraboo, WI 53913
Phone: 608-355-9950
Fax: 608-355-2922
Email: woodshop@tds net
Website: www.glenvilletimberwrights.com

Milwaukee Timber Company
585 Kossow Road
Milwaukee, WI 53186
Phone: 262-798-8986
Email: david@reclaimed-timbers.com
Website: www reclaimed-timbers.com

Reclaimed Lumber Company
585 Kossow Road
Waukesha, WI 53186
Phone: 262-798-8986
Fax: 262-798-9401
Email: david@old-barn-wood.com
Website: www.old-barn-wood.com

Schuler's Country Store and Workshop
533 N Main Street
Janesville, WI 53545
Phone: 608-754-4052
Email: info@schulercountry.com
Website: www.schulercountry.com

Traditional Woodworks and
Lumber Company
1679 38th Street
Somerset, WI 54025
Phone: 800-882-2718
Website: www.tradwood.com

Value-Added Products (VA)—Con.

Antiquus Wood Products
Phone: 800-852-9224
Website: www.antiquuswood.com

Reclaimed Forest
Email: info@reclaimedforest.com
Website: www.reclaimedforest.com